Philosophy and Practice

ROYAL INSTITUTE OF PHILOSOPHY LECTURE SERIES: 18
SUPPLEMENT TO *PHILOSOPHY* 1984

EDITED BY:

A. Phillips Griffiths

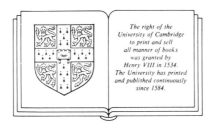

The right of the
University of Cambridge
to print and sell
all manner of books
was granted by
Henry VIII in 1534.
The University has printed
and published continuously
since 1584.

CAMBRIDGE UNIVERSITY PRESS

CAMBRIDGE
LONDON NEW YORK NEW ROCHELLE
MELBOURNE SYDNEY

Published by the Press Syndicate of the University of Cambridge
The Pitt Building, Trumpington Street, Cambridge CB2 1RP
32 East 57th Street, New York, NY 10022, USA
10 Stamford Road, Oakleigh, Melbourne 3166, Australia

Library of Congress catalogue card number: 85–47842

British Library Cataloguing in Publication Data

Philosophy and practice.—(Royal Institute of
Philosophy lecture series; 18)
1. Social sciences—Philosophy
I. Griffiths, A. Phillips   II. Series
301'.01   H61
ISBN 0-521-31231-0

H
6 1
.P54
1985 / 51,452

Printed in Great Britain by Adlard & Son Ltd, Bartholomew Press, Dorking

Contents

iii

Preface

The Royal Institute of Philosophy lectures for 1983–84 were arranged in consultation with the new Society for Applied Philosophy (which now has its own Journal). The contributors, but not the topics, were suggested by the Society; and it was therefore interesting to see, as the series unfolded (and the lectures are printed here in the order in which they were given), what a group of twelve philosophers and two philosophical lawyers conceived 'applied philosophy' to be.

It was not the policy of the new Society, and it has never been the practice of the Institute, to lay constraints on the content of the work of invited speakers. In this case, we were even more open to suggestions than usual; even the very topics were chosen by the invited speakers, assuming only that they were about philosophy and practice. Furthermore, we did not wish to limit them to a narrow notion of practice, as concern only public affairs or public or private morals; without, of course, wishing to exclude such matters. We intended 'practice' to be taken in a wide sense, as involving practical concerns which those who are not philosphers may have. I put it this way to exclude those practical concerns—for philosophy itself is a practice—which only philosophers would have: we wanted to avoid narcissism.

Having these fourteen essays before us, have we been given any help in deciding what applied philosophy is supposed to be?

Well, they are very disparate; and I find it impossible to apply any useful general description to them. My own response is this: I think there is one thing which I perceive one sort of applied philosophy to be: it is very important; and it is nothing new. (It is age-old in fact; but I limit myself to speaking of what is old or new over the last fifty years or so, in British philosophy.)

Some of those who welcomed the advent of the Society for Applied Philosophy did so because they were irritated, even outraged, by what they regarded as the aridity, the esoteric abstraction, the detachment from 'real issues', into which they thought contemporary British philosophy had fallen. Certainly, the sorts of considerations about substantive ethical or political issues dealt with by R. M. Hare, Ted Honderich, Don Locke and others in this volume were thought for a time to go beyond the scope of philosophy, which must limit itself to what fell under that unfelicitous expression 'meta-ethics'. But apart from that, I think we have been doing applied philosophy all along.

Preface

Let us look for a moment at what the critics of so-called 'Oxford philosophy' sometimes cite as the paradigm of aridity, the work of the late J. L. Austin. I remember, when at a seminar in Oxford thirty years ago Austin first outlined his investigation which later eventuated in his paper *Excuses,* Mr (now Professor) David Armstrong, taking advantage of his Australian immunity and perching himself on a high cupboard, challenged the formidable Austin, asking him 'And what particular philosophical problems is all this meant to solve?' Austin's reply was 'Roughly, all of them'. An exaggeration, no doubt. But *Excuses* and his previous seminar with Honoré, which so influenced the latter's work on law, I would claim to be of the first importance with regard to commonsense and legal appraisal of action.

What Austin was engaged in, and what all of these contributors some of the time and some of them most of the time are engaged in, is conceptual investigation. I do not say 'conceptual analysis', because this presupposes, or is at any rate too redolent of, a particular and questionable view of the structure of thought. Conceptual investigation is not only a matter of achieving clarity, though to do so is of the first importance. ('Clarity is not enough' it was once said: but it is plenty.) What people do must, unless they act mindlessly, depend on their conceptions, and their conceptions can be more or less coherent, and where coherent more or less explicit, and where implicit there is the greater danger of confusion. But conceptual investigation can also be creative. For example, Roger Scruton, starting from the conceptual distinction between intentional and non-intentional pleasures, develops a notion of arousal which deserves, in my opinion, to be allowed to give a new meaning to the word. (The *OED* definition gives no hint of reciprocity.)

As I say, conceptual investigation is not new. Perhaps it got a bad name, or was anyway obscured, by the school of linguistic analysis; for there were those who would have said that the only way to pursue conceptual investigation, if it could be distinguished from it at all, was by linguistic analysis. But the work neither of Ryle (throughout, but especially in his last book, *On Thinking*) nor the later Wittgenstein, can be so represented. Austin was thought by some to be trivializing when he said the first thing to do was to chase up a word and its cognates in the *OED*; but that can be a good way to start, so long as it is not also where we end.

Mr Warner's paper was highly appreciated by the audience at the Institute, and one member, who has made clear on many occasions his distaste for what he calls logical positivism or linguistic analysis, complimented him warmly, saying that Mr Warner's paper almost reconciled him to linguistic philosophy. Mr Warner was pleased, but also amused, remarking that he had had no idea that he was a linguistic philosopher. What Mr Warner is engaged in is conceptual investigation, an investigation into the concept of language. He is not entering into the arena of controversy about the most correct or desirable reforms of liturgical language; he is showing that there, as must be the case elsewhere, the ways in which language is conceived will give different directions to people's practical recommendations, whether they have made explicit, and thought through, their concepts or not. And they better had, or listen to those who do. If they get it wrong, they may be responsible for distorting not only the meaning of liturgical practice but our very religious consciousness.

I used to say, to some extent for the sort of reasons given by Dr Newton Smith at the end of his paper, and to the dismay of my colleagues who thought I was demeaning philosophy in the eyes of our university departments of Engineering and Business Studies, that philosophy is useless. This was hyperbole: in part I wanted to guard against a tendency, to use a witty spoonerism from a review in *Mind*, to sell my birthright for a pot of message. I can no longer say philosophy is useless if people will listen to it. But, if as I claim we have been doing applied philosophy all along, why talk of applied philosophy rather than just philosophy? Because there can be the investigation of specifically philosophical or metaphysical concepts such as substance, or universals, or the thing in itself; and the investigation of purely theoretical concepts in the sciences or in literary or art criticism; but there are concepts embedded in people's lives and practice, which would go on living if everyone who called himself a philosopher or a theoretician were dead, such as those of sexual desire, dishonesty and madness.

Dr Scruton's paper, *Sexual Arousal*, is adapted from *Sexual Desire, its Meaning and its Goal* to be published by Wiedenfeld, autumn 1985.

Philosophy and Practice: Some Issues About War and Peace

R. M. HARE

I am going in this lecture on 'Philosophy and Practice' first to say something about philosophy and then something about practice, in order to show you how they bear on one another. But I must start by paying a tribute to the President of the Society for Applied Philosophy, Professor Sir A. J. Ayer, who has kindly agreed to take the chair at this lecture. I can honestly say that he is more responsible than anybody else for putting me on the right track in moral philosophy. He did this by convincing me, when young, that the ways people were doing it at that time had no future. In the famous chapter on ethics in his marvellously readable and exciting book, *Language, Truth and Logic,* Ayer was thought to be trying to show that moral philosophy itself, and perhaps even ordinary first-order moral thinking, was a waste of time. From later work of his, and from his occasional pronouncements about moral and political questions, it is evident that the second of these slanders was false. But even on the theoretical side the lessons I learnt from his book were positive as well as negative. That is not to say that the negative lessons were unimportant. Some people have still not absorbed them, and continue to waste our time. But here are two positive points which you will find in Ayer's book, and which for me were crucial.

The first also occurs in Carnap and some other emotivists. Ayer says:

> It is worth mentioning that ethical terms do not serve only to express feeling. They are calculated also to arouse feeling, and so to stimulate action. Indeed, some of them are used in such a way to give the sentences in which they occur the effect of commands (2nd edn, p. 108).

This made me think that, even if moral judgments (or ethical sentences, as it was then the fashion to call them) do not *state* anything, as Ayer maintained, because they are not in the strict sense statements, it is going much too far to say, as he slips into saying, that they do not *say* anything (ibid.). When I tell someone to do something (for example to mind the step), I am saying something to him—something which he has to *understand* if my communication is to be successful; and there is no more reason for philosophers to neglect this kind of saying than any other. That this was only a slip is

1

clear from the fact that Ayer himself, like Carnap, has his own account to give of what 'ethical sentences' do say. Though I have never agreed with this emotivist account, and always resented it when people who did not understand the issue called me an emotivist (perhaps because they adopted a quite untenable emotivist account of the meaning of imperatives, as Ayer does in the passage I have quoted) I took the point that there were other things that moral judgments might be besides statements of empirical fact, or statements, in the narrow descriptive sense, of any kind. This set me thinking what could be their role in language; and of course the idea that there are many different language games, many different kinds of speech act, was already becoming familiar through the work of Wittgenstein and Austin—the latter, in particular, being impelled to attack what he called[1] 'the descriptive fallacy' by the work of the emotivists.

In looking for a non-emotivist account of moral judgments which could still survive the criticisms brought by the emotivists, I was helped by the second positive point I got from *Language, Truth and Logic*. When he is discussing the objection that it must be possible to argue seriously about moral questions because undoubtedly the discipline called 'casuistry' exists, Ayer says:

> Casuistry is not a science. It is a purely analytical investigation of the structure of a given moral system. In others words it is an exercise in formal logic (2nd edn, p. 112).

The ideas that moral judgments might be in some ways like imperatives, and that, nevertheless, they can be constituents in logical inferences and can therefore, presumably, enter into logical relations, set me thinking. I was determined to do moral philosophy, because I wanted to have some help with practical moral questions which troubled me, like the one I am going to talk about later, when I have finished reminiscing. Could it be that the task of the moral philosopher was to explore these logical relations, and on them base an account of moral reasoning?

It was clear to me from the start that moral judgments were not in all respects like the imperatives of ordinary speech. In my first book I pointed out the main differences, and said that it was 'no part of my purpose to "reduce" moral language to imperatives'.[2] But could it be that they shared some of their characteristics, notably that of action-guidingness or prescriptivity? This would already make it

---

[1] *Philosophical Papers* (Oxford University Press, 1961), 234; *How to Do Things with Words* (Oxford Univesity Press, 1962), 3.
[2] *The Language of Morals* (Oxford University Press, 1952), 2.

impossible to treat them just like ordinary statements of fact. These can, indeed, in a sense guide actions; but not in the sense in which imperatives or, as I thought, moral judgments do. So in his negative contentions Ayer was right. All this might be true, although they shared *other* characteristics with descriptive statements, in particular the characteristic known as universalizability: the feature that two acts, etc., cannot differ in their possession or non-possession of some moral property P if they have all their descriptive properties in common.[3] As I pointed out in my second book (*Freedom and Reason*, Ch. 2), an analogous feature holds trivially of descriptive statements too; but its possession by moral judgments is so far from being trivial as to be the foundation of any satisfactory theory of moral reasoning.

A lot of other features go with this feature of universalizability, among them the element in the meaning of moral judgments which since Stevenson's book *Ethics and Language* has been called 'descriptive meaning', and their undoubted possession of which still misleads people who ought to know better into thinking that they are *in all respects* like purely descriptive statements.

The idea that in moral thinking we are trying to find prescriptions which we are prepared to universalize to all exactly similar cases, even those in which we would be the victims, is of course a highly Kantian one. But it also led me in a utilitarian direction. For if you are trying to find such prescriptions when you are deciding what moral judgments to make, you will have to treat other people as if they were yourself. If you are not prepared to say that it ought to be done to you, you must not say that you ought to do it to somebody else. And so we have to love our neighbour as ourselves, which means treating his or her preferences as of equal weight to our own. And since the weight we give to our own preferences is positive, we shall be seeking the satisfactions of the preferences of all equally; and we shall have done our best if we maximize those satisfactions over all those affected considered impartially, which is exactly what the utilitarians are recommending. So Bentham's slogan 'Everybody to count for one, nobody for more than one'[4] takes its place, along with Kant's other formulations of his Categorical Imperative, as an equivalent expression to his first and main formulation in terms of willing the maxim of one's action to be a universal law.

There are well canvassed objections to utilitarianism. After I had satisfied myself, guided by Kant, that it had a firm basis in the logic

[3] See my paper 'Supervenience', in *Aristotelian Society*, Supplementary Volume 58 (1984).
[4] Cited in Mill, *Utilitarianism*, Ch. 5, *s.f.*

of the moral concepts, I naturally returned to these objections, to see what force they had. I very soon realized that they were nearly all the result of failing to recognize that our moral thinking takes place at more than one level. This is an old idea. It is to be found already in Socrates, who started moral philosophy. He distinguished between what he called knowledge and what he called right opinion.[5] In this he was followed by Plato and by Aristotle. Although the idea is overlaid in these writers by descriptivist ideas, the essential point can be taken over into a non-descriptivist system. The idea is that for much, indeed most, of the time when we think morally it is all right—indeed desirable and necessary—that we should not stop to give reasons for what we think, or work out all the pros and cons. The 'right opinion' of the morally well-educated person will guide him as well as any sophisticated reasoning process.[6] If one were clear enough about the 'that', there will be no need to have the 'why' as well.[7] This is true of the everyday level of moral thinking (what I call in my recent book[8] the 'intuitive' level).

But this level is not self-sustaining (as Plato and Aristotle well recognized, although many of Aristotle's self-styled followers have not). This is because we do need to know why the intuitions we have are the right ones (people sometimes have wrong intuitions); and so we need a higher level of thinking which will determine this. Aristotle is quite clear that for virtue, properly so called, practical wisdom (*phronēsis*) is required as well as the moral virtues.[9] Also, we often get into situations in which our intuitions conflict (I am going to illustrate this in a moment). Not only do the intuitions of different people conflict, but a single person's different intuitions may conflict with one another, so that whatever he does, he will be erring against deep moral convictions that he has. Only a higher level of moral thinking (I call it the 'critical' level) can then resolve the conflict.

The classical utilitarians Bentham and John Stuart Mill adopted this division of moral thinking into two levels in order to answer their critics. Whether they got it from Socrates I do not know. It provides an answer, because nearly all the standard objections to utilitarianism rely on an appeal to our common moral convictions: utilitarians are supposed to have to outrage these by requiring us to do things which either infringe people's 'manifest' rights or are in some other way 'obviously' wrong. The utilitarian can answer that of

[5] Plato, *Meno* 98b.
[6] Ibid. 97b.
[7] Aristotle, *Nicomachean Ethics*, 1095 b6.
[8] *Moral Thinking* (Oxford University Press, 1981), 2ff.
[9] *Nicomachean Ethics*, 1144 b31.

course we have these intuitions, and should have them, because it is highly desirable from the utilitarian point of view that people should be brought up in this way. Having been so brought up, they will have the intuitions, and these will lead them to do the right thing nearly all the time, if they follow them. If this were not so, the intuitions would not be the best intuitions to have; their upbringing would not have been sound. But if you want to determine what *are* the best intuitions, or the best upbringing, it is no use appealing to the intuitions you have been brought up with. They are what is in question, and they may not have been for the best. You have to do some critical thinking, and this is utilitarian. The best intuitions to have are those which, in general, will lead people to act for the best; and these are the ones which a sound upbringing will inculcate, and which wise moral thinkers will cultivate and respect. If they disregard them in the supposed interests of utility, they will most likely get it wrong and not act for the best, and therefore will not have been showing themselves good utilitarians. For it is almost impossible for us to calculate exactly the consequences of our actions, and there are many other dangers which attend the pursuit of expediency—dangers which a utilitarian who knows the moves in this argument can easily recognize. Once the levels of moral thinking are distinguished, nearly all these standard objections to utilitarianism collapse. For it turns out that a utilitarian also (even what is called an act-utilitarian) would bid us follow our intuitions in all clear cases, because that gives us the highest expectation of utility.

As I said, I took over this defence of utilitarianism from earlier thinkers. What came as a pleasant surprise to me was that the same manoeuvre also enables one to understand why people find it so hard to accept the kind of non-descriptivism which I had come to see as the only viable way of applying philosophical thought to practical problems. If you have had a stable moral education, as most of us have, you will think that you *know* that certain things are wrong. You *cannot doubt* that they are wrong. This is because you have been taught that they are wrong, and the teaching has stuck. If it was sound teaching, that is all for the best. So you will naturally give to these deliverances of conscience the status of *facts,* and will think that any philosophers like Professor Ayer who calls in question their factual status is morally subversive. Actually Ayer and his fellow-emotivists were the saviours of morality from the dead end into which descriptivists of various breeds were, and still are, trying to lead it. But people did not understand this; and his book was thrown into the fire or out of the window by the good and great.

In my recent book *Moral Thinking* I have been into all this in some detail, and it would be inappropriate in a lecture about philosophy and practice to go into the arguments and counter-arguments at length. This has therefore been only a sketch. I am going to content myself with merely affirming that a rational non-descriptivism can, and descriptivism of all kinds cannot, provide the person who is troubled about practical moral problems with a way of sorting them out. The reason why no kind of descriptivism can do this is that the essentially practical nature of morality is ignored by it. We need a way of reasoning about what we should *do,* and this no kind of descriptivism can provide.

I am going to illustrate the way that I advocate by discussing in the rest of this lecture one of the most troubling sets of problems of all (and the one that made me myself into a moral philosopher in the first place), namely problems about war. I am going to explain first of all why people become pacifists, and why they would not become pacifists if they did some more careful critical thinking. I shall then try to say in what sense patriotism is a virtue, and in what sense it is a vice. And I will leave a little time at the end to say something (not much, because I am no expert) about nuclear disarmament. A philosopher as such cannot hope to decide that issue, because it requires knowledge that philosophy by itself does not yield. But he can at least say clearly what the issue is; and that I shall try to do.

The two-level structure of moral thinking that I have been advocating puts us in a position to explain how a great many people now become pacifists. We are most of us nowadays brought up to abhor violence. This was not always the case, nor is it so in all cultures. But I take it for granted that critical thinking would justify this upbringing in our present circumstances. That people think like this leads to there being less violence in our life, and that is a very good thing. More harm than good would come if people stopped condemning violence, and instead cultivated the virtues admired by some football supporters (not, I am sure, including Professor Ayer, in spite of his love of the game). The very strong feelings which support this principle of non-violence readily extend themselves to cover all violence which is similar in its effects on the victim, no matter what its motives or justification.

But this is only an intuition, and might (indeed does) conflict with other intuitions which, again, most of us have acquired from our upbringing. I may mention especially ones which require us to protect the weak, and in particular those, such as our own families, to whom we are commonly thought to have special duties. These special duties too we recognize intuitively; and these intuitions can be defended in the same way by critical thinking, because it is a very good thing, in general, that we have them. A wise utilitarian educator would seek to inculcate into his charges both these kinds of intuitions: that is, both that which condemns violence, and that which bids us protect the weak, especially our own dependants. And it is very easy, and probably to a limited extent right, for this latter set of duties too to get extended into a general duty of loyalty to the group in which we find ourselves living, often our country. This is probably the best way for most people of protecting their dependants and themselves, namely belonging to a stable community with the power to enforce law and resist external aggression.

Thus it is that there builds up a conflict between the two principles of non-violence and loyalty, and pacifists and patriots come into confrontation. Some more unworthy motives commonly reinforce the feelings of both: the patriot often appeals to sentiments of national pride of the '*über alles*' or 'wider still and wider' variety; and the pacifist is often (I speak from experience of my own feelings when I was attracted by pacifism) moved by fear of himself being involved in violence at the dirty end. This is, indeed, a sign of grace; for it at least shows that we have a lively sympathy for the victims of violence, and understanding of their situation. Sympathy is a vital ingredient in moral thinking, because only if we have it can we be sure that in universalizing our moral judgments we are doing so with an understanding of what their acceptance in cases where we were the victims would mean for us, i.e. what it is like to be at the receiving end.

What I have to suggest is that critical thinking *can* sort out these conflicts, as it can others. That is what it is for. We ought to be aiming at a resolution of them which will allow us to retain modified forms of the principle of non-violence and the principle of loyalty, and to be clear about which should override which in particular cases. It will then be possible to be at the same time a patriot of the right kind, and, without being an extreme pacifist of the Tolstoyan sort, to go on abhorring violence in nearly all cases. At any rate, that is my own position, and I think it yields defensible answers to particular questions about war.

I am going first of all to discuss the justification for having a principle requiring loyalty. A superficial thinker might suppose that, by founding my account of moral thinking on the thesis of the universalizability of moral judgments, I have ruled out particular loyalties. If I have to universalize all my moral judgments, how can I say that there are duties to particular people or groups who are related to *me* in certain ways (duties to *my* children or *my* country). This is really a rather elementary mistake, but it is so common even among professional philosophers that I am going to take the risk of boring you and spend a few minutes explaining it.

To put it formally, the principle

> For all x and y, if y is the child (or country) of x, then x has certain particular duties to y

is universal in the sense required by the thesis of the universalizability of moral judgments. It starts with a universal quantifier, or pair of them, 'For all x and y...', and contains no individual constants (references to individuals).

The idea that universalizability forbids particular loyalties is due to a confusion of this universal proposition with another which is not universal in the required sense:

> a (some individual, say George) has certain particular duties to a's child (or country).

Here there is an individual constant, 'a' (standing in this case for a proper name). This second proposition *could* involve its holder in a breach of the thesis of universalizability; but only if he held it while refusing to universalize it. But he would not be breaking the thesis if he held it, but was prepared to universalize it by extending it to ascribe the duty to *anybody* in just the same situation. 'The same situation' must of course be taken as meaning that it is the same in all respects, including all the characteristics of people affected, and in particular their preferences—for otherwise we should find ourselves having to say that because a ought to do such and such to his child, who likes it (e.g. tickle his toes), b ought to do the same to his child, who detests it.

If the patriot is prepared to universalize the principle of his patriotism, he is in the clear so far as the thesis of universalizability goes. This does not mean (and about this too there has been much confusion) that, just because a certain judgment passes the test of universalizability, in the formal sense that a universal judgment can be *framed* which it exemplifies, it must be acceptable, If someone is prepared to universalize his judgment, it *qualifies* as a moral judgment (provided of course that it satisfies the other formal qualifications). But that in itself is not a sufficient reason for accepting it (it might be eligible as a candidate, but be rejected by all the rest of us in favour of other candidates by critical thinking). The general form of the solution to the problem of what moral principles to accept, among those that qualify, is this: we are to accept those which we can approve by critical thinking for general adoption; and we shall approve those whose general adoption will do the best for all those affected considered impartially, not giving any special weight to any interest because it is ours, and not giving priority *in the critical thinking* (though we may at the intuitive level, for reasons explained below) to those related to us in particular ways, who cannot be identified without reference to ourselves as those individuals.

This complete impartiality at the critical level can justify the selection of principles requiring partiality at the intuitive level, if those are the principles whose general acceptance will most conduce to the good of all, considered impartially.[10] The question, therefore, that we have to ask is, what these principles are, in the field of people's attitudes to their countries. The answer will depend on a question of empirical fact: what are likely to be the consequences of the general acceptance of such principles by those who are likely to be got to accept them? Of course there will always be rogue elephants, and the calculation of consequences must allow for their existence; but what we are talking about are the principles whose general acceptance by peoples of good will—and I am optimistic enough to believe that these will be in the great majority—will be for the best. The problem of what to do about the rogues is especially difficult when we are discussing nuclear weapons.

I will start my discussion of patriotism with the premiss that government is necessary. I could by critical thinking have justified the rejection of anarchism, but I will spare you that. Next, it does seem that the preservation of the political liberty of individuals and their meaningful participation in decisions of government by a democratic process requires the division of the world into territories of manageable size, in each of which its inhabitants have the responsibility for setting up and maintaining their own government. This is impossible if the inhabitants are for one reason or another (e.g. communal divisions) not able to share a common loyalty. That liberty and democracy are themselves good things I could show by a similar exercise of critical thinking, but there is not time for that.[11] I would say that the United States and India have reached something near the limit of size at which, by present techniques, democratic government can be carried on—the latter perhaps straining at the limit. And even for non-democratic systems like Russia and China there is a size-limit. Certainly world government is at present impracticable, if by that is meant a world body which is responsible for all the functions of government. There is nothing, however, to stop smaller 'states', as they are usually called, grouping themselves into larger units to which they assign some of these functions; the EEC is an example.

[10] See my paper 'Utilitarianism and the Vicarious Affects', in *The Philosophy of Nicholas Rescher*, E. Sosa (ed.) (Reidel, 1979).

[11] See my paper 'Liberty and Equality: How Politics Masquerades as Philosophy' in papers presented to conference on Liberty and Equality at Key Biscayne, 1983, J. Paul (ed.) (forthcoming).

If some such territorial division of responsiblity exists, as it does, and as it is best that it should, the question arises of the duties of the inhabitants of each territory (the citizens of each state) to each other and to the state itself. It seems to me (as a matter of empirical fact) that there are certain ways of carrying on by the citizens which will greatly increase the preference–satisfactions in aggregate of all the citizens considered impartially, and that these would be, by a sound critical thinker, included in a set of principles laying down (to use an old-fashioned phrase) the 'duties of a citizen'. To give examples: such duties would include the duty not to evade taxes, and in general the duty to obey the law and assist in its enforcement (which does not exclude *some* law-breaking in exceptional circumstances when good moral reasons can be given for it). They include a duty to secure and preserve good laws, in particular by giving an informed vote in elections and by taking a part in the political process; the duty to resist encroachment on liberty by government agencies; to be willing to undertake service to the community, and in general to display what is known, in another old-fashioned phrase, as 'public spirit'. All these duties could be justified by the same kind of critical thinking as I am advocating; but I am going to confine myself to the duty, if there is one, to bear arms in defence of the state.

That brings us to the area of conflict *between* states, and to the question of the extent to which patriotism, the support of one's own state to the possible detriment of others, or at any rate the giving of priority to loyalty to one's own state, is a duty or a virtue. The application of our method to this question is in principle simple and is the same as before. In critical thinking we are not allowed to give priority to the interests of any state, or its inhabitants, just because it is our state. But critical thinking may, all the same, recommend to us certain *universal* principles laying down duties which *any* citizen has to *his* state. Or we could specify these principles further, without making them less universal, by saying that certain duties exist only in certain kinds of states (for example in a tyranny the citizen might have a duty to rebel).

If any principle is a candidate, formally speaking, for inclusion in the list, it will be accepted or rejected according to whether its general acceptance is likely to advance the preference-satisfactions of all the inhabitants of all the countries considered impartially. Even some quite partial principles will pass this test. For example, it is for the good of everybody in all nations, on the whole, that people should be politically active in relation to the governments of their own countries, but not in relation to the governments of other countries. One reason is that we do not know enough about the consequences of our interventions in the politics of other countries to be sure that we are acting for the best. I say 'on the whole', because there are exceptions to this rule; but they are few.

When it comes to bearing arms, the situation is more difficult. But at least in times when weapons were not so frightful, we can find good arguments for saying that people did right to defend their own territories against aggressors; and in default of a probably impracticable system of 'collective security' (as it used to be called in the days of the League of Nations), I do not see how else international order could be preserved even to the limited extent that it has been. The effect of forgoing the organized use of force to repel aggression would be a rapid growth of disorganized and probably much more damaging use of force, which would result in the weak going to the wall and a relapse into anarchy.

What this brings us to is a kind of patriotism which is morally acceptable, because we are prepared to prescribe it universally to the citizens of all countries and not just of our own. It is forbidden, however, to support their governments, either by bearing arms or in any other way, in the pursuit of aggressive policies. If I were giving two lectures, not one, I would have taken some time at this point to show how such utilitarian critical thinking can develop what I have just said into something like a version of the traditional doctrine of the just war. The difference between me and most just war theorists is that they commonly base the doctrine on intuition, or on natural law (which is nothing but an appeal to intuition) or on supposed revelation. They are unable to give any reasons for their views, but a utilitarian can do this. Also, the principles of the just war are only intuitive *prima facie* principles; they are not necessarily applicable outside the range of situations for which they were developed. The views, however, may be the same in their content and practical implications—which is not to say that an absolutely clear and concrete formulation of these is yet available.

I should like to mention in passing that, if one looks at the patriotic attitudes that were widespread in most European countries before the First World War—patriotisms of the 'wider still and wider' sort—one notices (and perhaps some of my anti-utilitarian colleagues should be surprised at this) that a change to different attitudes has been brought about by what I can only call critical thinking on the part of the public. This is a confirmation of my theory about the two levels of moral thinking. People used to have those intuitions and those attitudes that led directly to the Great War (that was how the ruling classes in Britain and France and Germany and Austria were brought up). I am old enough to remember a generation in which such attitudes were dominant even in Britain. The appalling carnage of the war, floodlighted by a succession of

11

poets and novelists, convinced people that those attitudes had a very low acceptance utility, and they were abandoned except in Germany and Italy. Their abandonment, after the Second World War, became almost universal in the West. This was real moral progress, and it was the result of critical thinking, albeit largely inarticulate.

The task for the critical thinker now is to determine what should replace those attitudes. I am arguing that it should not be pacifism, as many people think, but rather a non-aggressive kind of patriotism which all can share, and which permits the use of force in self-defence. My reason is that this is the only attitude that will preserve international order and stability (which is a dominant element in the preferences of anybody who thinks seriously about it) from the countries that I called rogue elephants—I mean those whose governments do not share the same attitudes.

I should like to mention also that I wrote an earlier version of this lecture before the outbreak of the Falklands War, for delivery in the coming term to my class at Oxford. When the war started I began to wonder whether I should have to alter my views and my lecture as a result of it. But actually, by the time the war was over and I came to deliver my lecture, I did not see any reason to alter any of it except to refer to what had happened as an illustration of my thesis about patriotism. One thing I had done was to set myself a test to determine whether my opinion that we did right to resist the Argentinians was one that I would be prepared to universalize. I asked myself whether I thought that the Iranians were similarly justified in resisting the equally unlawful aggression of the Iraqis in the Gulf War. This was a good test, because I could not possibly accuse myself of bias in favour of the Iranian government, which is a regime as detestable as any. But I unhesitatingly answered that they were right to defend themselves; for unless those who are able to repel aggression do so, there will be no limit to aggressions in the world. The fact that on critical reflection I found that I could prescribe this universally made me think that my initial intuitions about the Falklands were the right ones. One can argue a lot about expediency and costs and benefits, and it is right to do so; but most good comes in the long run by having the kind of intuitions which made us resist the aggression of Argentina and the Iranians that of Iraq. In default of them any country that thinks it can grab anything will do so.

I am not, of course, arguing that the *subsequent,* and the *present,* conduct of the Iranians is justified. Having resisted the aggression, they should have been ready to negotiate a peaceful settlement; and so should we be if the Argentinians would reciprocate.

So I am happy with this kind of defensive patriotism as it applies to wars with conventional weapons. But of course the situation is altered when we come to consider nuclear weapons. For there the notion of defence fades, and we have nothing left but the threat of retaliation. I am not going to have time to go in detail into the question of nuclear disarmament, unilateral or multilateral. But perhaps I can say some things which will help to get the issue clearer.

The first is that, as I hope to have shown, pacifism in general is not acceptable (it has, in fact, a very low acceptance utility in the world as it is, given the existence of rogues). People become pacifists only because they over-emphasize one of the intuitions with which they have been brought up at the expense of all the rest. Now the leaders of the CND have a way of saying that they are not pacifists, and I am sure that this is true of some of them. The fact remains that without the spread of pacifist sentiment, and without the considerable stiffening given to the movement by a very solid core of pacifists in it, it would not have had nearly the following that it has. To give just one example, do you think that the Bishop of Salisbury's working party, which produced the report *The Church and the Bomb,* would have come to just the conclusions that it did but for the presence on it of Canon Oestreicher, a committed and extremely persuasive pacifist? If we are to take seriously the arguments of CND supporters, we have to subtract from them everything which appeals to pacifism as a premiss, for this premiss will not stand up; and we have to see what is left.

The second thing I wish to say is that, as we all recognize, nuclear war would be so frightful that the avoidance of it must be the preponderant aim of anybody who is thinking critically and trying to maximize the satisfaction of people's preferences considered impartially. But this is very far from establishing the unilateralist case, because it could well be that the weakening of the West's power to retaliate would make a nuclear attack more, and not less, likely. I have to testify that there have been three occasions since the Second World War on which I have been really frightened that somebody might start a nuclear war. The first was during the Korean War. The second was during the Cuban missile crisis. Both of these dangers passed, and I am persuaded that the possession by the United States of nuclear weapons was a stabilizing factor in those crises; and so, perhaps, was their possession by the Russians. The third is now; and what frightens me now, more than anything before except those two crises, is the growth of the 'Peace' Movement. If the resolve of the Western alliance is called in question, anything can happen. These are only my inexpert opinions; but the question certainly needs to be argued, whether unilateral disarmament would make nuclear war more or less likely.

The third thing I wish to say is that the very novelty of our present situation—the fact that nuclear weapons are so many orders of magnitude more frightful than weapons were even in the recent past—makes moral intuitions (of all sorts) an insecure guide; for they were formed as a result of past experience, and our present situation is so different. This of course applies to various patriotic sentiments that people have—for example people, like some in this country, and more, apparently, in France, who insist that we must have an independent nuclear armament because otherwise we shall be admitting that we are second-rate. *La gloire* is not now a sensible object of policy. But it also applies to some sentiments on the other side. I am by no means as certain as the Bishop of Salisbury's group was that intuitive principles about the just war can be applied without further thought to our present situation.

I should also like to mention in particular the argument that what it would be wrong to do it would be wrong to threaten to do. This seems to me to be a mere intuition, and one which cannot be sustained in all situations. It is a question of balancing the utilities and disutilities of possible alternative principles; and it seems to me that there could be, and well may be now, situations in which the expectations of utility, that is, of preference-satisfaction, would be maximized by making threats the carrying out of which would not maximize utility. If so, then a principle forbidding one to make such threats can at most be a *prima facie* principle; it can have exceptions. If it is claimed that the threat would not be believed because we are moral and will not carry it out, this shows insufficient understanding of human motivation. In face of the appalling disaster of nuclear war, deterrence is achieved by even a quite small possibility that the threat will be acted on.

Though I am not certain, I do think that, even with Hitler in 1939, who was a bit crazy, war would not have broken out if both sides had had nuclear weapons. And I also believe that if, or when, India and Pakistan have them, war on that subcontinent will be less, not more, likely, because they will then be afraid to indulge in the kind of more or less gentlemanly wars they have had in the recent past, for fear of starting something worse. I must add that the thought of Hitler, or even Mrs Gandhi and General Zia, having the bomb appals me; but nevertheless what I have just said could be true.

Although intuitions are not a secure guide in this unfamiliar labyrinth, they are at least some guide, inasmuch as our present situation is not *totally* different from those which people have faced in the past, and formed their moral convictions accordingly. Though the technical situation is quite novel, the human reactions of the various parties are depressingly much the same as before. Since the difficulties in deciding what to do arise not so much from technical and games-theoretical complexities as from the unpredictability of the human agents involved, intuitions about what they will do may be all we have to go on. And perhaps these factual intuitions are more reliable than any moral intuitions. If you ask me what Mr Reagan or Mr Andropov is likely to do in a certain situation, I at least have some idea. Moral judgments, which are what we are trying to make, must depend on our assessment of the probable consequences of alternative actions (those philosophers who pretend otherwise are irresponsible as well as confused). And in assessing them the philosopher is no expert. That is why I am not now going to say more about nuclear disarmament, except this: what we all have to decide is what attitudes to it, and to war in general, give us the best chance of survival.

Madness

ANTHONY QUINTON

1. Introduction

Madness is a subject that ought to interest philosophers; but they have had surprisingly little to say about it. What they have said, although often interesting and important, has failed to penetrate to the properly philosophical centre of the topic. They have concerned themselves with its causes and effects, with its social and ethical implications, but they have said little that is useful or definitive about what it is in itself. Preoccupied with its accidents, they have failed to engage with its essence.

They ought to have concerned themselves with madness just to the extent that they have taken themselves to be the custodians of the cognitive, of rational belief and valid reasoning. For madness is a cognitive defect, both as ordinarily conceived and, as I shall argue, in fact. Familiar idioms reveal the general prevalence of the assumption that madness is a cognitive disorder. We talk of mad people as having *lost their reasons*, as *being out of their minds* (using 'mind' here in the everyday sense of the intellect, the thinking capacity), of *having taken leave of their senses* (where it is common sense or judgment that is involved, not the perceptual functions).

Nevertheless, the proposition that madness is a cognitive disorder, however natural or instinctive it may seem, needs defence, for it is ruled out by such explicitly thought out accounts of the nature of madness as are available. The more professional of these tend to be statistical, to take what is, in matters of this kind, the coward's way out of defining the mad as those who are in some way abnormal, in the sense of forming a statistical minority. More thoughtful accounts of the nature of madness are to be found. One is the suggestion of Jonathan Glover (in Chapter 7 of his *Responsibility*) that, since the practical point at issue is whether to shut people up or not, or, at any rate, to take the management of their lives out of their own hands, the relevant consideration is simply whether people are likely to do themselves harm if not under supervision.

Others see madness as a personality disorder of a particularly intense kind in which disapproved-of emotions or desires lead to disapproved-of conduct. A sense of the arbitrariness of these disapprovals, heightened by the use of asylums as devices for the stamping out of dissidence in police states, encourages scepticism about the existence of a real distinction between the mad and the sane. The word 'mad' becomes, in Thomas Szasz's phrase, a 'derogatory label' attached by the powerful many to the defenceless few.

My thesis is, to put it more precisely, that madness is a systematic breakdown in the belief-forming mechanism or capacity of the mind, particularly in relation to those practical beliefs about oneself and one's immediate circumstances which most directly issue in non-verbal conduct. What reveals the breakdown is systematic unreasonable belief.

2. Philosophers on Madness

What have philosophers made of madness hitherto? Plato, in the *Timaeus*, draws a distinction between madness and ignorance as two different kinds of defect of intelligence. This at least takes an intellectualist or cognitive attitude to madness, but since madness and ignorance are not likely to be confused it is not otherwise of much significance. Locke draws a more important distinction between what he calls madmen and idiots, describing them in terms of his own fundamental conception of the mind as having, respectively, too many ideas and too few. What he is reaching towards is the current distinction between madness (and other forms of mental illness) on the one hand and retardation or mental deficiency on the other. Madness is a disease, something that happens to a mind; retardation is a constitutional handicap.

Hobbes and Voltaire are to be celebrated for their humanity and good sense in arguing for a naturalistic account of madness, in opposition to the prevailing theory of diabolic possession, endorsed by the Bible and, indeed, by the explicit words of Christ. But their accounts of madness itself are unenlighteningly statistical. Hobbes says that 'to have stronger and more vehement passions for anything than is ordinarily seen in others is that which men call madness' (*Leviathan*, part 1, c.8) and that 'all passions that cause strange and unusual behaviour are called by the general name of madness' (ibid.). This is an emotional theory of madness. The passions or emotions which Hobbes cites as constituting madness by reason of their excessiveness or statistically unusual nature are fury and melancholy, anticipations, perhaps, of paranoid mania and of depression.

Voltaire's theory is cognitive, but still statistical. It is also physiological. He says 'we call madness that disease of the organs of the brain which inevitably prevents a man from thinking and acting like others' (*Dictionnaire Philosophique*, article Folie). He infers from the assumption that a madman has the same perceptions as everyone else that the faculty of thinking is as much subject to derangement as the senses. In fact the mad have hallucinations as well as delusions, auditory ones being of great diagnostic importance in schizophrenia.

Kant gives the subject thorough consideration in his *Anthropology*. After distinguishing the madman from the idiot he indulges in a characteristic orgy of classification. Some interesting points can be briefly discerned amid the interstices of this machinery. He argues that therapy cannot help the mad since, locked in their own worlds of fantasy, they do not realize that there is anything wrong with them. In current terminology they 'lack insight'. The madman lives in a world of his own, like a dreamer; there is no public confirmation of his beliefs. Kant mentions in passing the fact that there is a hereditary element in madness, but does not make use of it.

Schopenhauer's account of madness interestingly anticipates Freud. There is nothing wrong, he contends, either with the senses or the intellect of the madman. What is adift is his memory. Finding his ordinarily remembered and actual past unbearable he creates for himself an imaginary and emotionally tolerable new one. In support of this bold theory of repression and compensating fantasy he claims that actors, who are compelled by their profession to perform outrages on their memories, are the human group in which madness is most often found. This imaginary piece of evidence would itself appear to be a piece of wish fulfilment. It should be noticed that although Schopenhauer says that madness is emotionally *caused*, he sees the condition as itself cognitive, as a matter of systematic false belief about one's past.

Descartes, taking a cognitive view of madness for granted, begins to go deeper into the subject, philosophically speaking, than anyone mentioned so far. As well as asking himself how he knows that all his beliefs have not been excited in him by a malignant demon, he raises, with almost parenthetical brevity, the question: how do I know that I am not mad? He then sidesteps it by saying that he would have to be mad to raise such a question. That implies, however, since he has raised it, that he must indeed be mad. For his purposes, at any rate, he does not need to pursue the question; its sceptical work can be done just as well by dreams and demonic deceit.

So far, then, as philosophers have reflected on the nature of madness they have not done so very thoroughly. But, for the most part, they have gone along with the assumption embedded in our common idioms for talking about it, in taking it to be a sickness of the intellect or reason, in adopting what I have called a cognitive theory of the matter. I shall now set out a theory of that kind in more detail and go on to consider actual and possible alternatives to it. Descriptions of the various forms of madness refer to a wide variety of manifestations, in thought, emotion and behaviour. As opposed to my view that the essential element in the whole complex is to be found in the domain of thought, the idea that peculiarities of emotion are what matters has its defenders, among them, as we have seen, Hobbes. In an epoch of principled hostility to the idea of an inner life, a behavioural conception of the nature of madness has an obvious appeal.

A suspicion that the picking out of certain emotions as definitive of madness is ultimately an arbitrary business underlies various kinds of scepticism about there being any objective difference between the mad and the sane. Sometimes this response to the problem has a right-wing flavour, as with Thomas Ssasz; more usually it comes from the left, as with R. D. Laing and Michel Foucault. A cognitive theory can resist such scepticism more readily than an emotional one. The difference between the true and the false, and between the justified and unjustified in the way of belief are less subjective and arbitrary than that between emotions that are socially acceptable and emotions that are not.

3. A Cognitive Theory of Madness

The first thing to do is to mark out as clearly as possible the field to which the theory under construction is meant to apply. I am not, to start with, concerned with retardation or mental deficiency, a constitutional weakness of the mind, but with mental illness or disease. Next by the word 'madness' I mean to refer to what psychiatrists, their textbooks and thus, following them respectfully, encyclopedias, call *psychosis*. This is comprehensive, large-scale mental disorder, as contrasted with more localized troubles like neuroses, 'personality disorders' (criminality, alcoholism, sexual deviance, for example) and comparable 'abnormalities'. A crucial distinction between madness and these lesser evils is that the mad generally, in other words for most of the time, lack 'insight'. They are not aware that anything is wrong with them or that they are in need of care and treatment. That is not to say that sufferers cannot be aware, in periods of remission, that they have been mad in the past or, as in the case of Charles Lamb's sister Mary, that they are about to go mad again in the near future.

The natural place to start looking for guidance is the clinical descriptions that are given of the various forms of psychosis. Three main varieties are currently recognized. The first of them is schizophrenia, taking several forms, from catatonic at one extreme to hebephrenic at the other. In all of them the sufferer is out of touch with or cut off from the common world and has retreated into a world of his own imaginative construction. One symptom of schizophrenia is held to be of particular diagnostic importance. That is the phenomenon of *insertion*, the delusion of being controlled by, indeed of receiving spoken orders from, some external intelligence, what is vulgarly called 'voices in the head'.

Schizophrenia is the most obviously cognitive of the psychoses. It is associated with a wide range of moods and emotional states and with a comparably wide range of styles of behaviour, from the wildly frenzied to the wholly passsive and inert. The common element is the schizophrenic's detachment from the real common world by a private system of false beliefs about himself and his circumstances.

The other main group of psychoses are the manic-depressive and the simply depressive. Wild behaviour and extravagant emotions, whether of elation or despair, are characteristic of these forms of madness. The manic individual has delusions of his own power and importance, of his quite superb intellectual brilliance. These are often political, as when he rings up presidents and prime ministers at grotesque expense and impossible hours of the day so as to remove the scales from their eyes with his unique set of infallible solutions to the problems of the world. The depressive individual, who may, of course, be the manic one a few days later, has delusions about the particular awfulness of himself, his circumstances and his prospects. In this case, unlike that of schizophrenia, the delusory belief is connected with a specific kind of emotional state and specific kind of conduct, whether absurdly self-inflated and overweening or desperately miserable and defeated. The primacy of the cognitive or belief aspect of the whole condition will need to be argued for.

Much the same is true of the third variety of psychosis, paranoia, which is ordinarily found in conjunction with one of the other psychoses. The essential belief here is that the sufferer is the victim of a large conspiracy, which may include everyone with whom he comes into contact and others beyond and behind them. The object of the conspiracy is to persecute him, to cause him pain, physical or mental, to humiliate, to disadvantage, even to destroy him. The associated emotional state is one of fear, suspicion and angry resentment which expresses itself in an appropriate style of behaviour: scowling, shrinking, hiding away.

In the general view of those who have most to do with the mad, then, there is to be found in each type of madness a comprehensive system of false beliefs. Where these beliefs are specifically about the sufferer's importance or desperate forlornness or organized victimization, there is a specific emotional state and a specific style of behaviour associated with the false belief-system. My central thesis is that the primary and crucial element in these groupings of belief, emotion and behaviour is the belief or, more precisely, system of beliefs.

The primacy of behaviour can easily be disproved. Behaviour is mad only if it expresses the standardly correlated emotions. In some cases, however, it arises from a quite different emotional background. It may be carried out by an actor or for a bet or to distract attention or to get released from military service. If so it can be entirely sane and reasonable, whether or not it succeeds in serving the purpose for which it was intended. The madness of behaviour, in other words, is derivative from that of the emotion it expresses. A particular form of behaviour, running away, for example, may be a reliable indication of fear. It may be, according to recent accounts of the nature of mental states, partly constitutive of it. But there is no fixed and regular connection between running away and fear. The ascription of fear to one who runs away can always in principle be defeated by some other explanation, perhaps the desire to answer a telephone no one else has heard or a twinge of boredom or an irresistible call of nature.

A first argument against the primacy of emotion in the total characteristic condition of a psychotic has already been alluded to in the description of schizophrenia. There simply is no specific emotion associated with it. The schizophrenic may be happy or sad, excited or impassive. It follows that schizophrenia cannot consist in the emotions that accompany it since these are to be found generally among the population at large.

The main argument against the idea that emotion is primary in madness is a further development of the same point and parallels the objection to the idea that behaviour is the primary factor. This is that the emotions of the psychotic are not *in themselves* indications of madness. There are readily conceivable situations in which any of them may be felt by an entirely sane person, even the extreme emotions that are specifically associated with manic-depression and paranoia. Consider a mother who finds out or comes to believe that a much loved child has just been horribly killed. If she did not experience the emotions typical in depressive psychosis we should conclude that there was something mentally wrong with her, a temporary, perhaps protective, state of shock. Similarly if she finds out or comes to believe that the child has just narrowly and surprisingly escaped a horrible death she ought to have the wild euphoria of the manic. Much the same is true in the case of paranoia. The point is made obliquely in the saying that paranoids often have some real enemies. The emotions of the paranoid are appropriate and reasonable in a Jew in Warsaw under German occupation or a present-day Russian dissident.

The emotions characteristic of a psychosis, manic depressive or paranoid, are signs of such a condition only if they are *unreasonable*, if they are utterly inappropriate to the circumstances in which the person who has them is. Just as apparently, because typically, mad behaviour is really mad only if the expression of the emotion that usually accompanies it, so apparently, because typically, mad emotion is really mad only if it is experienced in circumstances in which it is entirely inappropriate.

Emotions are not simply caused by beliefs, although beliefs do indeed cause them; they also embody beliefs. To be angry with someone is to believe that he has harmed one; to be pleased with oneself involves the belief that one has brought off something good (or could do so); to be hopeful involves the belief that something good is going to happen. As a first approximation it could be said that the inappropriateness to the circumstances in which the unreasonableness of an emotion consists is its embodying a false belief about those circumstances. My anger at someone is unreasonable if the belief it embodies about his having harmed me is false. Following on from this we might conclude that what makes the emotions of the madman psychotic is that his beliefs are false. The schizophrenic falsely believes his imagined private world is real. The depressive falsely believes that his prospects are dreadful. The paranoid falsely believes that every man's hand is against him.

But that needs qualification. In one way, indeed, if I falsely believe that someone has harmed me when he has done nothing of the sort, my anger at him—and any behaviour that results from it—is unreasonable. But that sort of unreasonableness is, as it might be put, objective. I am not shown to be an unreasonable person, even if I get angry with someone who has done me no harm (nothing that I would recognize as harm), so long as my false belief was itself reasonable or justified in the circumstances. Perhaps I misread or misheard as his a name in a letter or conversation which was that of someone who really had harmed me. I may have relied too much on a usually reliable informant. All the evidence I had might have supported the false belief that he had harmed me. If so my anger is subjectively reasonable even if not objectively so. It is appropriate to what I reasonably believe to be the circumstances, even if not to the circumstances as they actually are.

What is wrong with the beliefs of psychotics is not primarily that they are false, although they usually are. It is that they are unjustified. Emotions and, *a fortiori*, behaviour, are indications of madness only if they are expressions of defective beliefs, essentially of unjustified beliefs and so usually, but only consequentially, of false beliefs. We should consider the case of a man whose beliefs were subjectively unreasonable but nevertheless true. I might believe that someone had harmed me, without any reason for my belief, although he had in fact done so. In that case I am unreasonable, but, in a way, my emotion is not. People often say, truly or falsely, after winning some wild bet in a lottery or on an outsider 'I *knew* I was going to win'. If they believed they were going to win for certain they would be full of happy expectation. After the event we might say 'well, your confidence was justified', and so it was, in itself, as a belief; but they were not justified in being confident. In being concerned with madness, a condition of persons, not of propositions, the kind of reasonableness which is relevant to us is the subjective reasonableness of persons.

4. Emotion and Belief

Before going any further it may be right to stop to consider an objection to the assumption I have made that emotions embody beliefs. I am inclined to think this is correct since it is a natural development of the reasonable view that emotions have objects or are intentional, in Brentano's sense. One cannot just hate or fear or hope but must hate or fear someone or something, hope that something will come to pass. Fear entails belief in some approaching evil. Hatred and hope do not directly entail beliefs, but, nevertheless, more loosely imply them. Hatred is intense dislike and primarily a desire for evil to befall its object where that object is a person, perhaps for its non-existence where the object is a thing or event, in either case for the minimization, ideally the reduction to nothing, of its coming into contact with or affecting one. It seems at any rate conceivable that one should have a quite baseless hatred of someone, in the sense of being unable to identify anything about him in virtue of which one hates him.

Another line of objection to the view that emotions embody beliefs is that there seem to be objectless emotions, free-floating anxiety or Heideggerian *Angst*, for example. But it does not seem too artificial to say that in such a case the embodied belief is of a somewhat indefinite kind to the effect that *something*, one cannot say more definitely just what, is horrible and going to happen. (If Popper is right about the metaphysical nature of uncircumscribed existential propositions it would follow that Heidegger's *Angst* is indeed a metaphysical anxiety.)

It is not, however, necessary to hold that all emotions embody beliefs, only that those that are characteristic of madness, in the forms of madness with which specific emotions are associated, do so. I think it is clear that the elation of the manic, the despair of the depressive and the suspicious fear and resentment of the paranoiac are of the same uncontroversially belief-embodying sort as fear or, for that matter, of embarrassment (embodying the belief that one has made a fool of oneself) or regret (embodying the belief that one has done something in some way bad, whether morally or prudentially).

The manic's wild elation embodies a belief in his own supreme qualities of intelligence and, perhaps, virtue and in his power to bring off remarkable achievements with, so to speak, a flick of the wrist. It is not an objectless glee, as is shown by its leading its possessor into characteristically over-ambitious lines of conduct. The intense despair of the depressive involves a belief in his own worthlessness and perhaps his wickedness and in the incurable bleakness of his prospects. The fear, suspicion and resentment of the paranoid plainly presuppose a belief in the existence of a conspiracy directed towards his undoing.

The cognitive conception of madness I am proposing should be formulated, then, as the acceptance of unreasonable beliefs. We all accept unreasonable beliefs from time to time, indeed it may well be that we always have some unreasonable beliefs, with some of them persisting for a long time uncriticized and undisturbed. But that does not make us all mad. Two further qualifications need to be introduced. The first of these has been mentioned more than once in passing. This is that the unreasonable belief of the madman is systematic. The second is that the beliefs in question should be practical and directly relevant to the active life of the believer.

5. System and Practicality

The idea of system I have in mind is not a very precise one. What is meant is that the unreasonable belief that constitutes madness is neither short-lived nor localized, in the sense of being confined to some fairly narrow section of the whole range of someone's beliefs. Under the influence of drink or drugs one can have a broad array of unreasonable beliefs about oneself and one's circumstances (usually of a kind that is embarrassing to look back on later) which would not amount to madness unless it were to persist for a long time or indefinitely. One can also have unreasonable beliefs about some fairly narrow domain of fact that does not amount to madness, but at most to neurosis. Phobias, neurotic fears of some particular kind of thing or circumstance—crowds, spiders, flying, heights and so forth—clearly involve beliefs about the dangerousness of the things feared that are at least pitched unreasonably high. There are, after all, mobs, black widows, air crashes and crumbling cliff edges or church towers. Compulsions are beliefs of an unreasonable sort, for example about the dirtiness of the hands that someone with a washing compulsion cleans dozens of times a day. They too are neuroses whose unreasonableness is recognized by the otherwise reasonable person who suffers from them. But in the case of the psychotic the systematic extent of his unreasonable beliefs leaves no room for a main mass of reasonable belief to contrast with them and to provide a standpoint from which they can be criticized. It is to the systematic nature of his delusions that the lack of insight characteristic of the psychotic must be attributed.

Another, equally imprecise but equally indispensable, qualification is that the unreasonable belief-system of the psychotic should be practical, concern his everyday active life, his primordial business of looking after himself: waking and sleeping, steering clear of obvious dangers, eating and drinking so as to prolong life not bring it to an end, conducting relations with other people so as to avoid trouble and so on. The psychotic is a danger to himself and a danger, or at least a nuisance, to others in the same way as a retarded person, but for different reasons. The retardate does not know what to do or how to do it; the psychotic does not realize, because of his delusions, that things he knows perfectly well how to do ought to be done.

A lot of people believe a great deal of what may be called theoretical rubbish without being on that account in the least mad. Communication in seances with the spirits of the dead, miraculous spoon-bending, flying saucers are relatively inoffensive examples of the sort of thing I have in mind. Their main effect, one may hope, is to brighten the lives of those who believe in them, in the manner of fairy stories and tales of the uncanny or of astonishing voyages. A measure of suspension of disbelief, rather than outright acceptance, could have an intellectually therapeutic value, keeping the mind open, like other fictions, to possibilities one had not considered. They are unpractical in so far as they have little bearing on action, at least of a non-verbal kind.

Theoretical beliefs in a more respectable, academic sense of the adjective, about the distance from the earth of Alpha Centauri or the atomic weight of mercury or the causes of the collapse of the Roman empire can also be unreasonable without doing much damage. The only practical upshot they have for most people is verbal: in talk or in doing examinations. In themselves they do not give rise to emotion. I may hold on doggedly and angrily to an unreasonable belief of an academically theoretical kind. But that will not be because of the belief itself, but because of the historical circumstances of its adoption. I may have thought it up and committed my reputation to it. It is my true and reasonable belief that I am generally identified with it that endows it with an emotional force for me. Despite this not uncommon kind of obstinacy, it is often the case that theoretical beliefs are entertained hypothetically, in a speculative spirit. This methodological attitude is appropriate to the limited confirmability of theories. They should be held in a tentative spirit that is always ready to acknowledge a need to revise or abandon them in face of unfavourable evidence. That is the correlate in the academic or scholarly scientific domain of the playfulness or suspension of disbelief appropriate to the kind of humble theoretical folklore discussed a little earlier.

There is one large and important variety of belief-system that must be considered at this point, in which theoretical notions about the world, man and society are intimately connected with practical beliefs or at any rate prescriptions for conduct. These are religions and full-blooded political ideologies. Very often here too there is an analogue to the tentativeness proper to academic speculation and the playfulness proper to tales of the marvellous. Hume observed how surprisingly slight the effect of a proclaimed belief in hell is the actual conduct of those who profess it, which is often little different from that of those who do not. Lord Melbourne memorably approved of that. 'Things have come to a pretty pass', he said, 'when religion starts to invade private life.'

But much religious belief is, of course, serious and sincere and it typically protects itself from rational investigation by the principle that faith, which is, after all, something close to a euphemism for unreasonable belief, is a moral duty. Among the great religions Christianity occupies a kind of middle position between the Chinese form, in which there is no speculative, supernatural element to speak of, and the Indian form in which, both in Hinduism and in the less sophisticated types of Buddhism, the common world of practical everyday belief and action is held to be an illusion. Christianity asserts the existence of an elaborate supernatural order of things, but the reality of the created world is not denied. The Christian God, after all, incarnated himself in it. But apart from that and some lesser miraculous happenings, the common natural world is taken to be real on its own account in very much the terms in which it is conceived by everyday reasonable belief. Christianity adds a great deal of additional matter of belief to everyday convictions, but it does not conflict with or undermine them on the whole.

A significant residue of fanatical religion remains in which witches are identified and burnt, in which Moslems enthusiastically go to their deaths expecting an immediate move to paradise, in which Christian Scientists refuse medical aid for themselves and their children. At this level of intensity religion begins to look like collective psychosis. There is much more to be said on this subject and on the related topic of total political ideologies and, at a more modest level, about superstition. But ideologies and superstition resemble non-fanatical religious belief in adding to, rather than supplanting or suppressing, the reasonable beliefs about the world, about the believer himself and about the immediate circumstances of his life and field of his conduct which define his sanity. They do not, therefore, need to be further considered here.

6. Practical Beliefs and Evaluation

What I have called practical beliefs are, it might be objected, of a hybrid character, containing an unproblematically factual but also an evaluative element. Words like 'wonderful' and 'dreadful', 'good' and 'bad', 'harm' and 'advantage' occur in their verbal expression. But judgments involving these terms are intrinsically controversial, are not or are not simply cognitive in nature, express the preferences of their users rather than state what is objectively true or false. The unreasonable practical belief-system of the psychotic is not, then, as cognitive a matter as I have made it appear.

But the unreasonable aspect of the psychotic's characteristic beliefs is not the evaluative but the factual one. Behind the manic's elation lies the belief that he has a proposal which will bring peace to the world and is also wonderful, a proper object of elation. But there is nothing very questionable about the second, evaluative part of his belief. If he really had a proposal that would guarantee world peace who would question his right to be elated? The depressive believes that nothing he could do would succeed and that that is a bad thing, a proper thing to be depressed by. And so it is. What is unreasonable about his belief is its factual part, its judgment of his own potentialities. The paranoiac believes that everyone around him is in a conspiracy to frustrate him or destroy his reputation and also that if they succeed it will be very bad for him. Here again the evaluation is too obvious to question. What is wrong is his factual account of what is actually going on.

But although this objection fails to show that an account of madness in terms of systematic unreasonabble practical belief is only superficially cognitive it does raise a question that should be considered. In what has been said so far no mention has been made of the desires or preferences of the psychotic. Might it not be here that the essential core of madness is to be found?

It is quite true that the desires of the psychotic for the most part display his condition, although it may take time for someone else to recognize the fact. The mad are often 'rational', in so far as their beliefs, emotions, desires and actions hang coherently together. It is when we discover the systematic unreasonableness of his practical beliefs that we catch him out. Many desires are not ultimate, are not directed towards things we want as ends in themselves. They are for things we want because we believe that they will promote our achieving what we do want for its own sake. I want the waiter to come to the table, not because I enjoy the pleasure of his company, but so that I can order the meal. At the end of the chain of desires is a plate of food that I want for its own sake. Likewise, the paranoiac wants to get away from the other people in the bus shelter because he believes they are conspiring to kill him and he does not want to die. My summoning the waiter is based on the reasonable belief that it is a means to the end of getting fed. His flight from the bus shelter is an unreasonable means to self-preservation, because his belief that his fellow-shelterers are conspiring to kill him is an unreasonable one. Non-ultimate, or mediate, desires are in the same boat as emotions. Their unreasonableness, which makes them candidates for consideration as mad, is derivative from that of the beliefs that they embody.

That leaves ultimate desires, which, if they embody beliefs at all, embody only the belief that the attainment of their objects will be satisfying. Could it not be said of them that they can be and sometimes are for things which although satisfying to the desirer are nevertheless things it is mad to desire? Possible examples are the psychopath, and his brother, the coldly calculating criminal, the sexual deviant and the eccentric. The psychopath is 'without conscience', the suffering of others plays no part in the determination of his actions. In notorious cases he combines a persistent taste for cruelty and murder with a measure of blithe imprudence that leads to his getting caught. There is no question that his motivation is abnormal, exceptional and repulsive. But is he mad? Apart from the absence of any sort of altruistic concern for others he has the usual Butlerian apparatus of self-love and particular passions. He pursues his ends with a reasonable system of practical beliefs. I should conclude that he is nasty, but sane, as does common legal practice and common opinion. The calculating criminal is also sane, as distinct from the mentally deficient criminal, the passionate criminal (provoked beyond endurance), the criminal who commits his crimes under the influence of drink or drugs (which, I suggested earlier, produce temporary states of belief derangement comparable to madness).

In this connection the case of the major political criminal, like Hitler or Stalin, should be considered. It has been objected to the cognitive account of madness I am proposing that it would imply the sanity, probably, of Hitler and, almost certainly, of Stalin. (The second consequence is generally found less offensive.) Now there are aspects of Hitler's personality that seem psychotic. I am not thinking so much of the alleged episodes of rug-chewing as of the central position in his whole system of ends of his hatred of Jews. But, given its ultimacy and primacy among his purposes, he handled it rationally. For example, when, after his seizure of power, he expelled all Jewish professors, he was told that this would cripple German theoretical physics, which, it was correctly pointed out, would be of great military importance. He answered that he would rather Germany failed than succeeded with the help of 'Jewish physics'. All the same his hatred of Jews was not all that ultimate, it was permeated with ridiculous beliefs. But on the whole he was far too shrewd and crafty an operator to be described as mad. Those who, often passionately, think otherwise, tend to subscribe to three inconsistent propositions: Hitler was mad, only the sane should be punished, Hitler should have been punished.

Hitler was certainly a psychopath, and thus far mentally deficient, and a neurotic, in the light of his unreasonable, not simply contemptible, hatred of Jews. Sexual deviants and eccentrics, by which I mean people indifferent to worldly success that is within their power, and who choose to pursue some unusual or exceptional end of a harmless sort, living in isolation on nuts and berries, are neither. The sexual deviant may be quite right in his belief that he will get erotic satisfaction only from members of his own sex. The more generally agreeable forms of sexual activity involve the participation of others and that creates a need for protection, from violent coercion in the case of adult partners, from any sort of interference in the case of children, who can be coerced very easily and, where there is no coercion, may not know what is happening and so cannot be said to choose to take part.

The psychopath, who is without conscience, has a counterpart in the realm of prudence, the rash or reckless person, who, for the joys of skiing or motor racing, is ready to pursue them at great risk of injury or death. In English English it is that sort of extreme imprudence to which the word 'mad' is colloquially used to refer, while 'crazy' does the same job in American English. In the latter dialect 'mad' is the colloquial equivalent of 'angry'. It may be hard to decide, here as in the case of the criminal, just how far it is a matter of unusually balanced ultimate desires that is at work and how far a matter of unreasonable estimates of the likelihood of death or serious injury. I should maintain that a risk-taker who, as the phrase is, 'knows what he is doing', is perfectly mentally healthy, while one who, with ordinary desires, nevertheless acts more rashly than most people is to that extent neurotic, for I believe this accords with our reflective intuitions on the subject. Deviation in patterns of desire is not a sign of mental illness, deviation in practical belief is.

Madness, then, and, by implication, neurosis, is a specific kind of mental weakness or defect. It is to be distinguished from retardation or mental deficiency, which is a constitutional inability to learn, to acquire and retain beliefs and skills; it is not ignorance or stupidity of any kind, which is a shortage of beliefs and not a collection of bad ones; it is not illogicality or muddleheadedness, which is a failure to see the implications and incompatibilities of beliefs. It is a matter of having a set or system of unreasonable beliefs, comprehensive in the case of madness, localized in neurosis.

7. Scepticism About Madness

In defending a cognitive account of madness against an emotional or affective one I have had two ulterior motives. In the first place a cognitive theory makes the attribution of madness less disputable, more objective than the emotional alternative does. Unreasonableness of belief is a matter on which general argeement can be expected, while the characterization of certain unusual emotions and supposedly perverse desires as unacceptable is hard to defend from the charge of being arbitrary. Secondly, a cognitive theory sets up a distinction between the mentally ill and the socially deviant. To treat the latter as more or less mad is doubly undesirable. On the one hand it puts calculating criminals from Hitler downwards outside the reach of punishment; on the other it exposes homosexuals and eccentrics to the comparatively benign but still disparaging and potentially compulsion-inviting category of the mentally ill.

The objectivity of the distinction between the mad and the sane, which I am anxious to secure, has been challenged from both ends of the ideological spectrum. Thomas Szasz has been mentioned earlier for his view that to call people mad is to tie a derogatory label to them. Those we describe as mad, he says, differ only in degree from the rest of us. We all have problems of life; theirs happen to be particularly severe. The ideological point of his position is that people should not be encouraged to give in, to be rendered passive by institutionalization and subjection to treatment. They should be stimulated, rather, to pull themselves together and to take responsibility for themselves.

At the opposite extreme is Michel Foucault, who, in his *Madness and Civilization*, plays rhapsodic variations on a theme he states at the beginning—the mad conspiracy of men to call some of their number mad and to confine them. Between tracts of pretentious verbal posturing the idea is insinuated that for their own convenience and profit the holders of power carried out this imposture. Some rational fragments can be picked out here and there in the flux. Confined madmen were for long thought of as monsters and wild beasts. But that was due to the religiously endorsed idea that the mad were diabolically possessed and also to the idea that only rational beings are proper objects of moral concern. In repudiating the Cartesian tradition of intellectual hygiene for some dirty habits picked up from Nietzsche, he retains the French resistance to the idea that animals have rights, or even feelings. Of course the mad should be treated humanely, but neither distinguishing them from the sane, nor confining them for their own and other people's protection implies that it does not matter what is done to them in confinement.

A general merit of these scepticisms is that they raise the question as to whether the distinction between the mad and the sane is not some kind of put-up job. In the first place, it may be questioned whether the various forms of madness are diseases at all. Secondly, the usual ways in which sanity and madness are distinguished are unsatisfactory, although for quite different reasons. On the one hand there is the tight-lipped evasiveness of psychiatric professionalism, as revealed in textbooks. In imitation of the equally bogus rigour of ordinary pathology, disease is defined in purely statistical terms. On the other hand there are more or less affective accounts of madness, which define it in terms of radical failure of social adjustment or socially unacceptable behaviour caused by socially unacceptable emotions. The affective conception of madness I have already criticized. I shall now consider the claim that madness is a disease and then the idea that disease, mental or physical, is simply a matter of statistical abnormality.

Before leaving the sceptics I must explain why I have not included R. D. Laing among them. He, at least in his early work, gave an account of how people are driven into schizophrenia by disabling emotional pressures within the family. He held that the apparently senseless discourse of the schizophrenic can in fact be interpreted as a rational communicative response to the circumstances in which he finds himself. I am neglecting him because his main point is an account of what *causes* schizophrenia, not of what it is. It, like other forms of madness, may be emotionally caused, but that does not determine what it is. Even less does it imply that there is really no such thing. He does indeed go on to say that it is not what it is supposed to be. What casts doubt on any literary-humanistic theory of schizophrenia of this kind is the fact that it is to a considerable extent inherited. Even more striking, in view of the fact that most people are brought up by those from whom they get their genes, is the small variation in the incidence of schizophrenia as between one culture and another.

8. Is Madness a Disease?

The main argument for taking the various forms of madness to be diseases is their analogy to what are conventionally acknowledged to be diseases of the body. That argument does not raise the question of what a disease actually is, but it will be considered later. The mental and behavioural manifestations of madness—the unreasonable belief-systems, the absurd or unusual emotions and behaviour—would, if madness is a disease, be its symptoms. There is a close relationship between the ordinary sorts of madness I have been dealing with so far and the organic psychoses. The first and most powerful aspect of the analogy between madness and straightforward physical disease is that some kinds of madness, the organic psychoses, *are* physical diseases, or, at any rate, result directly from them.

A well-known and dramatic form of organic psychosis is paresis, the tertiary stage of syphilis, sometimes known as general paralysis of the insane, a complaint much favoured by cultural figures in the nineteenth century. More widespread is what is often called senile dementia, the mental collapse that can come with great age. Both of these are organic conditions since they are rooted in disorders of the brain, in cerebral lesions arising in one case from prolonged syphilitic infection, in the other from decay through the passage of time. The symptoms of these two conditions are very closely similar to those of functional schizophrenia, that schizophrenia which has no *known* physiological or organic basis. Other organic conditions of a more or less psychotic kind are delirium tremens, caused by alcohol, which is not easy to distinguish by way of its symptoms alone from the delirium of fever, and the dementia that arises not from old age but from injury to the head.

The boundary between organic and functional conditions, defined as it is in terms of what is currently known, is neither sharp nor permanent. A functional condition is one that is waiting for a physiological explanation, not one for which no such explanation can in principle be found. Over and above the close analogy between the symptoms of organic and functional psychosis a further reason for supposing that the functional psychoses of the present are the organic psychoses of the future is the fact that some functional psychoses, most notably depressive psychosis, respond to treatment with drugs. That is a more powerful consideration than may at first appear. For in this sort of case it cannot be argued that the drug serves merely as a symptom-suppressor, in the way that treatments for the common cold clear the nose and soothe the throat without getting to the root of the matter. The drug cannot get to the root of the matter unless there is a root of the matter to get to. If there is not the symptoms, or some of them, must actually constitute the disease.

Our ordinary notion of a disease is that it is a bad or abnormal condition which lasts for some time, perhaps a very long time. At the opposite extreme to things like cancer and tuberculosis are sudden attacks of pneumonia which can kill people off very soon after their onset. But even these last a few hours. If someone chokes on a bone or is suffocated or killed in a crash or by a fall a medical explanation is readily available for the cause of death. But the deaths are said to be due to accident or injury, not disease. Such deaths cannot be marked off from those due to disease by reference to the external cause of the body's malfunction and death because the lethal germs or viruses are just as much external as the choking bone or the fatal car. A reason for picking out longer lasting painful or fatal conditions as diseases is that their duration allows time for treatment.

The point of this digression is that we do seem to countenance the idea of momentary madness. Someone hit on the head or insulted or obstructed may be brought by it into a delirious, raving state that quickly passes. If this is correct it amounts to a marginal lack of analogy. A line of defence against it would be to say that the brain is the most delicate, complicated and volatile of all the organs of the body. It may be, too, that there are physical analogues: sudden, quickly passing bouts of fever.

A final reason for taking the analogy to justify calling the psychoses mental diseases is that some conditions that are unhesitatingly regarded as diseases of the body have obscure or unknown physiological bases, epilepsy and migraine, for example. They stand to the bodily diseases that have a known physiological basis as do functional to organic psychoses. I believe that all diseases, of the body and the mind, have a physiological basis. But that assumption is not presupposed by the view that madness is a disease. However, without it a certain whiff of the metaphorical clings to the idea that it is.

9. The Statistical Criterion of Disease

Pathology textbooks usually begin, before they plunge into the honest, scientific detail of the subject, with some gruff and embarrassed preliminaries of a definitional kind. The student is told that a disease is an abnormal condition of the body and is made clear that the word 'abnormal' is being used in a strictly statistical sense. The advantages of this are obvious. The field of study is demarcated in an irresistibly objective and uncontroversial way. Or, at any rate, it seems that that is so.

What it actually does is to pretend to have given a truly scientific account of the field, which turns out to let into it much that its exponents would never think of considering. For example, the possession of naturally blonde hair is common in Sweden but unheard of in Japan. It is the property of a small minority in the human species as a whole. Is it, then, a disease? Are having dense freckles, being over 80 inches tall, being left-handed? These last three conditions, unlike naturally blonde hair, are all a bit of a nuisance. Respectively, they make one look silly when middle aged, require one to crouch when going through doorways, necessitate special golf clubs. But at least introducing the idea of a *disliked* bodily condition is a move in the right direction. It recognizes an ineliminably evaluative element in the concept of disease.

The crucial negatively evaluated features in straightforward physical disease are pain, death and, more elusively, what is called dysfunction. The most obvious instances of disease are those bodily conditions which are either painful and will lead, if not corrected, to pain or death. Pain and death are unfavourably evaluated in almost all circumstances. But pain can trump death. When intense, prolonged and unstoppable it may make death relatively attractive. Dysfunction is harder to define. I cannot climb to the top of a gymnasium by a rope, but that does not constitute an illness. But I should be ill if I were unable to walk from where I am writing to the door (provided that I had previously been able to walk that distance); if I had never been able to do so I would not be ill but handicapped.

A statistical account of illness in terms of abnormality is, if anything, even less enticing in the mental case. The reason is that we are—to speak with somewhat vertiginous generality—much more alike physically than we are alike mentally. To bring that large contention down to earth a little: there is a real point to the idea of a normal body temperature. For most people most of the time it is 98.4°F. People whose temperature departs substantially from that figure become distressed, wish they felt as they more usually do in certain respects, find it hard to do things that they want to do and ordinarily can do without difficulty. Allowing for differences of sex and age, we are all anatomically much the same, within a moderate range of shapes and sizes.

Mentally, however, we differ much more widely. Different cultures, different personal histories, different tastes and interests and preferences cause us to follow very different styles of life, to approach the world with very different aims and to react to it with very different emotions. Because of our physiological uniformity statistical abnormality is not too bad a guide to physical ill-health. As the examples proved, it is not a sufficient condition. But in practice it is approximately a necessary condition. If someone is ill then his body is in a statistically abnormal condition. If that abnormality is connected to pain, death or dysfunction we have an adequate working criterion of physical ill-health.

Is illness always statistically abnormal? The idea that it is not could be named 'Auden's conjecture' in virtue of his line, 'this England of ours where nobody is well'. Operating under poetic licence he announces that no-one is well in England. Since there are plenty of different illnesses what he says is compatible with no disease ever affecting more than a small minority. Since there are well over twenty of them, the statistician's ninety-five per cent rule of normality can be complied with.

But is it possible for a majority to suffer from a particular disease? It could happen for a time, epidemically. A nation or the whole world could be temporarily afflicted for a while like a prison or a boarding school. Could some disliked bodily condition be suffered from by most of the people most of the time? Only, I suspect, if the identification of the disease was logically parasitic on the statistically abnormal character of most diseases. Otherwise it would be counted part of the general human condition, like getting tired after a long hard day.

Even if it is a necessary condition of illness, statistical abnormality is certainly inadequate as a criterion or definition unless an evaluative element is added. And the evaluative element must be of a particular sort, one that involves pain, death or dysfunction. A persistent, acquired condition of the body that is simply disliked, either by its possessor or by anyone affected by it, is not on that account a disease. An attractive child turns into an ugly adult. Its ugliness, although perhaps medically modifiable, is not an illness. Nor is early baldness, unless it is total and sudden. Nor are evil-smelling breath and body, even if not due to lack of hygiene.

The inadequacy of a statistical criterion of disease is even more patent in the case of mental illness. People with abnormally high IQs, calculating prodigies and the owners of enormously capacious memories are not insane. Nor are those with a compelling interest in Turkish carpets or real tennis or the breeding of decorative poultry. What is needed is some negative aspect to the abnormality. The wide range of mental abnormalities that falls under the consideration of the psychiatrist has little to do with pain (except in the sense of emotional distress, to which I shall return) or with death. It may be some kind of dysfunction, but that is even less clear a notion in the mental case than it is in the physical. To consider this problem the scope of the inquiry must be widened to include all mental illness, actual or alleged, neuroses and 'personality disorders', as well as psychoses.

10. What is Bad About Mental Illness

Neurosis differs from psychosis in two connected respects. A neurosis—phobia, obsession or compulsion—is a local or partial oddity of belief, emotion and conduct in relation to some particular kind of thing: high places, the possibility of being attacked from behind, washing the hands. This will co-exist with reasonable belief, emotion and behaviour with regard to other matters. Secondly, the neurotic recognizes this and deplores it. Like the physically ill person he will ordinarily admit that there is something wrong with him, even if he is unwilling to submit to treatment for one reason or another. The psychotic, just because his beliefs are systematically unreasonable, usually does not admit that there is anything wrong with him and cannot co-operate with the attempts of others to cure him.

What are called personality disorders are all localized in the way that neurosis is, but the attitudes to them of their possessors are very various. A good many alcoholics and drug addicts and some sexual deviants would like to have their personalities changed, and not just for the sake of convenience and so as to fit more smoothly into society. But many sexual deviants, all eccentrics and, I imagine, all criminals are unwilling to admit that there is anything wrong with them. They have insight in that they know what it is about them that brings social disapproval down on them, but they do not think these peculiarities ought to be eliminated and do not want them eliminated.

Perhaps it does not matter very much whether we see neuroses as illnesses or, on the other hand, take them to parallel those bodily deficiencies which, while not diseases, are medically treatable and, where disliked by those who have them, may be brought to treatment. Agoraphobia and washing compulsion could be categorized in the same way as an ugly face or early baldness. A reason for not doing so is the superficial and cosmetic nature of these disliked bodily defects. Their dysfunctional aspect is fairly trivial, more like conversational boringness or a stammer on the mental side.

The dysfunctions attributable to neuroses are more disabling, even though a neurosis can be accommodated, at some cost, in a life that is otherwise normal. So, given that the problematic mental conditions have no connection with pain and death, it seems reasonable to call them diseases too. If that is correct for neuroses it must hold all the more solidly for psychoses, since with them the dysfunction is very much greater. The total inability of the psychotic to manage his life does, indeed, bring pain and death in indirectly. If left to his own devices he may starve or may suffer and die as a result of dangers he is not in a condition to avoid or ward off.

Glover's proposal of a better criterion of mental ill-health than statistical abnormality exploits this fact about the extremely dysfunctional character of psychosis. He argues that, since the practical point of categorizing people as mentally ill is, in extreme cases at least, that of whether to institutionalize and to force treatment on them, the mentally ill should be defined as those whose consistent pattern of action is harmful to them. One objection is that this would make retardation a mental illness, but that could be circumvented by redrafting. He attempts to minimize the contestable and controversial potentialities of his central evaluative notion of harm by saying it is what is unpleasant, unwanted and deprives one of pleasure without any compensating benefit.

On Glover's criterion a religious zealot who refused medical treatment when physically ill would be not just disastrously mistaken but mad. The reckless people who drink and smoke too much or drive too fast are not just unwise but insane. Not only does his proposal imply that a lot of people are mad who are not, but the converse is at least a possibility. Could there not be a man who lived in a complete fantasy world, but who was so happy in it that it would be cruel to cure him? Admittedly his avoidance of harm would be a piece of good luck, perhaps that of living in some affectionate human setting in which he was cared for and looked after. He could not flourish in the real world unless so protected.

The disastrous consequences to the psychotic of the behaviour to which his madness leads are the bad feature which makes that condition madness and not its statistical abnormality. But the madness is not in the consequences; it is in the mental condition from which those consequences ensue. They could have arisen from sheer bad luck or undetected malice on the part of others and then there would be no suggestion that the victim was mad. In fact such disastrous consequences are most unlikely unless they are the results of madness. The state of mind that the disastrous consequences show, if persistent enough to rule out other explanations, to be madness is required to explain why the behaviour is so persistently disastrous.

Earlier I ascribed the charm of a statistical criterion to psychiatrists to its apparently objective and scientific character. But if it is inadequate how do psychiatrists manage in practice to pick out for treatment, in marked agreement with each other as to those who need it, patients who are not picked out for them by the criterion to which they ostensibly subscribe? The answer, clearly enough, is that their practice is better than their principles. In their training they learn how to diagnose madness and can give provisional accounts of that practice in the form of open-ended lists of symptoms, that is to say the 'clinical descriptions' from which I started and on which I have, of course, relied. They are not trained to take a step further back and to produce a justification for classing together as psychoses the assorted set of clinically described conditions they deal. They do not really need to until challenged by sceptical critics of the whole idea of madness. I have assumed that, in virtue of the wealth and intimacy of their experience, they know what they are doing when they diagnose people as mad. That does not entail that their attempts to summarize the principles embodied in their diagnostic practice have to be accorded the same authority.

11. Beliefs, Consensus and Descartes' Problem

My chief claim has been that madness should not be defined either in terms of the characteristic emotions of those identified as mad, nor in terms of their characteristic behaviour. Nor should it be defined in textbook fashion in terms of statistical abnormality or, again, functionally, as by Glover in terms of need for protection against a consistent behaviour pattern that is harmful to the agent. Madness consists in the systematic unreasonableness of a person's practical beliefs.

The effectiveness of the social practice of diagnosing some people as mad must, then, depend on some sort of consensus about the unreasonableness of the relevant, practical beliefs, to which, of course, the person under consideration can not himself be a party. He is bound to agree with the consensus if he is sane and disagree with it if he is mad, since, in both cases, he will have to say that his own system of practical beliefs is reasonable. To say that it is not is as good as self-refuting. What he says about the system is not exactly part of the system of his practical beliefs. But each of them informally implies its own reasonableness and so the whole lot of them, taken together, informally imply the reasonableness of the whole system.

Does this requirement of consensus reinstate the statistical criterion? In a way it does, but it applies to a different and more narrowly circumscribed range of material. As things are, and given that the relevant beliefs are practical in the sense I have described, the consensus is very broad. In the case of psychotics, at any rate, there is no serious doubt about the characterization of their beliefs as unreasonable. In the case of more localized peculiarities of belief, those of the fearful flyer, for example, there may be some opening for disagreement. But the possibility should be considered that the present state of affairs, in which the vast majority agree that the practical belief-systems of a comparatively small number of people are unreasonable, might not obtain.

Suppose that only a fifth of the population managed to precipitate the kind of consensus about the reasonableness of practical beliefs that is now much more widely shared. They could still regard themselves as the sane minority provided that no group as large as their own in the remaining four-fifths achieved a comparable consensus. As things are the sane inhabit a common world, while the mad live in worlds of their own, unable to communicate or co-operate effectively with each other or with the sane. In our epistemic democracy the mad are all fringe candidates of the most extreme variety. But if there were two belief-parties of much the same size we should be in a mess. Were such a state of affairs to seem to obtain it might inspire doubt in each party as to whether they really understood the remarks, and so had really identified the beliefs, of the other. We can understand what other people say only if we assume that most of what they say is true, at any rate (cf. my *Thoughts and Thinkers*, Ch. 8).

Another extreme possibility is intimated but not explored in the first of Descartes' *Meditations*. I have been considering the question how I, or anyone else, can reasonably conclude that anyone other than the inquirer is mad. Descartes touches on the question: do I know that I am not myself mad? It seems to me that others share my beliefs and regard them as broadly reasonable, at least on practical matters, and find my emotions and conduct not to be particularly surprising or absurd. But may they not all be humouring me? Or, to go a stage further, might my belief in their apparent endorsement of the reasonableness of my practical belief-system be only a large piece of my system of unreasonable practical beliefs.

It would seem that if one is mad one cannot know that one is or even seriously believe that one is. For to do so is to believe that one's capacity for forming reasonable beliefs has broken down, that one's system of practical beliefs is composed of unreasonable beliefs and also that, on that account, one's beliefs are different from those of most people, the epistemic consensus. But to do that is, in effect, to repudiate one's system of practical beliefs.

The belief that I am mad is, therefore, a more disturbing one than the belief that I am asleep and dreaming. Any evidence one could cite to show that one was not dreaming could simply be something that one only dreams to be at one's disposal. Likewise any evidence one might invoke to show that one was not mad might be just a lunatic fancy. But while one usually wakes up from dreams, madness is a more long-lasting condition. Sometimes there is remission in which people can look back and conclude, reasonably, that they were mad then but are so no longer. In that case the past mad self is, for most epistemological purposes, another person. On that basis they can reasonably predict the return of madness. On a smaller scale there can be moments of sanity when the psychotic makes a brief escape from his prison of delusion. But often madness is a dream from which the dreamer never awakes.

The thought that I am mad is also more logically disturbing than the belief that I am dreaming. For the belief that I am mad really does have the property ascribed by Malcolm to the belief (or assertion) that I am dreaming: it cannot be coherently framed. I can remember that I was mad. I can expect, or fear, that I will go mad. But I cannot believe that I am without undermining the grounds for supposing that my capacity to form reasonable practical beliefs has broken down on which the belief must rest.

Metaphors We Live By

DAVID E. COOPER

Aside from *aperçus* of Kant, Nietzsche, and of course, Aristotle, metaphor has not, until recently, received its due. The dominant view has been Hobbes': metaphors are an 'abuse' of language, less dangerous than ordinary equivocation only because they 'profess their inconstancy'.[1]

Attention was largely confined to those realms, like poetry, where this profession was especially frank. Kant's call for a 'deeper investigation' of metaphor in metaphysical and moral philosophy went almost unheard, and music as the food of love or dawn's rose-tinted hands, not the state as an organism or the accidents of a substance, remained the stock examples.[2] Several factors have changed this situation into one where 'friends of metaphor' abound. For one thing, doubts set in as to the possibility of crisply defining metaphor so as to put it aside for future and peripheral treatment. Derrida, for example, has stressed the difficulties of defining it outside of an itself metaphorical terminology of metaphysics—'ideas', 'transfer of meaning', and the like.[3] And loss of confidence in the analytic/synthetic distinction has muddled the enterprise of distinguishing proper from extended from figurative use. Another factor, brought home by Max Black, has been the appreciation of the role of metaphor in science; it may not only trigger, but model, construction of theory.[4] Third, linguists have confirmed to their own professional satisfaction Dumarsais' old dictum that one hears more tropes on a single day in the marketplace than in several sittings of the *Académie Française*; that metaphor has a pervasiveness and ubiquity that its reputation as an 'abuse' would hardly lead us to expect.[5] Finally, there were Roman Jakobson's seminal papers on common speech disorders, where he argues that their most vivid manifestation and partial explanation lie in the inability to handle

---

[1] *Leviathan* (Blackwell, 1960), 25.

[2] *Critique of Judgement* (Hafner, 1966), 198.

[3] 'La mythologie blanche', in *Marges de la Philosophie* (Editions Minuit, 1972).

[4] 'Metaphor', in *Models and Metaphors* (Cornell, 1962).

[5] Quoted in P. Fontanier, *Les Figures du Discours* (Flammarion, 1977), 157. For linguists' researches into the incidence of metaphor, see G. Sampson, *Making Sense* (Oxford University Press, 1980) Ch. IV.

David E. Cooper

metaphorical substitution and metonymic association.[6] With these last two factors, the study of metaphor enters the field of socio- and psycholinguistics.

A friend of metaphor, let's say, is one who holds at least the following:

(a) The study of metaphor is central for linguists. It is a deep deficiency in any theory of language that it does cater for metaphor, and not one that can be subsequently put to rights by tacking on an appendix

(b) Metaphor is not only a standard and ubiquitous feature of everyday talk, as Dumarsais saw, but unlike, say, the high frequency of hesitation or slurring in speech, this is no casual matter.

(c) The study of metaphor is important for the understanding of everyday thought and practice. People would not think and act the ways they do if they did not metaphorize as they do.

And let us say that someone is a true friend of metaphor if he adds:

(d) The study of metaphor is a component in social criticism. The ways we talk, think, and act are subject to assessment by virtue of the metaphors with which they are imbued.

Like all true friends, those of metaphor are deeply concerned at the waywardness of the object of their affection.

In its present state, the study of metaphor must be a philosophical one, for there lacks that agreement on metaphor's nature, criteria, and role required for it to be quietly passed over to the human sciences. There are questions about metaphor, indeed, which could never be handed over—ones about the relation between thought and language that the very possibility of metaphor presupposes. If the true friends of metaphor are right, the study is also one of practice, and a critical one at that. It is appropriate, then, that a plea for the study of metaphor should be heard in a series on 'Philosophy and Practice'.

Some people's enthusiasm for metaphor goes beyond friendship. There is a view that might be called 'pantropism', to the effect that all or nearly all we say is metaphorical. Nietzsche was a Pantropist if we are to believe his remark that literal talk is metaphorical talk whose figurative nature we have forgotten, like so many coins whose faces have become too worn to be recognized.[7] A view that falls not

[6] See especially 'Two Aspects of Language and Two Types of Aphasic Disturbance', in *Selected Writings*, II (Mouton, 1971).

[7] 'Über Wahrheit und Lüge im aussermoralischen Sinn', *Werke*, III (Ullstein, 1979) 314.

44

far short of this is urged in a recent book by Lakoff and Johnson, *Metaphors We Live By*. We find in it, at any rate, all the elements of friendship of metaphor. First, its centrality in a theory of language, for 'it seems inconceivable that any phenomenon so fundamental to a conceptual system could not be central to an account of truth and meaning'. Second, its non-accidental ubiquity: 'metaphor is as much part of our functioning as our sense of touch'. Third, the place of metaphor in thought and life: 'our ordinary conceptual scheme in terms of which we both think and act, is fundamentally metaphorical'. Finally investment of the study of metaphor with a critical role: 'a metaphor in a political or economic system . . . can lead to human degradation'.[8]

Much of the book consists in detailed exposition of some of these metaphors by which, according to the authors, we live. For instance, that of 'Argument as War'; the engrained tendency to talk of, think of, and treat argumentation as if it were a military confrontation. We *engage* in an argument by *defending our position* and *shooting holes* in our opponent's, so that we *kill* his argument *stone dead* and come out *winners*. This way of talking is reflected in the way argumentation is institutionalized—in TV debates, for example, with their champions of extreme and opposed views glaring across a table, chairmen trained to stimulate maximum controversy, and even a jury to award the honours of the day. Can we not imagine a people who metaphorize, and so treat, argumentation in a very different way; as a collaboration, perhaps, between travellers aiming at a common destination, so that a weakness in an argument is not something to exploit but a hitch to be repaired? Other examples given in the book include: 'Labour as a resource'—we call on a *reserve force* to *fill the gaps* in *manpower*; and 'Inflation as an enemy (or disease)'—we must *combat* it before it *poisons* the whole social *body*.

Neither the examples, nor the large claims being made on behalf of metaphor, would impress those who work with certain familiar ideas about the topic. According to the tradition deriving from Aristotle, metaphors are deviant utterances used to say what could have been said 'straight' (albeit, in some cases, with loss of effect). A modern version runs: someone speaks metaphorically when he uses words which mean one thing to mean something different, though suitably related; with the listener's task being to infer, via this relation, what the speaker means from what his words mean.[9] This view has several dampening consequences for the friends of

[8] University of Chicago, 1980. The lines quoted are from pp. 211, 239, 3 and 234.

[9] See, for example, J. R. Searle, 'Metaphor', in *Metaphor and Thought*, A. Ortony (ed.) (Cambridge University Press, 1979).

metaphor. First, metaphors cannot reveal anything significant about how we think, since they are always more or less close substitutes for the 'straight' utterances which properly express our thoughts. Second, anything approaching pantropism must be absurd, for we are not so Machiavellian as to indulge in this indirect and deviant manner of talking much of the time. The third consequence is that the bulk of cases cited by such friends as Lakoff and Johnson are not examples of metaphor at all. When I say 'He won the argument', no one takes me to mean anything but what my words mean, and for that very reason 'won' cannot be occurring metaphorically after all. Rather the verb 'win' is now a homonym, like 'table' or 'bank', which has an independant literal sense when applied to argumentation. The same goes for 'power', 'force', etc., when used to talk about labour. No doubt these new meanings derive, historically, from some earlier (and still present) ones, but as Saussure taught us, history does not determine synchronic description. We might call 'win an argument', 'manpower' and so on, '*dead* metaphors', provided we bear in mind that these are no more metaphors than dead husbands are still husbands. Certainly it is no more legitimate to call them metaphors than it is to call expressions like 'at midnight' or 'before 11 a.m.' metaphorical on the ground that the prepositions in question once denoted spatial relations only.

The superficiality of this familar view is exposed, in fact, by the final remark on prepositions. 'Before', 'at' and others, are genuine homonyms with both spatial and temporal denotations.[10] Two reasons for saying this are: first, the use of prepositions in the one domain does not mimic, at all systematically, their use in the other. If A happens before B, then B happens after A; but if I am standing before you, you are not standing after me. Second, use of the terms is not generative across the domains; that is, use in one domain does not suggest new, readily intelligible uses in the other. The fact that we are accustomed to spatial prepositions being transferred to the temporal domain would not, for example, help you understand me if I said 'I am underneath 11 a.m.'. Homonymy, in other words, exhibits neither systematic mimicry nor generative power. It is this, indeed, which makes it mere homonymy. Matters are quite different when we turn, say, to the military terminology of argumentation. First, such talk replicates with great consistency the structure of genuine military talk. An argument that I win is one that you lose; an argument full of holes is not, like sieve, a good one, but like a

[10] It is hard to agree, therefore, with Quirk and Greenbaum's claim that temporal prepositions have a 'metaphorical connection' with place ones (*A University Grammar of English* (Longman, 1973), 153).

soldier riddled with bullets, a useless one. Second, and more crucial, the way of talking is generative. Probably you have never heard the sentence 'The heavy battalions in the debate were only firing blanks', but you will grasp what it conveys, since it is a natural extension of a familiar system. Or consider, by contrast with the examples of prepositional homonymy mentioned, the fact that when I first heard someone say 'I'm really into Herman Hesse', I knew at once what he meant, because I was familar with a generative manner of talking about interests, enthusiasms, and the like, in terms of spatial immersion.

All of this suggests a crucial distinction to be drawn between metaphors *qua* individual utterances that we would ordinarily label as such, and metaphorizing—the activity of systematically talking about one domain in terms lifted from another, an activity that generates, *inter alia,* metaphors. That some of the past products generated, like 'win an argument', are too worn to still be called 'metaphors', does not mean they do not belong to a metaphorizing practice which retains the power to generate genuinely fresh metaphors. Nor does it mean they can be passed off as mere homonyms or 'dead metaphors'. (We can, parenthetically, allow for dead metaphors: ones like 'bookworm', say, which are not only faded but isolated from any systematic and generative practice.) Lakoff and Johnson are making a similar distinction to mine when they distinguish metaphors as linguistic units from metaphors, in a more fundamental sense, as the organizing concepts of which these units are typically the manifestations. 'Metaphors as linguistic expressions are possible only because there are metaphors in a person's conceptual system.'[11] (I prefer my less 'mentalistic' way of making the distinction.) An analogy may help: symbolic activity often, but by no means invariably, involves the use or production of discrete entities called 'symbols', which are one among several manifestations of symbolic activity. Just as it would be wrong to conclude that someone is not behaving symbolically from the absence of any symbols, so it would be wrong to conclude that someone is not metaphorizing from the fact that his utterances are not (any longer) metaphors. There is, so to speak, more to metaphorizing than metaphors.

I shall take it, without further ado, that metaphorizing—systematic and generative ways of talking about one domain in terms of another—is a pervasive feature of everyday language; and we must not be blinded towards this pervasiveness by the superficial observation that many of the utterances belonging to these practices are too

[11] Op. cit., 6.

David E. Cooper

familiar and worn to any longer be called metaphors in ordinary parlance. The question I want to raise is why our everyday talk is so pervasively metaphorical. Why, except for occasional effect, do we not stick to talking 'straight'? Only a small part of the answer could be provided by catachresis, the use of old words in preference to the invention of new ones for designating new referents. For if any expressions deserve the title 'dead metaphor', it is such catachrestic ones as 'bottle—cap' or 'table—leg'.

The literature offers two main answers to our question: the venerable 'aesthetic' answer and the currently more fashionable 'cognitivist' one. Hobbes explains metaphor as a 'special use' of language which aims 'to please and delight...by playing with our words'; and for that indefatigable taxonomist of tropes, Fontanier, its aims are 'plaisir et agrément'.[12] On this view, then, if metaphor is pervasive it is because men are so pleasure-seeking. For a modern like Max Black, however, the emphasis has switched to the cognitive. Metaphors are models we indulge in to help us understand the metaphorized domains, 'filters' through which the salient features and relations of those domains are allowed to shine. For Lakoff and Johnson, too, metaphor's 'primary function is understanding', for it enables us 'to get a grip or handle on' the recondite and the abstract through the familiar and the concrete. The personification of inflation as an enemy, for instance, 'has an explanatory power of the only sort that makes sense to most people'.[13] Popular these days is reference to metaphor getting us to see one thing as another, so that if it is a good one we see the thing better.[14] The two answers can in fact complement each other; for the very concretization of the abstract which is supposed to give metaphor its cognitive role is also, according to a tradition, a main source of poetic pleasure. It is no accident that Plato, enemy to empiricist orders of understanding, was also enemy to the poets.

I shall say little about the inadequacies of these answers, since I want time to develop an alternative approach. The 'aesthetic' answer has at least the virtue of ready intelligibility, yet it is surely incapable of explaining the genesis, let alone the persistence, of more than a fraction of metaphors. Time was—Homer's time, perhaps—when descriptions of verbal disputes in terms of battles may have give 'pleasure and delight', but it is long gone. And whatever sustains references to work or labour as an energy resource or power supply,

[12] Hobbes, op. cit., 19; Fontanier, op. cit., 160.
[13] Op. cit., 33.
[14] See, for instance, M. Davies, 'Idiom and Metaphor', *Proceedings of the Aristotelian Society* (1982), and my comment on this in *Mind* (1984).

it is surely not the 'plaisir et agrément' stimulated. When one thinks of the intentionally ugly and clashing figures of modern verse, the scope of the answer even in the field of poetry looks narrow. The 'cognitivist' answer lacks even the virtue of ready intelligibility, for its proponents rarely spell out the terms, themselves metaphorical, in which the answer is usually couched—ones like 'seeing...as...' or 'getting a handle on' or 'filtering'. And when they do attempt to do this, the results are often bizarre. Thus Black's claim that a metaphor models something in the precise way that one theory may model another in mathematics sounds absurdly over-elaborate for nearly all cases. And Lakoff and Johnson's claim that the 'enemy' metaphor of inflation 'gives us a handle on' inflation by providing an explanation 'of the only sort that makes sense to most people' is perversely exaggerated. It is true that some metaphors are produced where the aim is to provide sophisticated insight and understanding, but even here it is rarely the metaphors themselves which achieve this, but the 'straight' explanations to which the metaphors are striking overtures or codas. It is not Nietzsche's 'Truth is a Woman' or Lévy-Strauss, 'Food is good to think with' which furnish understanding, but the theories of truth and culinary symbolism to which the aphorisms lend colour.[15]

Besides their individual defects, the two answers are directed at the wrong question: the purpose of metaphorical utterances. For a start this is not a question to which there could be a general answer. Different metaphors are uttered with different purposes—to delight or distress, to illuminate or confuse—but many are not uttered with any purpose at all, and may issue instead from that unplanning 'passion de parler' that is also manifested by exclamation, rolling one's words around one's mouth, and singing them out.[16] The idea that a person speaks metaphorically only when his purpose is to mean something different from what his words mean is, as we saw, a bad one. In the second place, what needs explaining are not metaphorical utterances themselves, but our vigorous engagement in producing them. The distinction here is important and widely applicable. The purposes of gifts—the things given—are usually very different from the purposes of giving them. The aim of a toy, but not that of giving it, is to be played with. Now it would be silly to look for *the* aim of all gifts, but not silly to look for *the* significance of

[15] See S. H. Olsen, 'Understanding Literary Metaphors" in *Metaphor: Problems and Perspectives,* D. Miall (ed.) (Harvester, 1982).
[16] For this 'passion de parler' and a rousing attack on the idea of speech as first and foremost, intentional speech acts, see M. Merleau-Ponty, especially *Signes* (Gallimard, 1960), 24ff.

the practice of giving them. Likewise there is no such thing as *the* purpose of metaphorical utterances, but we may enquire into *the* significance of metaphorizing, into what our engagement in this practice reveals about men. This, at any rate, is my enquiry.

By way of approach, let us turn from metaphor for a moment towards some other phenomena: jokes, slang and myths. Many of the best jokes, we know, are not available to most people, so their teller is exploiting and to a degree forging a communication between himself and those with the appropriate shared knowledge, background, and sensibility to 'get' them. Slang, perhaps by definition, is talk in which only members of a community are at home; so that the outsider who indulges, like the business executive who dons nautical language along with a sailor's cap at the weekends, becomes an embarrassment, while if too many outsiders indulge slang has passed into common idiom. Myth too, has this connection with sense of community, to the degree that tribes and peoples have been able to distinguish themselves only in terms of their respective bodies of myth. There is something odd in the idea of a stranger 'accepting' a tribe's myth: how can he, it is not *his*. A feature, then, both salient and deep, of jokes, slang, and myth, is the sense of community both reflected and reinforced by participation in them: a feature we might call the 'cultivation of intimacy'. This feature is frequently displayed in the content or subject-matter of the joke, slang or myth. One of the most common kind of jokes are those directed against people outside of the audience to which they are officially addressed, thereby lending a unity, however weak and provisonal, to that audience. Think of racist and mother-in-law jokes. A striking characteristic of much slang is the chummy, cosy way in which things, especially things of destruction and danger, are spoken of by the speech communities, such as soldiers and prisoners, who encounter them. Weapons, for example, become 'Brown Besses' 'Brown Bills', 'Big Berthas', 'Tommies', 'Hot Dogs', and 'Big Fish'. And it would be hardly original to point out that the content of countless myths tends towards the cementing of identity and community, be they the autocthonous myths of the Greeks or those in which a tribe is placed in an especially favoured and protected relationship to some dangerous animal. The upshot in all these cases is similar: the cultivation of intimacy among members of a community—whether by pitting it against an outsider, by familiarizing and domesticating alien objects, or by highlighting mutual bonds among the members. The 'in' joke, 'the soldier's best friend', and the leopard which fastidiously decides which tribe to eat, all belong together in this respect.

The pervasiveness of metaphor, I suggest, is also to be understood in terms of this cultivation of intimacy.[17] It is no accident, surely, that the three phenomena just mentioned are themselves shot through with metaphor. For example, a whole style of humour, the 'mock heroic' consists in hyperbole, while favourite instruments of slang include personification and metonymic references to human beings—the 'brass', 'woodentops', and the like. And around myth a whole industry has grown up among anthropologists tracing the metaphoric and metonymic transformations of mythical elements. But the presence of metaphor in humour, slang, and myth is only one witness to the cultivation of intimacy that metaphorizing effects. Let me mention two other pointers.

Aristotle perceptively pointed out that the social acceptibility of metaphorical utterances can depend on who produces them in front of whom. 'People like what strikes them', he says, 'and are struck by what is out of the way.' Precisely because of this, slaves—who have no business striking their superiors—should speak 'plainly'.[18] The point, more generally, is that since metaphors evoke an intimacy between speaker and audience, it is an abuse of them when that intimacy is lacking. Second, it is noticeable that the groups of people who indulge most vigorously in metaphorizing about certain domains are those in the best position to speak 'straight'. No one, for example, engages more perfervidly in slangy, bellicosely figurative talk about argumentation than the professional logician. In a learned paper the talk may be of *reductio ad absurdum* or 'lacunas', but in the bar afterwards the talk is of 'knocking holes in' or 'blowing up' an argument. This ought to be puzzling for the 'cognitivist', since for him it should be the layman, groping for understanding of domains in which he is unfamiliar, who wallows in metaphor. But it is readily intelligible if the pervasiveness of metaphor relates to the reflection and cultivation of intimacy.

How is it that metaphorizing cultivates intimacy? Partly through its very nature, and partly through its most characteristic kind of content. Precisely because a metaphorical utterance is not 'straight', understanding of what it conveys cannot issue solely from general, shared linguistic knowledge—the ability, let's say, to assign truth-conditions to sentences on the basis of their components and

---

[17] I borrow this phrase from a stimulating paper by Ted Cohen, 'Metaphor and the Cultivation of Intimacy' in *On Metaphor*, S. Sacks (ed.) (University of Chicago, 1979). I also borrow from him the phrase 'friends of metaphor' and the fruitful comparison with jokes.

[18] *Rhetorica, Works IX* (Oxford University Press) 1404b.

composition.[19] Answers to the question of what the extra is, which is required for understanding, have generally been crude. The most popular has been that it's grasp of resemblance: it is because A resembles B that I take you to be conveying something about B even though your words are about A. What this ignores is that, since everything resembles (and fails to resemble) everything else, the resemblance must be one that is salient for both speaker and comprehending listeners. Such salience requires there to be shared perceptions, interests, and backgrounds including, not least, a shared tradition of metaphorizing in certain ways. When Foucault says 'Knowledge is an instrument for cutting', it is only those acquainted with the history of epistemology, those who can pit this metaphor against the traditional 'mirroring' picture of knowledge, who can share the point. Like the best jokes, the best metaphors tend to be recondite; for a basis for appreciation is a sense that the effort they call for is not one that can be made by all, but only by those whose communion this effort at once reflects and forges. As Dan Sperber puts it:

> Plus la métaphore est recherchée, plus l'évocation est profonde et individuelle, et plus le sentiment de communion dans le symbolisme est grand.

When someone produces a good, fresh metaphor that I grasp, 'something comes to pass, something comes to pass *between us*'.[20]

If metaphorizing is a cultivation of intimacy, we should expect to find this reflected in its content, as we did in the cases of jokes, slang, and myth. This expectation is not disappointed, for a survey of metaphors reveals an otherwise puzzling preponderance of ones with, so to speak, an intimate subject matter. I shall mention just three types of case. First, there is that type in which we personify intangible processes of an inimical kind: inflation, disease, and unemployment, for example, become enemies to fight, threatening to defeat us unless we marshal our forces in time. Sometimes the personification is so vivid as to generate pictorial renderings of the enemies: think of 'Mr Rising Prices' or those walking, talking migraines of TV commercials that get a good hiding from an army of two-legged tablets. Second, there is the battery of metaphors in

[19] Although I have joined in the usual talk of metaphor's 'conveying' something that the listeners 'understand', I agree with those writers, especially Sperber and Wilson, who find it misleading and prefer talking of what metaphors 'evoke'. See, for example, their paper, 'Pragmatics', *Cognition* **10** (1981).
[20] 'Rudiments de rhétorique cognitive', *Poetique* **23** (1975), 414.

which members of a nation are depicted as a family standing against others. One's country is a 'Mother- or Fatherland', to which one returns 'home'. What belongs to it is 'ours', and is marked off from what is 'theirs' by 'borders' and 'frontiers'. Other peoples may get relegated from the human family itself, metamorphosing into frogs, krauts, limeys, poms or some other animal or vegetable species. Finally, there are the many figures which metaphorize transactions between people as if they require and occur through physical union. A good example is what one author refers to as the 'conduit' metaphor, whereby thoughts, feelings and the like are represented as being conducted from one person to another through physical channels.[21] Your ideas, provided your words *carry* meaning, will *come through* to me, unless there is a *barrier* or some *static* between us, and may then *touch* or *move* me, *tugging at my heart-strings* perhaps.

The predominance of metaphors with an intimate content is no mystery if metaphorizing is viewed as one of those activities whose essence is the cultivation of intimacy. From this perspective, the paradigmatic case of metaphorizing will be a way of talking that is not merely appreciable only within a unitary group, but whose thrust is to depict that group in ways which highlight its community and set it off from those outside—the metaphorically charged slang of soldiers and prisoners, say. In both its relative esotericism and its content, such talk will emphasize and exaggerate the intimacy it thereby cultivates.

The perspective I am urging may seem to be badly at odds with something I was keen to stress earlier when I aligned myself with the 'friends of metaphor': namely, that much metaphorizing is *common* currency of everyday talk. Speaking of argument in terms of war, or of illness as an enemy, is hardly speaking esoterically. But how can the ubiquity of such talk be reconciled with the idea of metaphor as the cultivation of intimacy, for where on earth is that intimacy among speakers at large of which such commonplace metaphorizing could be the cultivation? If that idea were correct, shouldn't the natural home of metaphor, *pace* Dumarsais, be the sheltered corridors of the *Académie Française* and not the public agora of *Les Halles*? By stressing the ubiquity of many metaphors, do I not preclude that perspective which I have recently urged?

I think not, for the three reasons, of which the last is much the most interesting, since it propels us towards the critical discussion of metaphor. First, intimacy is not a matter, necessarily, of numbers. During the last war, everyday English became swollen with

[21] M. Reddy, 'The Conduit Metaphor', in Ortony (ed.), op. cit.

metaphor, of which Churchillian rhetoric about the beleaguered nation standing alone and endearingly defusing references to 'Jerry' and his 'doodlebugs' would be two obvious illustrations. What this suggests, of course, is not that metaphorizing is cut entirely loose from intimacy but that, under the special conditions, intimacy assumed nationwide proportions. Second, it is not the fact that people—some, many, or all—talk about one domain in terms of another which, by itself, constitutes metaphorizing. (If it were, the use of spatial prepositions as temporal ones would be metaphorical.) Rather it is this together with, primarily, the generative power to produce novel utterances, metaphors. Now typically these novel metaphors, generated by the metaphorizing way of talking, will be esoteric to a degree. All of us speak of winning arguments or fighting diseases, but not all of us produce or readily grasp the more complex bellicose jargon of professional logicians and doctors. Think, for examples, of the latter's 'magic bullets', 'blocking antibodies', or 'cell bombardment'. Hence we should not conclude that the link between metaphor and intimacy is severed by the ubiquity of some metaphorizing; for that ubiquity sustains, and more importantly, may be sustained by, the more esoteric extensions it generates—extensions, indeed, which it must generate in order to still count as metaphorizing.

The final point, the one that ushers in the critical discussion, is harder to state. I shall work my way towards it via the useful analogy with jokes. 'My wife', Woody Allen tells his audience, 'accidentally dropped a spoonful of her soufflé on my foot—thereby fracturing several small bones.' I want to say three things about this joke. First, it is one that everyone can 'get', but second—despite this—it is a conspiratorial joke. As Sperber, in his commentary on it, puts it, it 'evokes . . . a complicity of male chauvinists towards women who wish to do something well but ruin everything'.[22] The complicity or intimacy is forged by that attitude among husbands, towards their young wives, which makes it nugatory to spell out that the soufflé was a very heavy one—which, therefore, makes the joke possible. But third—and this is what reconciles the joke's universal appreciability with its conspiratorial nature—the conspiracy is make-believe. The culinary disasters of wives are not that frequent and could anyway produce only the feeblest sense of unity among the victims: and everyone knows all of this, which is why everyone, including the wives, can laugh. A common tactic of the comedian is to get the whole audience laughing at jokes which are officially addressed to only a part. Often he will address that part as if the rest of the

[22] Op. cit., 406.

audience were not there. 'Not a word of this to the missus...', he whispers, or 'When you get home to the wife tonight, fellers...'. This is only possible because the intimacy uniting the part of the audience—the husbands, say, or the drinkers, or the sons-in-law—is, and is known to be, mock. I said earlier that the cultivation of intimacy is a crucial dimension of humour; the present point is that this is not contradicted by universally appreciable jokes for, like the Woody Allen one, the pretence of intimacy may be a condition of the joke's possibility.

Much of this transfers to the nature of metaphorizing. A nice example, to continue with the chauvinist theme, is the ornithological terminology persistently used to talk about women. According to fashion, and to the nature of the women in question, they are birds, chicks, hens, crows or little geese, possessed of such features as flightiness, feather-brainedness, and being twitterers. There is nothing esoteric in this talk; it is not, say, the preserve of rugby players—yet it is conspiratorial. To echo Sperber, it evokes the complicity of male chauvinists towards women who wish, but fail, to achieve the august human dignity of men. What reconciles ubiquity with conspiracy is that this complicity is, and is mutually known to be, make-believe; which is why women can engage in such talk (almost) as much as men. Although, then, there is no genuine intimacy among males at large to cultivate, the persistence and effectiveness of this ornithological metaphorizing presupposes the make-believe that there is.

How do these latest remarks usher in the critical discussion of metaphor? Metaphors, of course, can be criticized along many different lines: stylistically, for example, as when one condemns a metaphor as 'mixed' or more 'cognitively', as when a metaphorical vehicle is accused of providing an unfruitful or misleading model of its tenor or subject. But I have in mind a more general dimension of criticism—a sociolinguistic one, if you wish—suggested by the perspective I have been urging. It is a notion of criticism with affinities to what the Frankfurt School meant by the term. For Marcuse and his colleagues, criticism was essentially a matter of exposing people's 'false consciousness' of their social world, and in particular the illusion that there is unity and harmony where in fact disunity and conflict rule; and to explain this less in terms of patently oppressive and propagandist institutions but through the everyday workings, in our society, of schooling, advertising, and in particular, *speech*.

I argued just now that metaphorizing, like humour, when it is not grounded in any real intimacy, may none the less require the temporary and mutually recognized make-believe of intimacy. Precisely because the pretence is recognized as such, it is generally a harmless one. Only the rare mother-in-law who is actually like the one lampooned in mother-in-law jokes is constitutionally incapable of laughing at them. But there is a vital distinction to draw between these cases of make-believe intimacy and ones of illusory intimacy. In neither case does the metaphor or joke cultivate a genuine intimacy, but in the latter case it feeds off and helps manufacture the illusion of this. The pretence of intimacy is no longer mutually recognized as such. What I mean by the criticism of metaphor is exposure of metaphorizing which cultivates such illusion.

Although the distinction is conceptually clear, it will not always be obvious which cases are of which type, and some, of course, will be in a grey area in between. Some of you, indeed, will think I have already given an example of the 'illusory' type in the ornithological talk about women. At any rate, some of you will think that this is not harmless make-believe but a reflection and reinforcement of an illusory unity among men bound by a derogatory attitude towards women as if they were creatures of a different species. That women engage in such talk is a sign, not of its harmlessness, but of how well entrenched a perniciously false consciousness may become. You may be right, but I prefer to take an example that illustrates the point more signally. Consider again, the militaristic metaphor of inflation as an enemy to be fought. Recent governments, none more vigorously than the present one, have invoked a thoroughly Chur-chillian rhetoric against inflation as the common enemy. We must gird our loins, tighten our belts, make sacrifices and battle on until the victory of stable prices is ours. Intimacy is cultivated, as so often, in a dual way; by both the content of the metaphor, with its stress on our unity in face of the invader, and by its use of a terminology originally employed by people who really are united in some intimacy—soldiers in battle. Now at least three remarks of the relevant critical kind may be made. The first is that, unless they reach Weimarian proportions, rising prices produce no marked homogenizing effect upon people, bring about no definite change in men's social intercourse with one another; so that the degree of community effected among people of a country undergoing inflation is extremely feeble. Second, the idea of general unity in the face of a common enemy is thoroughly fictitious, since there are large sections of the population who can benefit from inflation at the expense of others. Third, an effect of the metaphor designed or not, is to paste over those differences in people's economic positions that could be thought more important than whatever they share as victims of inflation. (Criticism as exposure of illusions of unity, it might be added, raises a moral question of some interest; for a partial point of the 'enemy' metaphor might be the seemingly desirable one of discouraging those with the muscle to benefit from inflation from flexing it. Certainly there can be no equation between criticism in the present sense and blanket condemnation. Here I shall only remark, rather blandly, that just as very strong reasons are required if we are to be silent over the fact that someone is lying, so they must be present if we are to acquiesce in metaphorizing that cultivates illusion.)

Intimacy as unity in the face of a common enemy is, of course, only one brand; and any generalization of the point I am making would have to encompass other varieties of intimacy which metaphorizing may serve to cultivate—for corresponding to these, there will be varieties of illusory intimacy. Other brands mentioned have been intimacy as membership of a family, as physical closeness and contact, and as clubmanship. And these naturally do have their illusory counterparts. To take the last case only, think of the 'clubby' metaphors beloved by advertisers and designed to create the impressions that much more unites the users of a product than simply that use. One joins the 'Martini set' unless one is a 'paid up member of the Skol-ars'; one flies 'Club Class' when going on one's 'Club Mediterranean' holiday; or receives books through the post from a 'Book Club' and becomes one of the *'Guardian* People' for 23p per day; and only this morning I received my 'Personal Millionaire's Club Membership Card' from the *Daily Express,* thereby making me one with several million others who could win some cash if we bother to buy the paper.

Hegel, rejecting 'cognitivist' and 'aesthetic' explanations of the ubiquity of metaphor, says it displays a 'need and power of the spirit and heart'.[23] And Heidegger notes it as significant that the first systematic treatment of the emotions was not in a work on psychology, but in Aristotle's *Rhetoric*—for it is in the devices of everyday speech that the nature of 'Being-with-others' is best revealed.[24] I have tried to identify the most general spiritual or emotional need to which metaphorizing answers: intimacy, whether between men and men or between men and their world (for, as Hegel also notes, metaphor is often deployed to satisfy the spirit's craving to 'seek itself' in external objects).[25] We talk and live in metaphors for the same reason that others talk and live in myths, and for the same reason that humour is a need: to cultivate, whether

---

[23] *Ästhetik,* **I** (Aufbau-Verlag, 1976). 393.
[24] *Sein und Zeit* (Niemeyer, 1979), 138–139.
[25] Op. cit.

3

authentically, through make-believe, or through illusion, a sense of intimacy.

Like much else that caters to a human need, metaphorizing can easily generate its own pathology. Hence, in addition to the paradigmatic metaphors which reflect and reinforce a genuine intimacy, there are those which merely pretend it, benignly or not. Because intimacy is a need, what appears to satisfy it will be clutched at, to the exclusion of the awareness of that real lack of intimacy which increasingly characterizes our modern existence. The stale metaphors in common circulation that abound today are a dimension of that 'idle chatter' (*Gerede*) which Heidegger diagnoses as a symptom of an 'uprooted consciousness', over-eager to take root in the thinnest soil. This pathology of metaphor—the stale, easy ones ready on the lips of all—reflects, perhaps, something deeper. As its paradigmatic best, metaphor testifies to a freedom of consciousness, to powers of imaginative construction, to insouciant independence of mind, and to Hegel's 'luxuriant delight in phantasy'.[26] The dead weight of stale metaphor presses down on this freedom; and with a load that grows heavier in a world that grows more public and less intimate—for that is a world in which metaphors which provide the illusions of intimacy find their market widening and their clientele less discriminating.

[26] Ibid., 394.

The Role of Interests in Science

W. NEWTON-SMITH

A series of lectures organized in part by the Society for Applied Philosophy and entitled 'Philosophy and Practice' is presumably aimed at displaying the practical implications of philosophical doctrines and/or applying philosophical skills to practical questions. The topic of this paper, the role of interests in science, certainly meets the first condition. For as will be argued there are a number of theses concerning the role of interests in science which have considerable implications for how one should see the scientific enterprise in general and in particular for how one assesses the claim that science ought to be accorded its priviliged position in virtue of its results and/or methods. And in view of the respect and resources accorded to science what could be of greater practical interest? It remains the case, however, that my interest may seem the inverse of that of the organizers of this series. For in looking at the role of interest in science, one is examining, so to speak, the extent to which the sphere of the practical determines what goes on in science. One is exploring ways in which the non-scientific impinges on the scientific. While my primary focus will be on the physical sciences, it will be argued that there is a significant difference between them and the social sciences; a difference which renders the social sciences intrinsically liable to penetration from outside. As will be seen, some of the particular arguments for this conclusion make pressing the question: what about philosophy? The answer, it will be concluded, is that philosophy is insulated from external influences to a considerable extent. In that lies both its importance and an explanation as to why much of it has little practical application.

The question is: what role do interests play in science? Certainly they play some role. Without an interest in prediction and control, the institution of modern science would not exist. And within science that interest affects the type of theories that are on offer. However, when this question is asked, usually by sociologists, they have in mind not interests (whatever they might be) that are properly scientific, but interests (usually self-interests) of individuals such as the desire for a successful career or the non-scientific interests of a group. For example, the interest of the Party in Eastern Germany in defending a certain interpretation of Marx has led to resources being deployed in favour of Lamarckian rather than Darwinian theories of evolution. This gives at best the roughest of indications of the terrain to be explored, namely, the role of the interests of individuals or groups other than properly scientific interests which they may have adopted. In what follows no analysis of the notion of interest or of the role of interests can be given. But what I have to say does not depend on any particularly contentious claims in this regard. The argument will be given sketched very briskly and spelt out in a number of forthcoming papers. In this paper my interest is in sketching a broad tableau.

Uncontroversially non-scientific interests (that is, interests other than those which are partly constitutive of science) do play some role. Scientists are not disembodied Cartesian egos motivated only by an interest in the pursuit of truth for its own sake and equipped with an algorithm for determining which of rival theories is most likely to give progress towards that goal. The availability of resources (largely decided outside the scientific community) play a major role in determining which areas of science get the attention. At the level of the broad tableau we all know the picture: Los Alamos, the race to the moon, ... That these projects got the resources rather than, say, agricultural science can only be explained by the non-scientific interests served by the fruits or expected fruits of such research. The finer brush strokes are harder: did the interests of brewers play a significant role in determining which areas of bacteriology were developed? Does the fact that decisions on where to spend medical research money is made by men of mature years rather than by women with young children play a role in deciding where it goes? That is, does it perhaps seem natural to them to spend it on heart research rather than prenatal or postnatal care because their experience is of friends with problems of the former kind? These questions obviously require micro-sociological investigations. The thesis that at the macro-sociological level that interests do play a role will be called *Boring Interests Thesis 1* or *BIT1* for short. In using this label I do not want to disparage the thesis. It is just that it is obviously true.

A more interesting area in which interests might be said to play a role would be in the matter of theory choice. My interests or my perception of my interests may play a role in the choice of the political party I vote for. May they not also play a role in determining which theory I opt for? In a world of diminishing academic jobs might it not be tempting to opt for one's professor's favourite theory? Might not some reference to the interest served be needed even in cases where I think I am doing this because he has shown me that there are better arguments for his theory than for any of its rivals? Few of us think that the entire explanation of the fact that certain Soviet scientists supported Lysenko was the perceived force of his arguments or that the erudition and ratiocination of

Cardinal Bellarmine over Galileo was the primary explanation of the failure of Galileo to win the immediate allegiance of the intellectual community. In these cases we are concerned with interests other than properly scientific ones playing a role in explaining a choice where the choice runs counter to what one would expect on normal scientific criteria and where the explanation of the lapse is not simply stupidity, carelessness or laziness.

One does find sociological accounts of theory choice according to which such factors play the main or only role in theory choice. Of course this thesis tends to destroy its own credibility if taken in the strong form. If it applies to itself we have no reason to take it seriously. If it does not apply to itself one wants an account of how sociology came to occupy the Archimedean point of rationality around which the vicissitudes of interests other than rationality hold sway. One is inclined to think perhaps uncharitably that it is in sociology that theory choice is most likely to be influenced by interests external to those interests (whatever they may be) that constitute the proper aim of sociology itself.

But even if taken in a restricted and non-paradox form to the effect that non-scientific interests are the main or at least an important determinant the thesis is most implausible in the case of the physical sciences. Applied to such sciences it takes a number of forms. I have heard it argued, for instance, that a game theoretic model which has scientists selecting theories so as to maximize career prospects best fits science. And the proponents of the so-called 'strong programme'[1,2] argue that social structures in some as yet to be explicated fashion determine causally the acceptance of theories, even of mathematical theories. We can see that such views are incorrect without looking at the details. For whatever the controversies about the nature of scientific progress, there is general agreement that there has been progress in the most minimal sense of the term, the instrumentalistic sense. There has been enormous increase in the predictive and manipulative power of contemporary theories of, say, physics and chemistry over the theories of some three hundred years ago. This success is so manifest through spin-off technology that not even Feyerbend[3] denies it. He does add that there are more fun things to do besides predicting and controlling

[1] B. Barnes, *Scientific Knowledge and Sociological Theory* (London: Routledge and Kegan Paul, 1974); *Interests and the Growth of Knowledge* (London: Routledge and Kegan Paul, 1977).

[2] D. Bloor, *Knowledge and Social Imagery* (London: Routledge and Kegan Paul, 1976).

[3] P. K. Feyerbend, *Science in a Free Society* (London: New Left Books, 1978).

the universe and points out that the scientist has had help from alchemists, witches and madmen. But deny it he does not.

We can consider the history of science schematically as a sequence of choices between, say, theories $T'i$ and $T''i$ where one of these is the winner and the other the loser. The sum effect of these choices is to give a particular route through a tree of alternative possible histories of science. The particular route taken has in fact brought, over-all, a massive increase in predictive and manipulative power. If the choice between $T'i$ and $T''i$ had been affected to any significant degree by factors external to science relating to someone's interest or some group's interest or perceived interests, it would be astonishing in the highest degree that choices determined in this way should conspire to produce the increase in observational success. It is not claimed that this is impossible, only that it would be most improbable to think that selecting theories with a view to pleasing the Party, the Church or one's supervisor would have increased observational success as a by-product. Therefore there are general grounds for thinking that in the physical sciences non-scientific interests have not played a very significant role in the choice of theories.

Let us call this thesis *BIT2* for *Boring Interests Thesis 2,* boring in this case because in a strong enough form to be interesting it is obviously false. If the idea that interests play an important role in theory choice can be so easily dispensed with, why have some thought to the contrary? The answer lies in an over-reaction to positivism. Kuhn and Feyerabend argue in their differing ways to the correct conclusion that there is no binding algorithm which determines the correctness of theory choice for any pair of theories relative to any given body of evidence. For the Kuhn of *The Structure of Scientific Revolutions*[4] and Feyerabend[5,6] all standards of theory choice are paradigm bound. Faced with the choice between paradigms there could be no rational standard of appeal and it seemed that the choice had to be determined by non-cognitive factors. For the more restrained Kuhn of *The Essential Tension*[7] there are paradigm neutral standards of theory choice. His list includes simplicity, predictive power, fertility, and plausibility among other factors. However, he argues, there is no guarantee, for example, that the criterion of simplicity will give a verdict in the case

[4] T. S. Kuhn *The Structure of Scientific Revolutions,* 2nd edn (Chicago: Chicago University Press, 1970).

[5] P. K. Feyerabend, *Against Method* (London: New Left Books, 1975).

[6] Feyerabend, op. cit., 1978.

[7] T. S. Kuhn, *The Essential Tension* (Chicago: Chicago University Press, 1977)

of any two theories. One theory may be more simple than the other in some but not other respects. And furthermore it may be that the criteria conflict: the results of a fertility test pointing in one direction, the results of a plausibility test pointing in the other. Let us call the operation of these two factors *Kuhnian Underdetermination* or *KUT* for short. *KUT* is simply the thesis that at any moment of time the actually available evidence and the rules for theory choice do not uniquely determine a best bet upon the available rival theories.

Unfortunately discussion of what happens in view of *KUT* takes place at a level of too great abstraction (at the level of macrosociology). For one hardly ever finds a case study in which it is established that there was an intractable debate in the scientific community which is best explained as one arising from different standards of, say, simplicity or from agreed standards pointing in different directions. The importance of this point cannot be underestimated. For taken in the abstract one is not unnaturally inclined to conclude that if the methods of science do not point to a choice, the choice must be the outcome of external, non-scientific factors (i.e. the interests or perceived interests of individuals, groups or societies). To the extent that we assume *KUT* obtains we will tend to conclude that non-scientific interests play a role in theory choice. However, if one considers case studies one finds it hard in the physical sciences to provide convincing examples of choices affected by *KUT* which were decided by such external factors. There are cases where two theories spar in the field together for a while: the 'methods' not according to decisive victory to one over the other. But one finds in such cases that no choice is made. Both theories remain competitors until the community recognizes the victory of one: a victory licensed by the methods of science and usually signalled by success at the empirical level. In so far as individuals have to make up their minds as to which theory to back in the interregnum, their choices are adequately explained by reference to hunches, guesses, and their sense of the situation based on past experience.

At this juncture let me introduce an analogy. Think of the master chef or the wine blender. Neither of these can fully reduce the exercise of their skill to an algorithmic system of rules. Indeed, one is not likely to get very far at all in trying to produce such rules. Yet we can recognize in the long run the skill of the wine blender. Some blenders take wines unpalatable on their own which in combination prove to be agreeable. Just because the choice of proportions cannot be rationalized by reference to a linquistically articulatable system of rules we are not tempted to explain the choice (or the variation in choices between different blenders) by reference

W. Newton-Smith

to social and/or pyschological factors. Why then should we be quick
to draw this conclusion in the case of science? No doubt there are
differences between the exercise of judgment in the case of gastronomy and the case of, say, astronomy but not so great as to sustain
this difference in treatment of the cases.

It is to be concluded, then, that external non-scientific interests do
not play any significant role in theory choice. The argument from
the increasing empirical success of science makes it most improbable
that they should. The supposition that they should arises from the
assumption that if choice cannot be rationalized by reference to an
algorithm of inductive logic, it must be determined by external
interests. But there is a gap between such factors as is clearly
illustrated in the cases of vineculture and gastronomy.

Both theses about the role of interests have been called *boring*. A
thesis which would definitely not be boring is that interests play a
role in determining the very content of science in the sense of determining what counts as an acceptable or good theory or explanation.
One version of such a thesis is: what counts as a good explanation is
relative to interests. That is, we cannot ask for the explanation of a
given phenomenon. We must rather ask for the explanation appropriate for a person with such and such interests. If anything like this
thesis is correct, given that science, both physical and social, is a
bundle of theories and explanations we are forced to the conclusion
that what counts as part of the very content of science is itself a
function of interests.

This thesis is outlandish. If interests determine what counts as a
good explanation or a good theory, what is the status of this theory
itself? Unless some theories are good in themselves or unless some
interest perspective is privileged (the working class, the philosopher-
king) the thesis is as self-defeating as the thesis that all theory choice
is a product of the operation of interests. A more restrained but still
exciting thesis has been advanced by Putnam[8] (p. 41) in the course
of criticizing the deductive nomological model of explanation
(hereafter cited as *DN*). Putnam argues that explanation is interest
relative and that the *DN* cannot account for this. While interests are
important to explanation they are so, it will be argued, in a quite
innocuous way.

The *DN* gives the following characterization of one type of
explanation (or good explanation):

An explanation E of a phenomenon P in a system S is an argument

[8] H. Putnam, *Meaning and the Moral Sciences* (London: Routledge and
Kegan Paul, 1978).

64

which has a description of E as a deductively valid consequence of a set of premises meeting the following conditions:

1. The premises are true or approximately true to a sufficient degree.
2. There are singular premises describing the initial conditions in S.
3. There are generalizations having empirical content which occur essentially in the derivation.
4. At least one such generalization is lawlike.

As the model stands it admits of clear counter-examples. Notwithstanding these I would argue that there is plenty of life in the model and that the best approach is to modify it rather than reject it. However that is a story for another occasion. I introduce the model because some, notably Putnam (pp 41–45), have offered objections which are supposed to simultaneously show that the DN model is unsatisfactory and that explanation is interest-relative.

Consider the following purported explanations which would indeed be explanations on the DN:

1. Why is this bird black?
   It is a crow and all crows are black.
2. Why did that stuff turn the flame yellow?
   It was sodium and sodium always does that.
3. Professor X is found stark naked in the girls' dormitory at 12 midnight. Explanation: (?) He was stark naked in the girls' dormitory at midnight−e, and he could neither leave the dormitory nor put on his clothes by midnight without exceeding the speed of light. But (covering law) nothing (no professor, anyhow) can travel faster than light.
4. A peg (1 inch square) goes through a 1 inch square hole and not through a 1 inch round hole. Explanation: (?) the peg consists of such-and-such elementary particles in such-and-such a lattice arrangement. By computing all the trajectories we can get applying forces to the peg (subject to the constraint that the forces must not be so great as to distort the peg or the holes) in the fashion of the famous Laplacian super-mind, we determine that some trajectory takes the peg through the square hole, and no trajectories take it through the round hole (covering laws: the laws of physics).

The first is anon., the second is Harré's[9] (p. 20), the third and

[9]R. Harré, *The Principles of Scientific Thinking* (London: Macmillan, 1970).

fourth are Putnam's (pp. 39–40). Putnam claims that neither the third nor four 'story' constitutes an explanation. According to him they do fit the *DN* and hence, he claims, the *DN* is a bad model of explanation. While it may in the end be a bad model, this argument of Putnam's does not give a good reason for so thinking. Explanations, according to Putnam, 'presuppose a range of interests', What is the explanation is relative to the interests of those seeking it. The Professor X story does not fit with our interest in prediction and control. That interest dictates an explanatory story told by reference to 'motives, or intentions, or neuroses, or anyway psychological causes...' The square peg example violates what Putnam calls 'methodological interests'. That is, given our methods for dealing with the world (we are not Laplacian super-minds) we want the simple geometrical explanation that 1 inch squares do not fit through 1 inch circles (given that the objects are not distorted).

Putnam is right to remind us that reference must be made to interests in understanding explanation. It is not, however, the case that this means that explanations become relative in a way that is incompatible with a hard notion of truth. Putnam seems to think it does. For he in fact uses the alleged interest-relativity to support the Quinean[10] idea of the indeterminacy of translation. Briefly, Putnam's claim is that the choice between rival translations should depend on which translation is part of the best explanation of the behaviour of the group whose language is being translated. But, claims Putnam, there is no such thing as *the* explanation of the behaviour of another group, there is only the explanation relative to our interests. For another group with differing interests translating the same language there will be differing explanations and hence differing 'correct' translations.

A correct appreciation of the role of interest in explanation can be brought out by considering two ways in which explanations of some given phenomenon may be in tension. First, the sentences used in specifying the explanation may be incompatible. For instance, one explanation offered of the null-result of the Michelson–Morley experiment was the absence of an aether. The other explanation was the presence of an aether which had a 'drag' effect on objects moving though it. In such cases the rival explanations will be said to be *incompatible competitors*. Secondly, there are cases in which the sentences characterizing the different explanations can be true together but offering one explanation rather than the other would be appropriate in some contexts. For instance, if I am asked why there

[10] W. V. O. Quine, 'On the Reasons for the Indeterminacy of Translation', *Journal of Philosophy* LXVII (1970), 178–183.

was a fire in my cottage in Wales I might truthfully but unhelpfully say to the insurance inspector that there was oxygen present. I might truthfully but misleadingly say to the police that there was a short-circuit in the wiring. I might say to my lawyer that I had miswired the place hoping to claim on the insurance. There is no doubt that interests are playing a role here. In such cases I will refer to the rival stories as *compatible competitors*.

It will be fruitful to introduce at this juncture the notion of what will be called a *Logical Space of Explanations* or, for short, an *LSE*. For any phenomenon *P* there will be a space of stories which might be told in answer to the question: Why *P*? The stories in an *LSE* are logically compatible and for each story there is some circumstance in which we would recognize it as the appropriate thing to say in answer to the question: Why *P*? *LSEs* can be constructed in a number of ways. As the example of the fire illustrates, the differing members (i.e. short-circuit, presence of oxygen, etc.) may draw attention to different aspects of the overall situation. Or as can be illustrated with the sodium example, the different members may vary in the depth of treatment accorded the subject matter. For instance, there will be circumstances in which the appropriate thing to say is simply that the substance was sodium and all sodium turns yellow in a flame. In a more sophisticated present context the appropriate thing might be to tell some story from quantum chemistry.

In the cases Putnam considers it is clear that interests play a role in determining what we think it appropriate to offer as an explanation. We select from an *LSE* the number it is most appropriate to offer. The fact that we could select something satisfying the *DN* model and find a context in which it is not appropriate does not cast aspersions on the *DN* model. The defender of the *DN* approach should offer it as an account of the conditions which must be fulfilled for membership in an *LSE*. All that then needs be done is to show for everything in the *LSE* there is a context in which we would recognize it as appropriate. To illustrate consider the crow examples which has been offered as a counter-example to the *DN* model. There are other members of the *LSE*: for example, there is some story about how the blackness of crows serves to spread their gene pool. What comes to mind most likely when we hear the example is some question which would be answered by that story. We do not want to be told that all crows are black. We know that and it adds nothing to our understanding. But in Oxford there is a notorious bird painter. Many birds are black because that is his favourite colour and he has been particularly active recently. I ask: Why is *that* bird black? You quite helpfully answer: "That's a crow. All crows are black. So don't worry about Bernie the Bird Painter. He's not been at it.' And similarly one can imagine a context in which the simple story about sodium was just the thing to provide. Perhaps a situation in which many gas supplies had impurities which produced a yellow flame regardless of whatever substance is put in the flame. Putnam himself has provided a context for the square peg round hole example. Just make us Laplacian superminds with a particular penchant for keeping track of things at the micro-level.

With imagination we can deal with his first example. Suppose it is a standing condition in some world that professors are always trying to get to bed with their students. In that world there is a particular taboo against this happening after midnight. Professors lose their tenure on violating this. Also, they have to attend faculty meetings every night that end at 11.50. It happens that they travel at speeds near that of light, slowing somewhat as they age. But do other things are normal speed. So why was Professor X there at midnight? Well he was there at midnight$-e$, you know they always cut it fine. And poor X didn't realize he was slowing down... I am not claiming that I have made this overwhelmingly plausible. My intention is the more restricted one of pointing out an invalidity in Putnam's argument. To refute the DN it is not enough to show that there is a context in which something satisfying the model would not strike us as a satisfactory explanation. The proponent of the model should maintain that it gives the conditions for membership in an LSE and that interests determine which member it is appropriate to offer. In this way we give interests a role to play without embracing any radical thesis about the role of interests in determining the content of science. One's theory of explanation which might well be that the DN determines membership of the LSE. No interests other than the purely scientific ones play a role in this. Other interests may well place a role in determining which member of the LSE is to be offered in answer to a demand for explanation.

Even if Putnam's thesis had been made out it would not have given us as exciting a conclusion as at first appeared. The discussion above has shown we can accord interests a role to play in the pragmatics of explanation without according them a role to play in determining the very content of science. This conclusion holds more specifically of the physical rather than the social sciences as will argued below.

To develop this we need to pay attention to a feature of explanation which can be illustrated with regard to Newtonian mechanics. That theory tells us that a body in uniform motion not acted on by forces will continue in uniform motion. If the body is accelerated the theory explains this by reference to impressed forces. No explanation is given by the theory of the continuation of uniform motion. This is what will be called a *natural state* for Newtonian mechanics. Natural states have to be determined. What filtered out other candidates for not really being natural states was prediction and control. In the particular case cited it seemed natural for a long time to suppose that a body ceased to move unless a force continued to act. But theories based on that presupposition simply were not as predictively successful as the Newtonian theories. The rival theories with different assumptions as to natural states did not come up with the empirical goods. One proceeds by conjecturing a natural state, embodies it in a theory and seeks empirical confirmation of the identification through the success of the theory. Selection of a natural state does affect the content of science for it affects what is explained and what is not explained. If interests played a role in this, interests would affect the content of science. In the case of the natural sciences, interests do not affect the determination of natural states. Or rather, no interest over and above the interest in prediction and control is involved. That state is natural which the best theory treats as natural where the best theory is the one giving the greatest degree of prediction and control.

This device is not so available in the case of the social sciences. We do not have in general a usable criterion based on prediction and control. I am not claiming that we will never have such success. For the purpose of my present question that is not relevant. It is only what we can do now that is relevant to understanding what we do now. I am trying to make sense of the idea that interests play a greater role in social science. One source of this is the possibility that interests determine what is a natural state. That is, the very constitution of the *LSE* might depend on what one takes as a natural state and that might depend on one's interests. One cannot abstract from the role of interests by controlling through prediction and control because that is not available now when we have to construct our *LSEs*.

To give some content to this idea consider the example developed by Steven Lukes[11] of the differences between liberal-pluralist theories of the state and neo-Marxist theories. These theories give different accounts of the increased role of the state in contemporary capitalist economics. For liberal-pluralist the increased role is part of the development of countervailing centres of power, the activities of which supplement the normal economic process. According to the neo-Marxist, on the other hand, the bourgeois state is the weapon of the capitalist class interests, the state role increases in order to

[11] S. Lukes, 'The Underdetermination of Theory by Data', *Aristotelian Society* Supplementary Volume LII (1978).

protect those interests and does so by producing a mystifying image of the state as the arbiter between classes—as the benevolent judge of the merits of the various pluralist forces. Notice that underlying these different explanations are different conceptions of what is natural. On the liberal-pluralist view the state is seen as natural, inevitable and basically beneficial and as restraining the conflicting passions that arise within it. That we have a state is not something that needs explaining. On the neo-Marxist view the state is not a natural entity. It exists as a tool of the ruling classes. One has to explain how it arose and what sustains it and one expects it to be a transitory state.

Each of these views is part of a theory. The theories differ in what is seen as natural and what is seen as requiring explanation. Neither theory can claim superiority on the basis of some overwhelming predictive and manipulative successes. The claim as to which theory has correctly identified the natural state is not going to be settled in any empirical way. Thus it does not seem far-fetched to think that one's assumption that one of these states is the natural one reflects one's own interests and is not the result of a binding methodological reflection. On any respectable scientific methodology, the correlation between class position and one's views on this matter are too close (even if not very close) for it to be a matter of coincidence. Beliefs about the natural nature of the state are simply not as randomly distributed over the classes as are beliefs about the weather tomorrow, the existence of quarks, or the truth of the four-colour theorem.

No pretence is made that the above is a convincing argument. It is intended merely to indicate an avenue of thought needing exploration. Some explanation is needed of the undoubted fact that non-scientific interests play more of a role in the social sciences than in the physical sciences. It is worth considering that the relative absence in the social sciences of what I have elsewhere called the *ultimate criterion*[12] means that interests do play a role in determining what counts as natural states and thereby in part determine the actual content of those sciences.

This situation is not analogous to that of the skilled experimenter or practised theoretician in physics. We do not have a recognizable group of experts whose judgments have proved in the long run to be productive. That being so, we can expect an input from interests into the content of social science: an input against which it does not look possible to control. The control we exercise in the case of the

---

[12] W. H. Newton-Smith, *The Rationality of Science* (London: Routledge and Kegan Paul, 1981).

physical sciences simply is not applicable. It might be tempting to think we could decide between the theories not by reference to prediction but by reference to explanation: select the theory that provides the best explanation. But this appeal is unhelpful. For the question as to which is the best explanation in the absence of a test from prediction will be just as vexed.

This paper has explored in a preliminary way the role of interests in science. To start a boring sense in which they do, called *BIT1*, was noted. This was in the determination of the areas of scientific investigation, in the deployment of resources and in the dissemination of results. I then considered whether interests might play a role in theory choice given Kuhnian under-determination. Because scientific method does not uniquely determine theory, it is formally possible that there is a gap to be filled by reference to interests. But I argued in very general terms that interests cannot play all that an important role in the physical sciences. We could not have achieved the predictive and manipulative successes we have if they did. The idea that interests might determine in part the very content of science was then explored. If explanation was interest relative in a sufficiently strong sense this would be so. We found, however, that while explanation has a pragmatic dimension which depends on interests, it does not do so in a way that allows interest to play role in determining content. However, it was suggested that interests do play a role in the determination of natural states in social science and would therefore determine in part the very content of science.

How in all of this does philosophy fare? Consider first *BIT1*. At the general level it is just as boring. Clearly external interests play a role in determining what strikes us as the important questions. We have a tradition and it constrains (but only) the choices open. I once encountered a communication from an American humanities association noting that its members were not doing as well as scientists in open competition for grants and urging that applicants model their applications on those of scientists. It would not surprise me to think that the interest, an interest I share, in the philosophy of language makes its presence felt at this particular historical era because it can be appropriately packaged. I do not accuse my colleagues of selecting topics to obtain grants. All we need assume is a random distribution of philosophical interests over the philosophical committees and the awarding of grants by those with an interest in 'scientific' sounding projects. Our interest in truth does not insulate us from external factors playing a role in the micro-determinations of which areas of truth to seek.

Things are going to be worse when we turn to theory choice in philosophy. We cannot cite any undeniable sequence of successes to keep the sociological wolves at bay. Nor can we cite general agreement on criteria of success that the temperate Kuhn sees operating in physical science. This creates a space in which the pressures of interests external to philosophy could operate. But we do not, I think, find that. We cannot so easily form a picture of a philosopher's political views from his writing on private language, the meaning of theoretical terms or the Law of the Excluded Middle. But we do expect to read a political position, an implicit array of values—moral, cultural, political—from, say, a sociologist's writings even when he or she is not explicitly concerned with such. Why is this so? The answer in part is that there simply is no discernible correlations between philosophical views on these matters and moral, cultural or political positions. The explanation as to why there is nonesuch cannot rest as it does in the case of the physical sciences on a situation in which the protagonists commit themselves to abide by the outcome of some methodology. We do not have a methodology and have more or less given up hoping for one. Why then are we not vulnerable in the way I suggested the social scientist is? The less superficial answer is that the absence of practical implications means that no one cares. No one cares implicitly or explicitly to manipulate the philosopher because no one can see how it makes any difference.

To develop this thesis which is not as cynical as the first gloss would suggest one needs ask what is the common thread linking philosophical activity. I see no other answer than the respect for critical faculties. Philosophical discourse, at least within our tradition, broadly speaking, is controlled by the demand for explication and argumentation. Such demands do not issue in a unique answer to a given question. That is why such diverse stories can flourish. The cultural importance of philosophy lies in the fact that it is an area of activity the point of which is to value, to take an interest in, the dictates of reason as applied to fundamental questions (truth, beauty, meaning, knowledge, etc.). If views about the nature of meaning made as much difference to how one lives as views about abortion, euthanasia, socialism, etc., philosophy would not have the character it has. In having a space in which rational criteria are to hold sway it is like science. It is unlike science in that many of its areas to not give rise to any practical consequences and so it is not subject to the pressure from outside that science is. Politicians care whether more resources are devoted to agricultural sciences than sciences with defence or attack spin-off. They do not care whether resources go into the 'science' of meaning or the 'science' of truth. The mere fact that is is difficult to trace the implications for how to re-order's one's life once one has given up believing in the analytic-synthetic distinction means that it is hard to see what situation would put pressure on one to hold one view rather than another.

Not wishing to conclude on such an apparently cynical note I end instead in paradox: the practical import of philosophy lies in its very impracticality. Because it does not have implications for practical life it can exist as a place in which the tools of ratiocination are honed to their finest. And in this it keeps alive the critical tradition. It inculcates values—explication and defence—the application of which outside philosophy has practical implications.

To illustrate one need only think of the fear the authorities in Eastern Europe have of philosophy. And this is not because of particular philosophical truths that are articulate, although mis-perceptions of this may play a role. For one sometimes finds a simple-minded equation of Marxism and philosophy. Marxism is powerful, if it is philosophy then philosophy is powerful and, if non-Marxist, dangerous. But at another level this amounts to an implicit recognition of what I am trying to say: philosophy keeps alive the critical spirit by creating a space in which that operates freely. The experience of its operation is transferred to spheres where decisions do make a difference. Decisions made with its guidance are less likely to be the outcome of the pressure of interests. The Eastern European authorities know this. The unfettered philo-sophical spirit is to be feared for it generates the critical temperament and much in some countries is not up to that critical scrutity In this way philosophy is of the greatest practical relevance.

The Society for Applied Philosophy can only exist because it is problematic to claim that philosophy has practical implications. Of course I do not want to deny that it is important for philosophers to draw out the practical implications of their theories, to take up neglected topics of practical interest. And I would offer my reflections on the role of interests in science as part of this project. But at the same time I want to insist that the practicality of philosophy comes at second remove from its very impracticality and we should not be embarrassed by this. In its very remoteness and impracticality lies its charm and its importance.

Dishonesty and the Jury: A Case Study in the Moral Content of Law

RICHARD TUR

It must be considered that a man who only does what everyone of the society to which he belongs would do is not a dishonest man.[1]

A lack of confidence in the ability of a tribunal correctly to estimate evidence of states of mind and the like can never be sufficient ground for excluding from enquiry the most fundamental element in a rational and humane criminal code.[2]

1. Introduction

Section 1(1) of the Theft Act, 1968 enacts that 'a person is guilty of theft if he *dishonestly* appropriates property of another with the intention of permanently depriving the other of it ...'. The concept of dishonesty, which also features in the definition of a number of deception offences, has been the focus of a sustained controversy between leading academic criminal lawyers and the Court of Appeal. The Theft Act, 1968 was based largely on the work of the Criminal Law Revision Committee and it established a new criminal code, provided a completely fresh start, defined theft (and related offences) in simple and clear language and got rid of 'the immensely and unnecessarily complicated structure, full of difficult distinctions of a purely technical character and bristling with traps for the judges, magistrates, prosecutors and police ...'[3] which had emerged over centuries.

The Committee devoted little of its report to dishonesty but regarded it as 'very important' and 'a vital element in the offence'.[4] 'Dishonestly' was preferred to 'fraudulently and without a claim of right made in good faith', the parallel phrase in the earlier law, because 'dishonesty' is something which laymen can easily recognize

---

[1] *Boswell's Life of Johnson* Oxford Edition (London, 1904) Vol. 1, 456.
[2] Per Dixon J., *Thomas* (1937) 59 C.L.R. 279, 309.
[3] J. C. Smith, *The Law of Theft*, 4th edn (London, 1979) para. 2 (hereinafter *Theft*).
[4] Eighth Report of the Criminal Law Revision Committee, Cmnd 2977, 'Theft and Related Offences', para. 39.

Richard Tur

whereas 'fraud' may involve technicalities which might have to be explained by a lawyer. The Committee thought that 'dishonesty' could stand without definition and, indeed, some members would have preferred not to define it at all. However, the Committee thought it appropriate to preserve two well-established rules of law. First, that theft is inconsistent with a claim of right made in good faith. Secondly, that a finder of property cannot be guilty of theft where he believes that the owner cannot be found by taking reasonable steps. Consequently the Theft Act, 1968 provides by section 2(1) that a person's appropriation of property of another is not to be regarded as dishonest if he appropriates the property (a) in the belief that he has in law the right to deprive the other of it; (b) in the belief that he would have had the other's consent if the other knew of the appropriation and its circumstances; and (c) in the belief that the owner cannot be discovered by taking reasonable steps. Section 1(2) provides that an appropriation may constitute theft even if it is not made with a view to gain and section 2(2) states that an appropriation may be dishonest notwithstanding a willingness to pay for the property. Clearly the Act leaves dishonesty largely undefined and, since the sections mentioned refer only to theft, dishonestly as it relates to deception offences is left wholly undefined.

This approach did not meet with universal approval even before the Theft Act passed into law. Sir Brian McKenna, writing in 1966,[5] remarked that there would be the same objections to the undefined adverb 'dishonestly' as already obtained regarding the undefined adverb 'fraudulently'. He welcomed the partial definition of dishonesty but asked 'why does it stop short of certainty by leaving it to the jury to decide whether any other excuses will be permitted?' Either 'fraudulently' then and 'dishonestly' now added nothing to the phrase 'without a claim of right' in which case the partial definition in section 2(1) could be regarded as exhaustive or the term embodied more than the phrase in which case the extra content could be 'brought into the open and stated expressly' thereby producing an exhaustive definition. Since no exhaustive definition is provided the jury will have 'to apply their own standards of honesty' with the result that different decisions may occur on like facts, e.g. an employee's use of his employer's money with an expectation of returning it[6] or a stockbroker's use of A's money to finance B's purchase, expecting to replace it in the ordinary course of business.[7]

[5]'The Undefined Adverb in Criminal Statutes' [1966] Crim.L.R. 548, 552.
[6]*Williams and Wife* [1953] 1 Q.B. 660.
[7]*Banyard* [1958] Crim.L.R. 419.

The learned author therefore concluded that 'it is surely better that these questions should be decided not by juries but by Parliament'.

All this prefigures a view, forcefully and repeatedly expressed by leading academic criminal lawyers such as Professors Elliott, Glanville Williams, Griew and Smith which is informed by two propositions that they all share; first, a Benthamite conviction the certainty is 'the grand utility of the law';[8] secondly, a contempt for the jury as profound as Bentham's own. He thought its influence 'uncertain, unconjectured, feeble, broken, discordant; it is the stability of a house divided against itself. It is different in different places; you can never be sure of it two days together. He who is saved by one jury may be sacrificed by another; the hero of today may be the victim of tomorrow.'[9] Consequently all four insist that dishonesty ought to be exhaustively defined by law and that means, failing legislation, by the judges. The judges themselves, however, have held that dishonesty is a question of fact for the jury.[10] Of course there are differences of detail amongst these commentators as to the precise definition of dishonesty and, indeed, Professor Elliott would go so far as to dispense with dishonesty altogether in the definition of theft.[11] Again, moral fervour varies. Professor Glanville Williams especially criticizes 'the poor level of self-discipline now prevailing' and the 'lax notions about the right of property'.[12] Thus for some of the commentators it is not merely that jury decisions may be capricious but also a commitment, in the name of law, to a morality higher than that of ordinary decent people which sustains the opposition to dishonesty remaining a question of fact for the jury.

In choosing the title for today's lecture I was conscious that it is not original. It is the same as that adopted by Professor Griew for his inaugural lecture at Leicester University about ten years ago. There the similarity ends because I seek (a) to defend the institution of the jury; (b) to maintain that dishonesty should continue to be an element in the definition of theft; and (c) to support the Court of Appeal in its continued resolve that dishonesty should be a question of fact for the jury and not a question of law for the judge. Consequently what I have to say runs counter to the orthodox mainstream of current academic criminal law.

---

[8] Cited in Mary P. Mack *Jeremy Bentham: An Odyssey of Ideas, 1748–1792* (London, 1962), 59.

[9] Box 35, p. 6, cited Mack, *Jeremy Bentham*, 422.

[10] *Feely* [1973] Q.B. 530; *Ghosh* [1982] Q.B. 1053.

[11] 'Dishonesty in Theft; A Dispensable Concept' [1982] Crim.L.R. 395.

[12] Glanville Williams, *Textbook of Criminal Law*, 2nd edn (London, 1983) 726 (hereinafter G.W.).

Richard Tur

II. The Jury—For and Against

As to the jury, Professor Griew condemns it as the 'biggest friend of the criminal classes';[13] he remarks that 'it cannot be rational to trust...twelve strangers of unknown quality'[14] because that would exhibit 'a faith in their competence that is both blind and gratuitous'.[15] He concludes that 'we may not be able to abolish the jury, but at least we should keep it in its place'.[16] A contrary view is expressed by Lord Keith of Kinkel in *Stonehouse*; 'a lawyer may think that the results of applying the law correctly to a certain factual situation is perfectly clear, but nevertheless the evidence may give rise to nuances which he has not observed but which are apparent to the collective mind of a lay jury'.[17] Again, Professor Zander subjected the opinion of Sir Robert Mark, sometime Commissioner of the Metropolitan Police, that juries acquitted too many accused persons to quite devastating criticism.[18]

III. Dishonesty in the Definition of Theft

As to dishonesty remaining part of the definition of theft, Professor Elliott advocates that 'the cleanest way to avoid the risks [of 'uncertainty and capriciousness'] is to remove the word "dishonestly" from the definition of theft'.[19] But in *Feely*, Lawton L.J. observed that 'we find it impossible to accept that a conviction for stealing whether it be called larceny or theft can reveal no moral obloquy. A man so convicted would have difficulty in persuading his friends and neighbours that his reputation had not been gravely damaged. He would be bound to be lowered in the estimation of right thinking people.'[20] Thus the criminal law should not be astute to extend criminal liability to conduct which would not be condemned as dishonest according to the standards of conventional morality.

In *Feely* the manager of a betting shop had taken £30 from the till for his own purposes, contrary to his employer's instructions. He had a right of set-off for this amount in respect of money owed to him by his employer. The trial judge directed the jury that 'even if he were

[13] *Dishonesty and the Jury* (Leicester, 1974), 7.
[14] Op. cit. 20.
[15] Op. cit. 18.
[16] Op. cit. 24.
[17] [1977] 2 All E.R. 909, 940–941.
[18] Sir Robert Mark, 'Minority Verdict', in Mark, *Policing a Perplexed Society* (London, 1977), 53–73. Michael Zander, 'Why I Disagree with Sir Robert Mark', *Police* (April 1974), 16.
[19] [1982] Crim.L.R. 395, 404.
[20] 973] Q.B. 530, 541.

prepared to pay back the following day and even if he were a millionaire...makes no defence to this offence, if someone does something deliberately knowing that his employers are not willing to tolerate it is that not dishonest?'[21] The Court of Appeal emphatically rejected this attempt by the trial judge to define dishonesty as a matter of law: 'We do not agree that judges should decide what "dishonesty" means...Jurors, when deciding whether an appropriation was dishonest can be reasonably expected to, and should, apply the current standards of ordinary decent people. In their own lives they have to decide what is and what is not dishonest. We see no reason why, when in the jury box, they should require the help of a judge to tell them what amounts to dishonesty.'[22] The Court of Appeal therefore quashed the conviction, not because the appellant had not been dishonest but because the question of his dishonesty had not been put to the jury and it was at least possible that, had the question been put, the jury would not have regarded the conduct as dishonest. 'It is', the Court of Appeal observed, 'possible to imagine a case of taking by an employee in breach of instructions to which no one would, or could reasonably, attach moral obloquy...[and] a taking to which no moral obloquy can reasonably attach is not within the concept of stealing either at common law or under the Theft Act, 1968 . . . .'.[23] Of course, 'people who take money from tills and the like without permission are usually thieves; but if they do not admit that they are by pleading guilty, it is for the jury, not the judge, to decide whether they have acted dishonestly . . .'.[24]

Feely is unpopular with the academics. Professor Glanville Williams sees it as the point at which 'the rot commenced'[25] and Professor Elliott states baldly that the Court of Appeal was 'quite simply wrong'.[26] Therefore these commentators advocate that conduct to which no moral obloquy could reasonably attach, judged by the standards of ordinary decent people, should none the less be stigmatized as theft. To see that this is so it is convenient to translate the definitional requirement of dishonesty into a 'defence' of honesty. Thus any appropriation of property of another with the intention permanently to deprive is theft unless the conduct is honest. As the law stands honesty is partially at large in that the term includes not only belief in legal right, belief in consent and belief that the owner cannot be found but also an undefined residue which is to be

---

[21] [1973] Q.B. 530, 536–537.
[22] [1973] Q.B. 530, 537–538.
[23] [1973] Q.B. 530, 539.
[24] [1973] Q.B. 530, 541.
[25] G.W., 725.
[26] [1982] Crim.L.R. 395, 399.

determined pragmatically by the jury. Thus, as the law stands, the jury always has the opportunity to acquit on a charge of theft if it does not regard the conduct of the accused as dishonest. Hobart J. observed in 1609 that '. . . all laws admit certain cases of just excuse'.[27] I add that what may constitute a just excuse is so context-dependent that exhaustive definition in advance must necessarily limit the range of circumstances which might excuse. We simply cannot decide such borderline issues, abstractly, in advance and therefore we cannot legislate for them.

Professor Elliott's proposal is, in effect, the addition of one more excusing condition, namely that the appropriation is 'not detrimental to the interests of the other in a significant practical way'[28] together with the abolition of any further undefined residue. Thus theft would be wholly and exhaustively defined by the law and the jury's role of deliberating upon the honesty or dishonesty of the conduct would vanish. Consequently the opportunity to find that the circumstances gave rise to a just excuse would also vanish. Thus even if a jury believed, and reasonably believed, that no moral obloquy could attach to an appropriation it would, were Professor Elliott's proposal implemented, be unable to acquit unless the conduct fell foursquare within one of his heads of honesty, namely, a claim of right, a belief in consent, a belief that the owner could not be identified, and insignificance. The inevitable consequence of Professor Elliott's proposal and, indeed, of any proposed exhaustive definition of dishonesty, is that some accused will be convicted even where a jury considers them morally blameless.

The idea that the law may be presented as a body of rules exhaustively determining all conditions of liability and all excusing conditions is frequently, though erroneously, associated with legal possitivism. Professors Simpson and Dworkin have attacked what they what they take to be the all-or-nothing model of rules espoused by Professor Hart in particular and by legal positivism in general.[29] Professor Simpson insists that the common law is simply not like that and that the positivist account reveals less the nature of law and more the rational expositor's aspiration to present the law as if it were a coherent and comprehensive code. Professor Dworkin challenges this model of rules on the grounds that there are principles beyond the rules which qualify the application of the rules to fact

[27] *Moore* v *Hussey* 1609 Hob. 93, 96.

[28] [1982] Crim.L.R. 395, 410.

[29] A. W. B. Simpson, 'The Common Law and Legal Theory', in *Oxford Essays in Jurisprudence*, Second Series, Simpson (ed.) (Oxford 1973), 76–99; Ronald M. Dworkin, 'The Model of Rules', *University of Chicago Law Review* **14**, (1967), 35.

situations as they occur. Thus even if all the conditions stipulated in a legal rule obtained in fact the normal legal consequence may be defeated by the existence of some additional circumstance not referred to in the rule. Thus, to use Professor Dworkin's own illustration, a will, valid according to the definition contained in the relevant legal rules, may be deprived of effect by the circumstance that the beneficiary murdered the testator. Thus the principle that no man should profit from his own wrong qualifies and limits the scope of the rule. Further, it is by no means clear that it is possible for anyone, other, perhaps, than Professor Dworkin's imaginary, super-human judge, Hercules, exhaustively to list all the potentially defeasing conditions. As Professor MacCormick observes, 'even if we were to write out all the statutory rules, including in them all the exceptions hitherto imposed by the courts...we could not be confident that we had succeeded in listing the sufficient conditions for the validity of a determination....'.[30] If this is true, the positivist aspiration (as presented by Professors Simpson and Dworkin) is incapable of practical realization simply because the just excuse or defeasing conditions which qualify all laws are incapable of exhaustive definition in advance of particular concrete applications.

Whatever the independent merits of such observations (and they are considerable) it is clear that Professor Hart did not commit the offences charged. He insisted that 'we should not cherish, even as an ideal, the conception of a rule so detailed that the question whether it applied or not to a particular case was always settled in advance, and never involved, at the point of application, a fresh choice between open alternatives'.[31] This is in part due to our relative indeterminacy of aim and our relative ignorance of fact and partly because of the limits of language which is always more abstract and general than the concrete and particular facts to which it applies. Professor Unger catches the point exactly: 'Language is no longer credited with the fixity of categories and the transparent representation of the world which would make formalism plausible in legal reasoning...'.[32] Professor Hart occupied himself with the 'open-texture' and 'problems of the penumbra' and remarked that 'here [within the framework of relatively well settled law], if anywhere we live among uncertainties between which we have to choose, and...the existing law imposes only limits on our choice and not the choice itself'.[33]

[30] (1974) 90 L.Q.R. 102, 125.

[31] H. L. A. Hart, *The Concept of Law* (Oxford, 1961), 125 (hereinafter *Concept*).

[32] R. M. Unger, *Law in Modern Society* (New York, 1976), 196.

[33] 'Positivism and the Separation of Law and Morals', *Harvard Law Review* **71** (1957–1958), 593, 629.

Richard Tur

Professor Hart had no doubt that rules are not all-or-nothing in character and he insisted that 'even a rule that ends with the word "unless..." is still a rule'.[34] But clearly a rule that ends 'unless...' does not 'even purport to set out conditions that make its application necessary'.[35] As Professor MacCormick says, we should 'avoid claiming that our formulae can or should be stated with the logician's precision as an "if and only if" rule laying down necessary and sufficient conditions'.[36] Consequently the formulations to which legal science can aspire are necessarily defeasible in the face of ineffable circumstance. The content of the formulations produced by the legal scientist can only be more detailed and precise than the data they purport to describe by virtue of invention or misrepresentation.

Howsoever innocent Professor Hart may be of the charges it does appear that the professors who oppose the Court of Appeal's approach to dishonesty are guilty of such 'naive positivism'. They believe that it is possible to establish an exhaustive criminal code which forecloses upon new choices at the point of application. Indeed, some of their number participate industriously in an unofficial criminal law codification 'commission'.[37] Of course if one believes, with Bentham, that a science of legislation is possible, then one may seek to devise and promulgate an exhaustive criminal code determining, in perpetuity, all conditions of culpability and exculpation. From such a perspective, the common sense of juries and the intuitions of judges are obstacles to be eliminated and not data to be accommodated. The codifier presupposes rationally defensible values which, owing to their rationality and the authority of reason, may legitimately be imposed upon society from above by the legislator or from outside by the academic. Thus the current standards of ordinary decent people may be dismissed as 'lax'[38] and the judgments of the Court of Appeal dismissed as 'wrong'.[39] There is, however, no agreement that values are rationally determinable and the moral basis is simply assumed by the rational codifier just as Mill's famous 'proof' begged the central question in issue.[40] Indeed, one might turn Mill's 'proof' on its head whereby Mill was 'right in saying that ethical theory must contain one principle that cannot be proved, for to prove it would involve deriving it from some more basic principle,

---

[34] Hart, *Concept*, 136.
[35] Dworkin, *University of Chicago Law Review* **14** (1967), 26.
[36] (1974) 90 L.Q.R. 102, 123.
[37] [1981] Crim.L.R. 281.
[38] G.W., 726.
[39] [1982] Crim.L.R. 395, 399.
[40] Mill, *Utilitarianism* (London, 1863) Ch. IV.

which latter would then be part of the theory'.[41] Given the Benthamite predeliction, it would be no surprise if, like Bentham, the professors on their eighty-second birthdays were 'still codifying like any dragon'.[42]

IV. Judge versus Jury

As to the question whether the issue of an accused's dishonesty ought to be a matter for the jury or for judges, Professor Smith submits that 'standards of honesty should be laid down by law, not left to the vagaries of jury decisions'.[43] To this there are several responses. First, certainty and predictability are not the only desidera for a system of criminal law. Justice is also desirable. In this context 'justice' requires that decisions be tailored to all the circumstances of the particular case. Even if one insists that justice involves treating like cases alike, it follows that unlike cases should be treated differently. General rules of law, no matter how comprehensive and detailed they aspire to be, inevitably abstract from the particularity and concreteness of individual cases with the result that differences between cases may be smoothed over and therefore ignored. Thus both generality and certainty oppose justice which requires that all the circumstances of the case be taken into consideration. As Lord Devlin observes, 'When . . . a man is on trial for his liberty, predictability is quite unimportant. What is wanted is a decision on the merits'.[44]

Secondly, albeit *ad hominem*, Professor Smith is not himself noted for his faith in judges. Thus he writes, 'the House of Lords has a dismal record in criminal cases . . . can we really afford the House of Lords as an appellate court?'[45] This observation is not without some justification and had the situation since the Theft Act, 1968 included dishonesty in the statutory definition of theft been that judges had 'been busily fleshing out a legal concept which the draughtsman had drawn in outline only',[46] the vagaries apprehended by Professor Smith may well have been avoided only at the price of a harsh and inappropriate consistency; that is, by the imposition of an extrava-

[41] Everett W. Hall, 'The "Proof" of Utility in Bentham and Mill', *Ethics* **60** (1949); see, too, Glover, 'Moral Disagreements', in *Causing Death and Saving Lives* (Harmondsworth, 1977), 23–26.

[42] Mack, *Jeremy Bentham*, 4; *Works*, Bowring (ed) (London, 1838), XI, 33.

[43] Smith, *Theft*, para. 116.

[44] *Trial by Jury*, revised edn (London, 1966), 157.

[45] [1981] Crim.L.R. 393.

[46] Elliott, [1982] Crim.L.R. 395, 395.

gant judicial conception of honesty bearing little or no relationship to the 'current standards of ordinary decent people'[47] and, purporting exhaustively to define dishonesty, denying flexibility and therefore just excuse in the face of circumstances not anticipated in the framing of the definition. There is no obvious advantage in avoiding 'vagaries' at the price of consistency for its own sake, just as there is little point in our all being treated equally if we are all treated like dogs! Alternatively, had judges been fleshing out a legal concept given in outline only in the legislation, the vagaries of jury decisions might simply have been replaced by the vagaries of judicial decisions. Professor Smith would certainly acknowledge that different people have different views as to 'dishonesty', and that judges have no special insight as to its meaning.[48] It is no coincidence that Bentham himself waxed indignant on 'Judge and Co.' 'It is the judges . . . that makes the common law. Do you know how they make it? Just as a man makes laws for his dog. When your dog does anything you want to break him of, you wait till he does it, and then you beat him for it. This is the way you make laws for your dog; and this is the way judges make law for you and me.'[49] Consequently judge-made law is uncertain; 'wherever jurisprudential law reigns certainty is impossible; it has no ground to stand on. Jurisprudential law is sham law; to ascribe stability to this creature of the imagination is to ascribe stability to a shadow. Statute law everywhere has a tenor—a determinate collection of words; there is the will, and there the expression of it.'[50]

Thirdly, and this is the crux of my argument, treating dishonesty as a question of law for judges rather than as a question of fact for the jury breaks the nexus between current morality and the criminal law and thereby destroys 'the protection against laws which the ordinary man may regard as harsh and oppressive'.[51] Indeed, 'it must be considered', observed Johnson, 'that a man who only does what everyone of the society to which he belongs would do, is not a dishonest man'.[52] But if we do seek to ensure that no man be convicted of crime and stigmatized as a thief where he only does that which other men of his society would do, the decision as to the nature of dishonesty should lie with a jury of ordinary people and depend upon their agreement rather than be vested in a single judge

[47] *Feely* [1973] Q.B. 530, 538.
[48] Smith and Hogan, *Criminal Law*, 5th edn (London, 1983), 491: *Theft*, para. 116.
[49] *Works*, Bowring (ed.), V, 235.
[50] *Works*, Bowring (ed.), VII, 309.
[51] Lord Devlin, *Trial by Jury*, 160.
[52] *Boswell's Life of Johnson*, Vol. I, 456.

whose own morality may be higher and might legitimately be expected to be higher than that of the ordinary man and whose solitary appreciation of conventional morality is unlikely to be more or even as authentic as that of the unanimous or nearly unanimous view of twelve ordinary people. As Sir William Holdsworth wisely observed of the jury system, 'It tends to make the law intelligible by keeping it in touch with the common facts of life.'[53]

Of course, if dishonesty were to be a question of law for the judges rather than a question of fact for the jury, then it would also be a question of legal science for the professor of law. It is, however, by no means clear that professors of law are necessarily more in touch with conventional morality than are judges and it is at least possible that some professors of law may be as remote from conventional morality as judges are and may have as little sympathy with or confidence in the morality of the ordinary man. Professor Elliott, for example, is concerned that a jury might share a defendant's opinion that it is not dishonest for a punter knowingly to benefit from a bookmaker's mistake on the basis that bookmakers, unlike grocers, are fair game.[54] Yet Professor Elliott also believes that 'the conviction as thieves of people who take little loans of money for temporary purposes is unedifying'[55] and he therefore proposes as compensation for the removal of dishonesty from the definition of theft a limiting condition such that it is not theft where an 'appropriation of property belonging to another is not detrimental to the interests of the other in a significant practical way'.[56] This, however, appears apt to exclude not only the borrower but also the petty pilferer. Professor Smith, however, though equally scandalized by the proposition that book-makers might be fair game, takes a more stringent line on insignificance observing that 'a belief has sometimes prevailed in the army and other large organizations that it is "all right" to take small items of property belonging to the organization ... [and that] it would be preferable if the judge could direct the jury that the pilferer was acting dishonestly'.[57]

Professor Glanville Williams adopts perhaps the most stringent position of all; current standards are 'lax';[58] the jury will not be more 'decent' or 'honest' than ordinary people and unanimity tends in the direction of a standard lower than average. In any event, honesty,

[53] Holdsworth, *A History of English Law*, 7th edn (London, 1956), Vol. 1, 349.
[54] [1982] Crim.L.R. 395, 399; *Gilks* [1972] 3 All E.R. 280, 283.
[55] [1982] Crim.L.R. 395, 406.
[56] [1982] Crim.L.R. 395, 410.
[57] Smith, *Theft*, para. 117.
[58] G.W., 726.

the moral value underpinning the Theft Acts, has nothing to do with current standards. 'Honesty means three things, all of them largely independent of prevailing mores: (a) respect for property rights; (b) refraining from deception, at any rate where this would cause loss to another; (c) keeping a promise, at any rate where the promisee has supplied consideration for the promise or will suffer loss if it is not kept. The most important of these meanings for the law of theft is the first.' Professor Glanville Williams takes the view that 'what must be found is a definition of dishonesty (outside the specific situations mentioned in section 2) that will not depend exclusively on general opinion....'[59] For Professor Glanville Williams this definition is 'disregard for property rights' but he says of Professor Elliott's proposal couched in terms of insignificance that 'we can at least be certain that almost any definition making the position independent of current social attitudes would be better than the rule in *Ghosh*'.[60] If the people are Professor Glanville Williams's Caesar, then, like Bentham, he appeals not to Caesar as he is but Caesar as he ought to be.[61]

Since the learned professors do not agree among themselves what dishonesty is, it is unlikely that making the issue a question of law whereby judicial or legislative decisions might be informed by the fruits of academic insight, deliberation and theorizing would eliminate the vagaries which the academics attribute to jury decisions. What is more likely is that the issue of dishonesty which is currently a matter for the robust common sense of ordinary people, would become progressively more intellectualized. Sir William Holdsworth caught the sense of this perfectly: 'If a clever man is left to decide by himself...he is usually not content to decide each case as it arises. He constructs theories for the decision of analogous cases. These theories are discussed, doubted or developed by other clever men... The interest is apt to centre, not in the dry task of deciding the case...but rather in the construction of new theories, the reconciliation of conflicting cases, the demolition of criticism of older views. The result is a series of carefully constructed, and periodically considered rules which merely retard the attainment of a conclusion without assisting in its formation. It is only the philosopher, or possibly, the professor of general jurisprudence, who can pursue indefinitely, these interesting processes. Rules of law must struggle for existence in the strong air of practical life. Rules which are so refined that they bear but a small relation to the world of sense will

[59] G.W., 730.

[60] G.W., 730.

[61] *Works*, Bowring (ed.), X, 73; 'The people is my Caesar. I appeal from the present Caesar to Caesar better informed.'

sooner or later be swept away. Sooner, if, like the criminal law or the commercial law, they touch nearly men's habits and conduct; later, if, like the law of real property, they affect a smaller class, and affect them less nearly. The jury system has for some hundreds of years been constantly bringing the rules of law to the touchstone of contemporary common sense.'[62]

V. Dishonesty Beyond Theft

The issue is, however, further complicated by the inclusion of dishonesty as a defining element in a range of additional offences involving deception. These include obtaining property, obtaining a pecuniary advantage, procuring the execution of a valuable security, obtaining services, securing the remission of a liability, inducing a creditor to wait for or forgo payment, and obtaining an exemption from or abatement of liability. The partial and negative definition of dishonesty and the qualifications as to gain or readiness to pay apply only to theft and consequently the meaning of dishonesty for all these offences is entirely at large. Some commentators have seen in this circumstance yet another defect in the law. Professor Elliott observes that the relation between dishonesty in theft and dishonesty in the other offences was 'obscure from the beginning but has become more obscure'[63] and that this increased obscurity flows from the judge's determination to treat dishonesty as a question of fact for the jury thereby 'making a rod for their own backs'.[64] But quite what the objection is, is itself obscure. Of course, if dishonesty were to be a question of law it would be possible to impose consistency right across the board but it is not obvious that dishonesty should have the same meaning in the wide range of circumstances now under consideration. It may well be that a claim of right always negatives dishonesty in theft but may not always negative dishonesty in deception or excuse forgery or blackmail. Thus one might wish to say that where a man believing himself to have a legal right to property merely takes possession of it that man is not dishonest but if, rather than merely taking it, he deceives another into parting with it or obtains it by means of forgery or blackmail, the moral justifiability of his conduct is an open question. Thus, where force or fraud occur, honesty is less plausibly to be found. As to blackmail one might conclude that even a claim of right does not justify

[62] Holdsworth, op. cit., Vol. 1, 349.
[63] [1982] Crim.L.R. 395, 398.
[64] [1982] Crim.L.R. 395, 395.

demands with menaces. The situation with deception and forgery is less clear. Perhaps both should be treated analogously with theft whereby a claim of right would always be a complete justification. Perhaps they both should be treated like blackmail whereby a claim of right would never be a justification. Arguably they might occupy a middle position whereby a claim of right might be a justification for obtaining by deception or even for forgery in some circumstances but not in others.

This raises the apparently paradoxical spectre of an honest deception but it is, perhaps, not absurd that in some circumstances deception could be a morally legitimate strategy.[65] In *Salvo*[66] a used car dealer sold a Valiant to K, taking a Falcon in part exchange; Salvo then sold the Falcon to T. Later Salvo discovered that K had had no title to sell the Falcon and he, Salvo, was put to expense to perfect T's title. Later Salvo repurchased the Valiant from K, paying by cheque, intending subsequently to dishonour it, which he did, all on the grounds that this was the only way he could get the Valiant back. Although convicted of dishonestly obtaining property by deception his conviction was quashed on the grounds that a claim of right could be a defence even where property was obtained by deception. If so, the proper arrangement is to leave dishonesty in deception cases entirely at large for the jury which, as it happens, is, indeed, current legal practice in England.

Professor Smith helpfully compares theft, forgery and blackmail: 'It appears then that if D believes he is entitled to a sum of money (and even if he is entitled to it); (i) he is guilty of forgery if he demands it with a forged instrument; (ii) he is guilty of blackmail if he demands it with menaces; but (iii) he is not guilty of theft if he appropriates it'.[67] He then asks whether obtaining offences should be grouped with forgery and blackmail on the one hand or with theft on the other and he submits that 'they belong with theft'.[68] Now, whatever the merits of Professor Smith's arguments it is to be noted that this grouping of obtaining offences with theft is a choice not necessitated by statute, nor case law, nor by logic. And even if obtaining offences are more like theft than forgery or blackmail, it does not follow that they fall to be treated exactly as does theft with

---

[65] The notion of honest deception raises parallel difficulties to an honest lie, see G.W., 729; or honest graft, see David Ward, 'The Ethnic Ghetto in the United States; Past and Present', *Transactions of the Institute of British Geographers* (New Series) **7** (1982), 262, and Riordan (ed.), *Plunkitt of Tammany Hall* (New York, 1963).

[66] [1980] V.R. 401.

[67] Smith, *Theft*, para. 182.

[68] Ibid.

regard to a claim of right or dishonesty. Essentialism is the vice of believing that for one word there is but one meaning. Applied to dishonesty, essentialism is especially vicious. Dishonesty is context-dependent. Thus what might constitute dishonesty in theft may differ from that which constitutes dishonesty in deception offences in significant respects, notwithstanding a strong family resemblance. These differences may make a moral difference. This itself legitimates leaving an undefined residue for the pragmatic determination of the jury. Hale observed: 'the variety of circumstances is so great and the complications thereof so mingled that it is impossible to prescribe all the circumstances evidencing a felonious intent but the same must be left to the due and attentive consideration of the judge and jury'.[69] Equally, the range of circumstances is so great and the complications so mingled as to render exhaustive definition of dishonesty impossible and it, too, should be left to the attentive consideration of the jury.

VI. Subjectivism

An additional problem when one looks at a concept such as dishonesty relates to the traditional categories of the criminal lawyer. Crimes are conventionally divided into two major clusters of elements: *actus reus* and *mens rea*. *Mens rea* has been criticized by judges, for example by both Stephen J. and Cave J. in *Tolson* as 'misleading' or 'uncouth'[70] and *actus reus* attracted the strictures of Lord Diplock in *Miller*.[71] None the less, these concepts provide the basis for the exposition and analysis of the criminal law. A problem is that some concepts, and dishonesty is but one example, straddle the boundary and this problem is exacerbated where a belief prevails that every concept is exclusively *mens rea* or *actus reus*. Thus Professor Smith regards 'dishonestly' in the Theft Act as a separate element in the *mens rea*.[72] There is without doubt a significant element of truth in this because the requirement of dishonesty involves not merely the objective circumstance that the accused's conduct does not conform to prevailing standards but also that he acted 'with a consciousness of wrong-doing'.[73] Consequently there is also a significant element of truth in Professor Smith's observation

[69] 1 P.L. 500.
[70] *Tolson* (1889) 23 Q.B.D. 168, 185; 181.
[71] [1983] 2 W.L.R. 539.
[72] Smith, *Theft*, para. 181; cf. 5th edn (London, 1984), paras 122–124.
[73] Thomas, *The Institutes of Justinian* (Oxford, 1975), 265.

4

that 'dishonesty is a subjective concept'. The rigid dichotomy of *mens rea* and *actus reus* and the 'evangelical zeal'[74] with which some academics pursue subjectivism, being 'in total subjection to the subjectivist bug'[75] raised the possibility in the academic mind that perhaps dishonesty was *wholly* a subjective concept. That, in turn raised the spectre of the 'Robin Hood defence', that is the possibility that an accused might be acquitted of theft because he believed it honest to steal from the rich and give to the poor. If this were so then the entire law of theft would be subverted for it would be a case of every man his own legislator. Professor Glanville Williams remarks that subjectivism of this extreme variety 'gives subjectivism a bad name'.[76] Indeed it does and one might suppose that some of the professorial opposition to the concept of dishonesty was informed by the aim of protecting subjectivism from apparent absurdity. However, rather than seek wholly to objectify dishonesty in the law in order to avoid the apparent absurdity of subjectivism one might accept that dishonesty is a dual concept, encompassing both subjective and objective elements. In *Caldwell*, Lord Diplock gently mocked English academic criminal lawyers for being 'obsessive'[77] about the subjectivist–objectivist dichotomy and he remarked that 'questions of criminal liability are seldom solved by simply asking whether the test is subjective or objective'.[78]

Rather than acknowledge the dual nature of dishonesty, the commentators, perhaps because of their disdain for 'Judge and Co.' and for the jury, anticipated that the law would develop in such a way as to establish the 'Robin Hood defence'. They were therefore astute to read such nonsense into the decisions of the courts when the issue of dishonesty arose. Thus in *Gilks*[79] they perceived an acknowledgment that the defendant's belief that bookmakers were fair game might constitute a defence and in *Boggelyn v Williams*[80] they believed their suspicions to be wholly vindicated. In that case the defendant whose electricity had been cut off reconnected the supply. He knew that the supplier did not consent but he notified him of the reconnection and believed reasonably that he would be able to pay at the due time. The court rejected an argument that the defendant's beliefs were irrelevant, holding that they were, indeed, crucial to the question of his honesty. It does not follow, however,

[74] See Wells, [1982] Crim.L.R. 209. 210.
[75] Cross, (1975) 91 L.Q.R. 540, 541.
[76] G.W., 727.
[77] [1981] 1 All E.R. 961, 965.
[78] [1981] 1 All E.R. 961, 967.
[79] [1972] 3 All E.R. 280.
[80] [1978] 1 W.L.R. 873.

nor did the court state that the relevance of the defendant's belief rendered his belief dispositive. The courts have never held that a man's moral *values*, bizarre or not, may constitute a defence. What they have held and held repeatedly, albeit with occasional laxity of expression and some tergiversations, is that a man's *belief* that his conduct is not dishonest according to the current standards of ordinary decent people may well excuse on a charge of theft or of a deception offence.

The Court of Appeal has restated the position in *Ghosh*.[81] A jury must first of all decide whether according to the ordinary standards of honest and decent people what was done was dishonest. If it was not dishonest by these standards that is the end of the matter and the prosecution fails. If it was dishonest by those standards then the jury must consider whether the defendant himself realized that what he was doing was by those standards dishonest. If the answer to this question is 'No' the prosecution fails; if 'Yes' it succeeds on the issue of dishonesty. This statement reveals very clearly the dual nature of dishonesty. The first question is wholly objective. The second question is subjective. It appears, further, that an acquittal under the second question could well be justified by reference to the general principle that an accused falls to be judged on that state of facts which he honestly and *bona fide* believed to be the case.[82] The defence of mistake of fact is well established in English criminal law and much applauded by the subjectivist lobby.[83] It will not suffice that the accused claims simply not to know what the current standards are. In order to succeed he will have to assert a positive, albeit mistaken, belief that current morality did not stigmatize his conduct as dishonest.

The facts of *Greenstein*[84] illustrate the possibility of an acquittal under the dual test re-affirmed in *Ghosh*. The defendants made a practice of applying for very large quantities of shares sending a cheque far in excess of the amounts in their bank accounts. They had no authority to overdraw but they expected to be allocated a relatively small number of shares and receive a 'return cheque'. By

[81] [1982] Q.B. 1053, especially 1064. The facts of the case were that a surgeon obtained fees from the NHS by falsely representing that he had performed an operation. He claimed that the money obtained was the balance of fees already owed to him.

[82] *Prince* (1875) L.R. 2 C.C.R., 154, 157, per Brett J., 'The first point therefore to be considered would seem to be what would have been the legal position of the prisoner if the facts had been as he believed them to be...?'

[83] *Morgan* [1976] A.C. 176; *David Raymond Smith* [1974] Q.B. 354; see Smith and Hogan, *Criminal Law*, 5th edn, 188–190.

[84] [1976] 1 All E.R. 1.

paying this cheque into their account they enabled their original cheques to be honoured either on first presentation or very soon thereafer. The point of this complex manoeuvre, known as 'stagging', was to receive a larger number of shares than they would otherwise have been allotted because where demand outstrips supply shares are allocated in proportion to the numbers applied for. Now it is quite possible to regard this manoeuvre either as dishonest or as an ingenious stroke of business acumen; 'there is nothing illegal in stagging'.[85] The jury found the defendants guilty as charged but it is likely that it was influenced by the fact that the defendants had pursued this course of action repeatedly even after warnings that it was unacceptable to the issuing houses and to their bank. If one supposes a single instance of stagging in the absence of any warning a defendant might plausibly argue that what he did was not contrary to the standards of ordinary decent people and that if it was he positively believed that it was not. After all, the practice was well enough established in his community to have been given a name and it therefore follows that he was not the only person using the stunt. A jury might well conclude on such facts that although the practice was dishonest, the defendant believed it to be honest and therefore acquit. The more an accused's belief diverges from the current standards the less is a jury likely to accept that he actually held the belief asserted. 'It will be a rare day when a jury is satisfied as to the existence of an unreasonable belief.'[86] The more dubious the deliverances of current morality, the more likely is a jury to accept the belief asserted. That seems to me to be eminently correct. It strikes the appropriate balance between objective and subjective elements and it prevents the conditions of criminal liability being more stringent than those of moral culpability. It would be wrong for the law to seek to be more precise than the conventional morality which it reinforces and reflects.

VII. Law and Morality

Professor MacCormick observes that the criminal law is *necessarily* geared to the protection of legitimate interests according to a certain dominant political morality.[87] Punishment he holds to be 'an

[85] *Ghosh* [1982] Q.B. 1053, 1057, citing *Greenstein* [1975] 1 W.L.R. 1353, 1359.
[86] Per Dickson J., *Pappajohn* (1980) 111 D.L.R. 1, 20.
[87] 'Against Moral Disestablishment', in MacCormick, *Legal Right and Social Democracy* (Oxford, 1982), 18–38, at p. 30.

expressive and symbolic act'[88] evincing moral disapproval. 'It sets the seal of public disapprobation upon the wrongful act of which the offender has been found guilty ... [it] expresses the state's condemnation of the deed done.'[89] Further, 'an attitude of condemnation or disapprobation is *per se* a moral attitude'.[90] Both Durkheim and Lord Devlin emphasized that the cohesiveness and solidarity of any large and complex polity requires some common morality.[91] Of course it would be fanciful to suggest that a social morality lies fully armed within the common consciousness of the members of a society. None the less, in order for a society to exist at all there must be some shared basic morality. That shared basic morality is incorporated into the law which not only reflects but also articulates, refines and makes more precise the requirements of the morality of a society as it applies to particular cases.

The moral value underlying theft is honesty. In incorporating the moral value of honesty the criminal law should prohibit that which is clearly dishonest and permit that which is clearly honest. Only thus can the 'criminal law ... support morality, not contradict it'.[92] Once it is clear that the criminal law supports moral values and that criminal punishment evinces a moral judgment on the conduct of the accused, borderline cases fall into perspective and are readily dealt with. Such borderline cases are inevitable by the very nature of the concept of dishonesty. In the real world conduct passes by degrees from the completely honest to the blatantly dishonest and somewhere in the middle a grey area obtains calling for fine judgment. These borderline cases cannot properly be dealt with in advance because they are invariably complex on their facts. Thus the law ought to leave these cases to the trial court or jury. These know the facts and can therefore properly measure such cases against the moral standard. Such cases are in moral terms doubtful. The law cannot be more precise than the morality it reflects without becoming artificial and remote. And if the law serves moral values which are artificial and remote from ordinary standards, imposed, for example, by exhaustive definitions of moral concepts such as dishonesty dreamed up by a commission of academics, the law itself will fall into disrepute.

It may appear that such a proposal for borderline cases renders the law uncertain and, indeed, this is so but the uncertainty is that of the

---

[88] Ibid.
[89] Op. cit., 32.
[90] Op. cit., 33.
[91] Op. cit., 34.
[92] Canadian Law Reform Commission Working Paper 19 (1977).

human predicament itself and cannot realistically be legislated away. In any case if the law is as I have described it, it embodies the common teachings of morality and 'everyone is required to live up to such common moral principles. He who knowingly skates on thin ice cannot reasonably complain that no sign-post marks the precise spot at which he may fall through. Those who disregard the common moral teachings do so at their peril.'[93] In practice, however, where the immorality of conduct is a matter of reasonable doubt it is unlikely that a jury will be unanimously or almost unanimously of the opinion that the accused was sufficiently immoral to justify his being punished and the genuinely borderline case will result in an acquittal.

The commentators have advocated *a priori* rationalist (and, indeed, critical) morality in which everything is cut and dried in advance and all determinations are foreclosed upon by exhaustive definitions. Consequently the robust common sense of juries and the intuitions of judges are obstacles to be eliminated. A counter-model of morality involves constructing the best moral theory one can on the basis of one's intuitive judgments in particular cases rather than deriving solutions from principles unequivocably given, self-evidently, in reason. Of course no theory can accommodate all intuitions and the constructive model of morality allows one to discard recalcitrant intuitions as misconceived but one cannot merely discard intuitions out of hand. Out of this attempt to reconcile conflicting intuitions emerges moral principles which themselves are susceptible of refinement and qualification in the light of further instances and dilemmas. This dialectic of principle and instance is reflected within the legal process itself which throws up an inexhaustible supply of examples in the light of which principles may be tested, qualified and refined. Law is, on this view, the institutionalization of the constructive model of morality. Consequently the intuitions of judges and the collective decisions of juries provide data which *prima facie* are to be accommodated rather than simply dismissed out of hand. On such a view the law, especially the criminal law, reflects and supports some conception of a just social order.

This continuity of positive law and positive morality presupposes no Holmesian 'brooding omnipresence in the sky',[94] and it concedes only that law is necessarily moral in the purely formal sense whereby it seeks to determine how one ought to behave.[95] The content of the

---

[93] Per Lord Morris, *Knuller* v *D.P.P.* [1972] 2 All E.R. 898, 910.
[94] Per Holmes J., *Southern Pacific Co.* v *Jensen* (1917) 244 U.S. 205, 222.
[95] Kelsen, *Pure Theory of Law* (Berkely and Los Angeles, 1967), 65.

law is not, however, necessarily moral if by that is meant that to be moral it must conform to values proceeding from some *a priori* rationalism. The moral content of the law flows from the detailed, patient interplay of doctrine and decision; of principle and precedent. On such a view law is the dominant and, indeed, most fully articulated system of positive morality in a community and it is therefore an appropriate arena for applied moral philosophy. It is true, as Professor Smith observes, that 'it is the business of the law to establish standards'[96] but it does not follow from this that the legislature informed by the rationalist codifier is the sole source of the standards which the law does establish and nurture and arguably 'the current standards of ordinary decent people' have at least as strong a claim to inform the content of law as have the rationalist values imposed *ab extra* by reformers and expositors of the law. Only by leaving an undefined residue to the judgment of the jury can we be confident that the law runs in harmony with conventional moral values and that changes in such values will be accommodated and therefore that no one will be convicted of serious crime whose conduct is not deserving of moral obloquy.

VII. Conclusions

I take the concept of dishonesty as an example of standard-bearing concepts generally. Other examples are 'immoral purposes' in section 32 of the Sexual Offences Act, 1956[97] and the common law notion of a 'disorderly house'.[98] In my view such concepts are not and cannot be exhaustively and exclusively defined by the law. Rather, they reflect extra-legal standards of social conduct. The existence of such concepts in the law suggests a general thesis, namely that any functioning legal system necessarily incorporates and reflects values immanent in the community which it serves. Such a thesis supports these propositions: law is simply too important a matter to be left solely to lawyers; not all law is 'lawyers law' and one should guard against an academic tendency to convert questions of practical moral philosophy into technical questions exclusively determined by the law; where standard-bearing concepts feature in the legal universe of discourse, moral philosophers have a significant contribution to make; and, since law necessarily involves questions which are irreducibly moral, the law provides the most detailed and best

[96] Smith, *Theft*, para. 117.
[97] *Grey* [1982] Crim.L.R. 176.
[98] *Tan* [1983] 2 All E.R. 12.

authenticated data for practical moral philosophizing. Finally, a distinction taken by Bentham, Austin and Mill between 'positive' and 'critical' morality and more recently canvassed by Professors Cooper and Strawson distinguishing what I call 'essential social morality' and 'extravagant individual morality' calls for further scrutiny[99] because the essence of the controversy between the academics and the judges is not morality (writ large) versus mores (writ small) but the critical morality of a self-selecting group versus the positive morality of ordinary people. That discusssion, however, awaits another day.

[99] Cooper, 'Two Concepts of Morality', *Philosophy* (1966), 19–33; Strawson, 'Social Morality and Individual Ideal', *Philosophy* (1961), 1–17; see, too, Urmson, 'Saints and Heroes', in *Essays in Moral Philosophy*, Melden (ed.) (Washington, 1958), 198–216.

Positional Goods[1]

MARTIN HOLLIS

In days gone by, when we had something called Rapid Economic Growth, we used to worry about it. We worried especially about its social costs and its technical limits. If growth meant gearing people to efficient production, we would have to be geographically and socially mobile. That threatened our old ways of community life, with their neighbourhood values and extended families. There were more obvious costs too, like chemicals in the air and highways through the landscape. Furthermore, the cornucopia need not be bottomless. To sustain its effusions, nature might have to be pillaged until we ran out of trees or oil. Technology might hit bottlenecks so severe that costs began to outrun benefits. That would mean thwarting the new expectations which economic growth had aroused and which were its motivating force. But, for all that, our island race faced the horrors of affluence, abundance and goodies for all with a stiff upper lip.

A late thought in the discussion was that there could also be *Social Limits to Growth*—the title of Fred Hirsch's powerful book,[2] making the point. There can never be goodies for all, he argued, for the striking reason that many of the goods, which we all want, are positional. This is a deeply subversive idea. A positional good is one which a person values only on condition that not everyone has it. Prizes, for instance, are worthless, if shelled out to all, and much of what we seek has this exclusive character. Goods are also symbols, especially if generated by turning us into a meritocracy, and, as Don Alhambra sang ruefully in *The Gondoliers,* 'if everyone is somebody, then no one's anybody'. The cornucopia is bound to fail us for this self-defeating reason. Hirsch summed up the catch pithily by remarking that, 'if everyone stands on tiptoe, no one sees better' (p. 5).

His case made a large impact and the notion of a 'positional good' has gained wide currency. But events have overtaken the analysis, thanks to a savage recession, which has put the snags of growth out of our heads. This is an unreasonable sequel, since it has turned out to be possible to enjoy the snags of economic growth without having the growth. Also we

[1] Warm thanks are owed to Derek Parfit for his unstinted and very helpful comments on the original draft and to Amartya Sen and others present when it was discussed in Oxford, where I was being partly supported by a grant from the British Academy, for which I give thanks also.
[2] London: Routledge & Kegan Paul, 1977.

seem to be proposing to climb out of recession by making ourselves yet more meritocratic and this must mean that any resulting goodies will be treated as rewards. So the task of absorbing the idea of positionality into social theory, ethics and the philosophy of action remains as interesting as before. This paper will make a start.

Scarcity for scarcity's sake is the pure form of a positional good. Numbered lithographs, for instance, are each priced higher the fewer of them there are, since they are valued partly because they are scarce. Everyone could own a mere print but not everyone can enjoy a numbered guarantee that not everyone has one. This is social scarcity, involving a direct link between value and exclusion. Status and power are more abstract examples but more pervasive ones too. To have high status is to have higher status than others: to have power is to have power over someone. This is the stuff of meritocracy and it may even extend to ethics, if, for instance, to be good is to be better than the next man and to be holy is to be holier than thou. That may be going too far—we shall see.

Hirsch himself was an economist and used the idea of social scarcity to persuade his colleagues that, within the familiar textbook economy, there was a whole 'positional economy' waiting to be explored. To do it, he added a second kind of scarcity, one due to the effects of crowding. Scarcity for scarcity's sake results, he thought, from motives like 'envy, emulation and pride' and, where these are present, the positional element in value is irremovable. Incidental scarcity arises when the value of the good merely happens to vary with the number of people who have access. It subdivides into physical congestion, as with the pleasure of motoring, which depends on how crowded the road is, and social congestion, as with the fun of conducting an orchestra, with a second conductor to take turns. The scarcity is incidental in the sense that more roads would restore the pleasure or a second orchestra the fun. Since resources are usually limited, however, it is a very common form of scarcity and means, in effect, that almost everything in any budget has some positional aspect.

In order to generalize the idea beyond economics, I propose to add another distinction, one between 'vertical' and 'horizontal'. Hirsch's scarcities are vertical in the sense that they depend on other people who want the good losing out in the attempt to get it. The status seeker wants more of the prestige, the motorist more of the road, the conductor more of the orchestra's time. A different sort of positional element occurs with complementarities. The conductor needs an orchestra. Within the orchestra, the brass needs the woodwind; the first flute needs the second flute. A good is horizontally positional, if its value to its possessor depends on other people having other goods. In O. Henry's story 'The Gift of the Magi' a poor couple have only two treasured possessions. The man has inherited a gold fob watch and longs for a fine chain to hang it on. The woman has a beautiful head of shining hair and longs for a set of tortoise-shell combs to adorn it with. Because they love each other deeply, he secretly sells his watch to buy the combs; and she secretly sells her hair to buy a platinum chain. The story ends consolingly, 'But in a last word to the wise of these days, let it be said that of all who give gifts these two were the wisest'. But, if I may leave this higher moral for later, the coarse reckoning is that each finished with a good which was of no value because its complement was missing. The distinction is thus between goods of competition, whose positionality is vertical, and those of co-ordination, whose positionality is horizontal.

Armed with these ideas of pure and incidental, vertical and horizontal, let us consider some questions of rational choice and social distribution. A famous remark from J. S. Mill's *Utilitarianism* will serve as a point of departure. While discussing the sort of proof which the principle of utility is capable of, he observes, 'each person's happiness is a good to that person and the general happiness, therefore, a good to the aggregate of all persons'. This catches very well the spirit not only of utilitarianism but also of a family of Enlightenment attempts to connect the wants of each person to the good of all persons. The best known application of this spirit is perhaps Welfare Economics. At any rate I shall begin there.

The generic problem is to find a warrantable rule for converting individuals' preferences into a social choice. Let there be n individuals, each with a full and consistent ranking of the feasible states of the economy (or outcomes of the social choice). The search is for a rule which will order the states (or at least pick a best state) in a way responsive to the preferences. 'Responsive' is usually construed with the aid of four conditions, suggested by Kenneth Arrow in *Social Choice and Individual Values* (1951). Worded loosely, they are Universality (the rule must work whatever the individual preferences), Pareto Optimality (if all prefer x to y, the social choice cannot be y over x), Independence of Irrelevant Alternatives (social choice between x and y shall depend solely on individual rankings of x and y (not, for instance, on rankings of x and z)), and Non-Dictatorship (the social choice shall not be automatically dictated by the preferences of any individual or sub-group). Arrow's startling proof that no possible rule can be guaranteed to meet all four conditions has not undermined the approach. Welfare economists continue to look for a rule which will meet conditions close to Arrow's and they are joined in their search by, for instance, theorists of political voting systems and liberals wanting to formalize the notion of individual rights as a workable constraint on social choice.

Martin Hollis

To isolate the issues raised by positional goods, let us assume that there is an x which each individual wants most but only if not everyone has it. For instance, suppose that three tramps are about to spend the night in a park where there is one small bench. The bench is just large enough for one person to sleep or for two to sit in fair comfort or for three to squeeze miserably. Each tramp would most prefer to have the bench to himself and would rather sit in comfort than be squeezed. Moreover, each would rather spend the night on the ground than share the bench with two others, although also preferring to sit with one other than to lie on the ground.

These conditions yield a partial ordering. To get the rest of it, we must know how each would rank outcomes where the bench was occupied but not by him. Let us suppose for the moment that none is envious by nature and so would rather have the bench used by someone than by no one; and, to round it off, by one rather than two. Writing '0' for 'occupy', we get this table:

Outcomes				Rankings		
(A)	(B)	(C)		A	B	C
0	1	1		1st	4th=	4th=
1	0	1		4th=	1st	4th=
1	1	0		4th=	4th=	1st
0	0	1		2nd=	2nd=	6th
0	1	0		2nd=	6th	2nd=
1	0	0		6th	2nd=	2nd=
1	1	1		7th	7th	7th
0	0	0		8th	8th	8th

To bring the positional problems out, I assume finally that the tramps are mirror images of each other and in particular that all have the same intensities of preferences, so that the situation is wholly symmetrical.

What can we say about the social choice? The Pareto Principle rules out *111* and *000*, since there are six ways to improve on those for all. Nothing more follows simply. Let us agree, however, for purposes of argument, that the social choice 'ought' to be single occupancy of the bench. We can make this so by stipulating that the total utility for one occupant and two on the ground is greater than for two on the bench and one on the ground. The question now becomes how the tramps, considered as rational individuals, can arrive at it. To be precise, it is two questions. How might the best outcome emerge? Why should it be stable?

I do not find it plausible to suggest that the distribution of positional goods can be left to an Unseen Hand. There is no equilibrium of the copy-book kind to be had, where the market clears with effective demand satisfied and further supply unprofitable. With positional goods there is usually scope for a further transaction, at least if the next deal need not bear the resulting loss on the previous ones. For instance weekend cottages in rural villages are a positional good. If there are too many, they blight the charm of the village, whose native life is part of the invaders' pleasure. If extra ones are built, they soon obstruct each other and ruin the landscape. There is an optimal number. But is still pays the next newcomer to buy one or to find a builder whom it pays to build one, since the loss in amenities is borne by those already in occupation. Here an Unseen Hand makes mischief by expanding the market so as to erode the value of the positional good. In theory the process continues until the village has become too unattractive to be worth an extra unit to anyone and by now the positional good is no longer a good. That is no doubt why planning regulations are usually invoked, to put a stop to the mischief.

Similarly each of the tramps prefers an outcome where he has the bench to himself. But, faced with one where he is a loser, he then prefers half the bench to a place on the ground. The best outcome is thus unstable, if left to an Unseen Hand. Admittedly there is a lower limit, since (according to the table) each will opt for the ground, if he expects both the others to opt for the bench. This result is stable; but it is inaccessible, if left to an Unseen Hand. Just ask which tramp is to be the meek fellow who shall inherit the earth. The symmetry of the setting, with each tramp's ranking a mirror image of the others', prevents anyone's choosing '1', unless all do; and prevents rational predictions, since each must reckon on what each expects each to reckon that each will reckon that each. . . . Nor is this a case where the rational way to defeat the Cunning of Reason is to act irrationally, since there is no randomizing strategy, which can survive others' suspicion that it is being used. The best outcome does not emerge or, if it does, is unstable and the positional good cannot be realized.

Where an Unseen Hand fails, a theory of contract may perhaps succeed. The tramps can rationally contract to draw lots for who is to have the bench to himself. Each has the same good reason to agree, since he cannot be left worse off than by the Unseen Hand and has a one in three chance of winning. (Indeed a lottery might still be a rational arrangement, even if we had touched the tramps with envy, so that each slightly preferred an empty bench to one which he had no place on, provided that a one in three chance of success outweighed the envy.) A contract for a lottery creates a kind of 'original position', where each votes self-interestedly for the General Will, since he does not yet know exactly how he will fare in practice. The proposal preserves the positional good, distributes it fairly and commands the rational assent of each individual—or so it would be fashionable to claim.

101

Raffles are all very well for casual amusement in a society which makes its main distributions in some other way. But there are snags to making social theory with them. After the lots have been drawn, the situation is changed, because the tramps no longer have equal power. The losing tramps in fact have the greater power, since they can make the night wretched for the others, whereas in life at large, no doubt, it is usually the winners who get the power as well as the other prizes. But, in whichever way power is redistributed, the game changes. This is not to say that asymmetrical outcomes must be unstable, since rational men will not upset an outcome without reason. But it is to point out that it is one thing rationally to agree to a contract and another rationally to abide by its results. The same point arises with Prisoner's Dilemma games generally, to trouble the apparent reconciliation of social order with private interest. There it is traditionally met by appeal to fear, to enlightened self-interest, to natural symapthy or to morality. I shall next comment briefly on these four moves, not to add to the large main-line discussion but to bring out the peculiarity of positional goods.

In Hobbes' *Leviathan* fear is used to prevent free-riding. It is administered by a stark central authority, keeping each citizen so much in awe that he willingly forgoes his chance of free-riding in return for a guarantee that others have forgone theirs. There is need for fear, because Hobbes adds more about motivation than a bald definition of rational choice and a bald set of preference orders contains. Indeed he adds enough envy, emulation and pride to suggest that many main benefits of society are directly positional. If so, it is hard to see how *Leviathan* can offer an outcome both stable and tolerable. A state of equal peace benefits all equally and, to that extent, fear prevents greedy men cutting their own throats. But the state of peace lets men get on with a struggle for differentials and relative advantages—the restless pursuit of power after power which ceaseth only in death. In this positional struggle relative losers are liable to become absolute losers. If so, the outcome is no longer stable because it satisfies all rational players and remains stable only through a fear which has destroyed universal benefit which it polices. This is not meant as a verdict on *Leviathan*, which has many intellectual resources. But it is meant to show the rational outcome of a positional game can upset the conditions which made it a rational outcome. When this threatens, fear is not an adequate preventative.

The second traditional appeal is to enlightened self-interest. Here rational strategies are given more scope. It is done by muting the conflict of interests, reducing the positional element in the goods sought and making human motivation less a matter of envy, emulation and pride. This helps by saving rational men from driving harsh, short-term bargains and from consuming what reason prefers them to invest. The teeth of the Prisoner's Dilemma are drawn by providing a lasting social environment, where the game is played repeatedly and losers in one game can be promised a win in another. It is no longer a one-shot affair but a series, where short-run gains do not pay. No doubt some do better overall than others but rational men are content, provided that the worst off still does better than he would have done under any other feasible arrangement. If it is asked why each tramp should prefer that someone has a place on the bench, even if he himself was unlucky, there is now a possible answer. The answer also explains why he should rationally abide by the outcome. He does so, in effect, because it will be his turn tomorrow.

But I find the answer facile, while motivation remains self-interested and any serious element in the goods sought positional. We are not dealing with men of honour and it begs the central question to rely on a lasting social environment. The loser may not get his turn tomorrow; and by then he may be powerless to refuse to play. Consider work, for example, both as an exchange of labour for income and as an expression of human dignity or identity. In traditional theory, rational egoists regard effort as a cost, to be undertaken only for reward. The division of labour occurs, because it is in the interest of all. The employer pays today, since otherwise the worker will not work for him tomorrow. All are best suited by a labour market which clears with all employed who could be and each receiving the equivalent of his marginal product. No doubt there is much to query about this picture but I wish to focus on just one aspect of it. It does not treat jobs as positional goods. In the present industrial labour market, however, they are (indirectly) positional goods. As they grow scarcer, those who have them organize to keep them and, in controlling access, can raise the rate of pay. Those who dispense them can meet the bill, provided that output per man rises. So productivity deals suit both parties, helped along by negotiated redundancy and wastage. There is, however, an invisible third party to each deal, those who would have been employed. They get the dole, to be sure, some of them perhaps even receiving more than they would in a labour-intensive economy struggling against foreign competition. But the dole does not buy self-respect. Yet the unemployed would be worse off without it. They are locked into a game which has changed subtly during the series. A crucial benefit has become positional. Whereas it should have been rational to continue the game because no one could do better for himself, it has become rational for some only because they could do worse.

The point of the example is not just the cynical one that the enlightened self-interest of the haves of course distributes positional goods so as to suit the enlightened self-interest of the haves. It is that the notional contract among rational egoists, behind a veil of ignorance before holding the lottery, must reckon with effects of the game on the game itself. The contract countenances inequality and so makes it possible to have positional goods. Why should rational men all acquiesce? The answer, addressed especially to the losers, is supposed to be that a smaller share in a larger cake will be larger than an equal share in a smaller cake. But, if larger shares include greater power, inequalities are cumulative and the terms of the game will be renegotiated as the pattern emerges. These sub-contracts will give everyone a little more than they might have got at the moment but some much more than they were expected to have. In theory this should have been foreseen at the original position and allowed for in the contract. But the original contract is not among omniscient beings, distributing a fixed bundle of goods over time. It has to consist of a set of rules for allocating whatever goods are produced as the society develops, the rules being designed to encourage production as well as to regulate distribution. So the emergence of positional goods cannot be prevented and, I submit, a theory resting on the enlightened self-interest of rational egoists will result gradually in there being absolute losers.

If this is not conclusive, at least it is the sort of reasoning which has prompted many thinkers to hold that, unless some streak of altruism in human nature is postulated, there cannot be stable solutions to the Prisoner's Dilemma. So, thirdly, there are appeals to natural sympathy. Each tramp prefers someone to have the bench, not because it will be his turn tomorrow but because someone is thereby better off without loss to anyone else. If the tramps are sympathetic and fair-minded, perhaps they will abide by the results of the lottery amicably enough. This view of human moral psychology has some force against the cruder versions of egoism. But it does not challenge the central thesis of egoism, that each man is moved by his own wants and interests. It merely includes some benevolence in the wants, making it easy for egoists to subscribe to the Pareto principle. Consequently there is still no reason why anyone should take a loss for the sake of others. Benevolence is an apple which rots in a barrel containing apples of discord and will not withstand the discord introduced by cumulative inequality. This may seem a very terse comment on a long chapter in political theory but egoism is both a psychological theory and a thesis in the philosphy of mind and, as the latter, it is unaffected by challenges to cheap versions of the former. The most sympathetic man will stand on tiptoe when those in front of him do.

Fourthly, then, it is tempting to appeal to the idea of morality, by making it the mark of a rational man to take a moral view of his situation. The appeal is standardly at two places. One is to make the rational man assess the merit of distributions without regard to his own personal share. The other is to ensure that he abides by a contract agreed to. With this help a neat solution seems to emerge for the tramps. The first step is to introduce a notion of social choice, got by abstracting the problem from the persons and asking merely how many tramps shall occupy the bench. Inspection of the preference orders shows the impersonal answer to be either one or two; and the choice between these options can be made by considering the intensity of the preference which each tramp has for sleeping over sitting, bearing in mind that two can sit but only one lie down. (I am still supposing that all have the same intensities of preference.) The second step is the lottery and, having forfeited his moral right to complain if he loses, each will rationally abide by the result. This is all neat and tempting but it raises a hard question about the relation between moral and rational. Since the question is too large to tackle head on, I shall try to see what can be learnt specifically by considering the positional element.

Both steps would be more persuasive, were the good not positional. The social choice, presented as inferred from the actual preferences, is indifferent as to who gets the good. But none of the tramps is indifferent. Each would rather that two sat, if he was one, than that one slept, if it was not he. Even if each prefers sleeping to sitting very intensely indeed, he still prefers his sitting to someone else's sleeping. A similar situation can arise in free-rider problems, when each prefers (1st) that he rides free, (2nd) that no one rides free, (3rd) that someone else rides free. But here it could be claimed right and reasonable that no one has a free ride. With a positional good, however, some but not all must have it, and the basis of the inference to 'some' from each man's 'not someone else' is unclear.

Equally, granted that there are to be some losers, why precisely does each forfeit his right to complain by agreeing to the lottery? Is it because, having done all he can to further his own interests, he should not bewail his fate? Or is it because he must recognize, as a rational man, that complaint would be morally and hence rationally unjustified? If the reason is that he cannot do more to further his self-interest, fairness is to be seen simply as a procedural device for getting self-interested persons to co-operate. If the reason is moral, we must take care not merely to assume that the truly rational man is moral or the truly moral man rational. At any rate the difference can be put crisply enough with the aid of higher-order preferences. In both versions considerations of fairness guide each tramp to take an

Martin Hollis

attitude to his own preferences in the light of others'. Strategic self-interest bids him submit to an impartial ruling for the sporting chance of at least half a loaf rather than a strong prospect of no bread. Morality bids him prefer to contribute to an outcome fair to all. One invitation is to realism, the other to idealism. In the longer term, the former tells the rational man to shape his character so that he can profitably play games with others. The latter tells him to shape it as he would ideally wish it to be. These are different kinds of advice with a different rationale. I daresay that the rationale behind learning to play fair for the sake of strategic self-interest is plain. But the link between fairness, morality and rational autonomy is more puzzling.

It is especially puzzling for positional goods—so much so that someone may again want to deny that moral goods can be (at least directly) positional. Morality is commonly held to involve impartiality and universalizability. The latter seems to require that a man should not do what not everyone so placed should do. But, if a good is positional relative to a group of people identically placed, not all of them can have it or bring it about. There is something to worry about here, I think, but it needs to be carefully isolated. Universalizability does not demand flatly that every moral agent behave exactly alike. The Kantian does not suppose that, if anyone should marry, everyone should. The Utilitarian can advocate occasional breaking of promises without having to recommend that they never be kept. For the well-trodden example of the college lawn, which can usefully be walked on by up to but not over half of the inmates, it is easy to bid each cross the grass, provided that few enough others do. In general, then, even co-ordination problems requiring a combination of different or conditional actions can be solved by universal, conditional injunctions without moral objection. The crucial point, however, is that solutions are morally of benefit to all. Happy marriages coexist with happy bachelors, just enough promises are broken to serve the general good and the college lawn gives pleasure to everyone. Positional goods, on the other hand, often involve advantage.

The morally interesting cases are those where there is discrimination among relevantly similar people. Prompted by talk of economic goods, I have been speaking mainly of distributions but positional moral problems can also occur in the production of a good state of affairs. For instance, when exactly three hundred men were needed to conquer the Midianites, the Lord told Gideon to let his troops drink at the river and to pick out all and only those who lapped water from their hands; and there turned out to be exactly three hundred (*Judges*, 7, vv. 1–7). This, let us suppose, was discrimination without difference, decided on because any morally perspicuous criterion would have produced the wrong number of men singled out. The example sets a problem for theodicy and I use it to point out that conflicts between general good and individual justice are not peculiar to utilitarianism. Let S be a good state, produced when some but not all do '0' and better than the states produced by all or none doing '0'. To generate S, all who are ϕ shall do '0' and all others do '1'. The general good (howsoever defined) requires that ϕ be a characteristic of the right number; individual justice demands that being ϕ be a moral reason for attracting the reward or penalty (honour or dishonour) of doing '0'. Since these requirements have quite different sources, I see no reason to think that they are bound to coincide. Where they do not, a positional moral problem occurs.

The abstract threat becomes real as soon as incidental scarcities and horizontal complementarities are allowed an impact on moral choice. For example, in a perfect world there would no doubt be enough kidney machines to go round. But the National Health Service is short of them and, let us suppose, irremediably so. (The problem, which I am trying to discuss, is bound to show up somewhere; so let it be here.) One person has access only if another is excluded. The queue can perhaps be roughly ordered by excluding, for instance, those terminally ill with other diseases; but, I assume, the number of people with a strong claim still outruns the number of places. If so, the problem is not solved by ruling that places be assigned only to those able to benefit fully. However 'benefit fully' is defined, there will be too many persons. To this case of incidental scarcity, let us add a horizontal element by noticing that some of those needing dialysis also have, for instance, diabetes. This group benefits from a kidney machine only if treated for the other condition too.

The example is meant to challenge a common approach to ethics from two quarters. Ethical theorists are inclined, I think, to start by looking for the solution to ethical problems which would be best if all complied with it. For instance, rule-utilitarians are prone to argue that each of us should follow whatever rule would yield the best results, if followed by all. A stock objection is that this can be rotten advice in a world where not everyone does in fact follow the best rule. Thus, if treatment for diabetics were withdrawn, they should presumably lose their claim of kidney machines, even though it would be better if the treatment for diabetes were restored. For, in that world of imperfect compliance, they would then be excluding persons better able to benefit. This is a point about imperfect compliance, rather than about horizontally positional goods, but the latter occasion of it should make us take it more seriously.

107

The other challenge comes firmly from the positional element. A rule, which would be for the best, if followed, by all, will not deliver positional goods. Perfect compliance with a simple rule, governing a positional good, overshoots the area of the Bell curve, where the positional good is realized. (By a 'simple' rule, I mean one without conditional clauses—a matter to be taken up in a moment.) It is no good dividing the total time available on kidney machines through by the total number of persons who would benefit, if the result is that no one benefits enough. Instead the time must be divided into units first and then the people be found, with some relevantly similar persons thereby excluded. This runs counter to some cherished beliefs about ethics but it follows from the premise that the good is positional and the entitled demand in excess of supply.

What simple rules cannot achieve it may be that conditional rules can. The form of them will be that each person shall do x, provided that the total number of persons doing x is not thereby raised above n. Practical problems aside, however, such rules are morally awkward, because they do not ensure that each person gets his moral deserts. In utilitarian terms they threaten the link between the happiness of each and the happiness of the aggregate of all persons. More generally they stop us supposing that two rights cannot make a wrong. The best social choice need no longer be one which somehow offers at least something for everybody. Conditional rules do, I think, advance matters by giving each an imperative which will not destroy the positional good. But they do nothing to reassure us about the snug fit between to good of each and the good of all.

Kidney machines are an example of incidental scarcity and horizontal complications. Does the moral economy also include direct scarcities? Hirsch's directly positional goods are attended by motives like 'envy, emulation and pride' and look as if they are goods only in the economist's sense that people do in fact value them. But the category seems to me to be wider.

Firstly, there are positional virtues, which would need review if practised by all. If everyone were generous, kind, long-suffering and unselfish, the costs of such goodness would diminish. So would the occasions for it, since the number of recipients in need would diminish too. Caring for the sick is virtuous only if there are sick to care for. But this shows at most that some virtues depend on there being an imperfect world to practise them in. Similarly there is no call for turning the other cheek, unless some lewd fellow of the baser sort has smitten the first one. But this merely reminds us that virtues are for foul weather. A deeper thought may surface, however, if we reflect that adversity shapes the moral character. In a perfect world perhaps on one would develop a moral character and we would all be the poorer for the lack. I shall not pursue this bracing sentiment here.

Secondly, there are virtues which could be practised by all but only with disastrous results. Thrift is a famous example—*en masse* it destroys the economy. This is another case where the Unseen Hand makes mischief and I have nothing to add to what distinguished thinkers have noticed under this heading, except to repeat that Unseen Hands are incompetent to distribute positional goods.

Thirdly, there do seem to be some virtues with the inbuilt comparative needed for a vertical dimension. If it is a virtue to put the interests of other before one's own, it must be a comparative virtue. For, were all to try to the full, each would be quickly frustrated and no one's interests would be served. It is not a virtue to insist on being the last person through a door, if social life is thereby paralysed until all doorways are demolished. Unselfishness has to be the virtue of being less selfish than the next man, without being too competitive about it. Intellectually this is the most intriguing category but, witness my frivolity, I cannot think of examples which need taking seriously. At any rate motives like 'envy, emulation and pride' are not essential. Action done from motives which we usually applaud can sometimes defeat its own ends, thanks to positional elements. There are implications for ethics here, which are worth exploring.

It emerges, I hope that *Social Limits to Growth* is a title which understates the scope of Hirsch's positional economy. There are related limits to the scope of any social system which relies on competition, whatever its rate of growth. Winners need losers. This is partly, I fear, because the park bench becomes cosier, if ringed by people tossing and turning on the ground. But it also for the more amiable reason that, where the sum of even unexclusive demands out-reaches the supply of satisfactions, goods become positional. Lack of economic growth is liable to reduce supply faster than demand.

Nor are the limits merely social, as distinct from moral. Positionality subverts the plausible thought that collective choices are to be justified by showing them directly responsive to individual claims. The point comes out simply *à propos* of Arrow's conditions. 'Universality' means that preferences for positional goods cannot be kept out. 'Pareto Optimality' is all very well *ex ante*, when each tramp does not yet know whether he will be lucky in the lottery, but *ex post* some will find that they dislike the result. It is unclear to me quite how this matter of perspectives is to be absorbed into theory of collective choice. 'Irrelevant Alternatives' (or any other Invariance condition) becomes distinctly tricky for positional goods, since their value depends on the rest of the distribution. 'Non-Dictatorship' is awkward, given that positional goods may have to be so distributed that only some people get their preferences satisfied. That all leaves much to ponder not only for social and democratic choice but also for any moral decision involving several persons.

There would be more to say if I had more time and could see my way more clearly. The source of trouble is definite enough. It is that positional moral coins are minted by individual choice but have a value depending on the number and variety in circulation. This puts collective good in tension with individual justice in an abstract way which is prone to have real and ugly human consequences. Yet we cannot deny that there are positional goods, some of them moral. If no one stands on tiptoe, some see worse than they should. May I invite contributions to a sort of Moral Theory of the Back Row?

Were You a Zygote?

G. E. M. ANSCOMBE

The usual way for new cells to come into being is by division of old cells. So the zygote, which is a—new—single cell formed from two, the sperm and ovum, is an exception. Textbooks of human genetics usually say that this new cell is beginning of a new human individual. What this indicates is that they suddenly forget about identical twins.

These result from the cleavage of a cell cluster into two cell clusters at some very early stage, which may be within a week of formation of the zygote. In the early 1970s Jerome Lejeune put the outer limit for such cleavage at thirteen days. The multiplication by cell division has not got very far at that stage; not, it seems, as far as thousands, whereas 'The human adult who started life as a single cell has about 10^{14}, or one hundred quadrillion cells'.[1]

All this means that if I ask you 'Were you a zygote?' you might intelligently reply 'No, I was an identical twin'. Then I could say that you and your twin jointly were once a zygote.

A human zygote is alive, and is a human thing, a new beginning of human life, and not a part of any human being. We might say it is a human *being*: a whole new human entity. But there is an objection because what we mean by *a* human being is *a man* in the sense *a member of the human race*. It is a Mensch, if we are talking German, an ἀνθρωπος in Greek, a *homo* in Latin. English suffers from not having a distinct word just for this. I will save myself from having to break into German, Greek or Latin, by adopting the word 'human' as a noun to be used in this sense.

Let me state an argument against the human zygote's being *a* human. Suppose the cell cluster divides and twins result. I'll call the zygote 'A' and the twins 'B' and 'C'. Neither B nor C is identical with A. Therefore *either*:

(1) A, not yet divided, was somehow already two. So A can have been already a pair of humans, B and C.
   or
(2) A was just one human, and became two by an extra one growing out of it.
   or

[1] Levitan and Montague, *Textbook of Human Genetics* (Oxford University Press, 1971).

111

(3) A was a single human, which turned into two by splitting, as one amoeba splits and turns into two amoebas.
or
(4) A, though a whole human substantial entity, was not a human yet; nor was it a pair of humans.

So far as I know there is no sufficient evidence for (1). Certainly some ten years ago Professor Lejeune confessed to having no evidence on the point. 'In man we have no data.... In...[some races of armadillos] the eggs do split every time into four embryos...always the same number...So we know looking at the armadillo and the race it belongs to, how many twins are genetically imprinted in the first cell. In that case we know the determination of the number of twins has occurred at the very moment of fecundation. In humans we do not know.'

If the opinion that twinning is already imprinted in the first cell *is* true of humans, as it may be, then various problems do not arise. Philosophically, if this were true, we would not have to ask about the odd logical status of the zygote—this human entity which is an individual substance, not part of one, and not *a* human.

(2) also would be acceptable for not raising any such obscure conceptual issues. But once again, there seems not to be evidence.

The third possibility, namely that one human splits into two, I am disposed to reject out of hand. But it needs more discussion. The obvious objection is that in the case of the amoeba there's no doubt we start with one amoeba and it splits into two amoebas. But in the human case it precisely is the question whether what we start off with *is* a human. What account could we give of its becoming two humans? Neither of the two humans that eventually develop can be identified as the same human as the zygote, because they can't *both* be so, as they are different humans from one another. We might indeed say that each *had* been the same human as the zygote was, and so also the same human as the other, though they are not the same human as one another now. But what has become of the human that both of them once were identical with? Has he—or it—simply ceased to exist, as we might say the parent amoeba ceases to exist on splitting?

It is true that present non-identity of B and C does not prove that B and C *were* not identical with A and so with one another. All the same, that does not prove that B and C *may* each have been identical with A. And, whether A is a human entity or an amoeba, there is the obvious objection that before A split into B and C, B and C did not exist.

Should we say that the amoeba, and any cell that divides, doesn't cease to exist, but continues as two, not one? That the amoeba exists in, or as, any simultaneous set of its descendants? That a single zygote cell which multiplies likewise exists in thousands of millions of its descendants? It is sometimes said: we are all Adam. Is that true in the sense—if there is one—in which the amoeba is all its descendants? No: for the amoeba did not die, but Adam died.

What has multiplied like amoebas is *cells*. We could say to a total collection of cells in the pair of twins: all you cells were once one cell. That would be parallel to the amoebas all having been one amoeba. However, it is because the cells *make up* two humans that we can say those *humans* were once one cell. With amoebas, there isn't this intervening term: we start with an amoeba and end with a collection of amoebas. In this way, then, even if the zygote *is* a human, the case of the zygote and the later twin humans is not parallel to that of the amoeba and the later set of amoebas.

Would there be at least this parallel: the amoeba doesn't die, and neither does the human who is a zygote when the zygote multiplies? No! For, assuming that the single human persists through some cell divisions up to the cleavage of cell clusters into two cell clusters which are two separate humans, that human exists in the descendent *cells* up to that cleavage; but the amoeba through division exists in descendent *amoebas*. There will be no parallel ground for saying that the human exists in the 'descendent humans' (as I will call the twins). For the humans are 'descendant' only because they are composed of descendent cells. And in the sense in which the supposed single human persists through a multiplication of cells, it does not persist through the cell cluster's being cloven into two distinct *humans*. It is no more: for nothing but persistence through a multiplication of cells is there to count as its persistence, and that cannot so count, because what it counts as after cleavage is the persistence of two new humans, Yet might we not say a parallel thing about the amoeba and the descendent amoebas? We might; but as an amoeba is one cell, the persistence through cell-division is in the amoeba simply persistence of amoeba-life through division. So the multiplication of cells *is*, formally, the multiplication of amoebas.

II

Let us consider whether I could truly say: I was once a sperm and an ovum. That is, the sperm and ovum from whose union I came were jointly I. The objection to this is just that the sperm and ovum were not one substance. That is, on a count of individual substances they come out as two until they have formed one cell.

I do not mean that each cell is a substance; most are only parts of substances. That they are so is proved by the fact of cell differentiation which soon begins to happen as they multiply by dividing. Cell differentiation is for the sake of the kind of structured, organized living material whole that gets formed through it. The kind of living thing that gets formed as a result of multiplication and differentiation of cells determines the differentiation and organization of them to the extent that this happens in a normal manner. Everywhere in a textbook of genetics the norms of health and reproduction of undefective specimens of a kind provide the aegis under which the enquirers have worked and the exposition proceeds. Note, for example, the occurrence of the term 'syndrome' in a large work on human genetics. Normally or successfully operating physiques and powers do not constitute 'syndromes'.

If a human zygote is not itself a human, then the way in which the human kind determines its way of developing is not a matter of a species to which it already belongs as a member. It is a matter of one to which belong those individuals whose gametes united to form the zygote, and into a member or members of which it will develop if it develops normally.

If a zygote was the beginning of a new human substance, and I (singly) was that zygote, then wasn't that zygote the beginning of *this* human being? Yes; but if there can be a human substance without its being a human, then either *this* individual human substance did not begin then or at one time *this* individual human substance did indeed exist but wasn't yet a human. So I wasn't yet *a* human? That seems correct. The development from something that was a single human substance only means that I was always *something* human. As for identical twins, they were jointly something human, and then each severally something human. One can become two, then, but two cannot turn into one such that you could point back to the two and say: that's the existence that was the beginning of the existence of someone.

This needs some qualification; because two lumps of clay become one by being pressed together. The one lump had been two, and its present unity is that of spatial continuity. Two cells, a sperm and an ovum, can also become one. Would it then be true to say the zygote had been two cells?—as, to say the lump of clay had been two lumps?

No; for the latter coming-to-be-one is no substantial change but only one of deletion of boundaries. The same clay continues to exist, however pressed together or separated into lumps. But with fertilization a single—new—organism comes into existence. It has a new genetic make-up. This turns it into the immediate material for development of a member or members of whatever species its parents belong to. The two lives of the sperm and the ovum have ended because they have turned into an individual with a new life, the life carried by the zygote.

Here life=existence. In starting to live, this thing has started to exist. Thus if asked whether the zygote had been the two former cells, one should say: materially, yes; but in form and existence, no. Not in form, because the new living thing is of a new kind from what they were. They weren't organisms only needing nutrition to grow into a certain pattern. And not in existence because the life—its being alive—is not their being alive. But there can occur that cleavage of the multiplied cell cluster which leads to identical twins. Here the division *is* like the division of a lump of clay into two. At this stage the life is divided into two only because the living thing is cloven into two; and hence only inasmuch as it is so cloven. We cannot say yet that we have here two distinct animals. But we can say that we have two materially distinct carriers of the life that started with the formation of the zygote.

Punishment, the New Retributivism, and Political Philosophy

TED HONDERICH

This paper will in good part concern six arguments taken as making up what is called the New Retributivism.[1] It will also have to do with a seventh retributivist argument, and with the unexamined idea that reflection on punishment can lead a life of its own, independently of political philosophy. Both that idea and the arguments bear on the main question of whether punishment in our societies is right or wrong. It is a question not worn to a frazzle, as is the one of *how* it is that punishment is right, which piously presupposes that it is. My answer to the impious question gets very little wear in this reactionary and, as it sometimes seems, vengeful time. For a particular reason, it will have to go undefended here.[2]

First a definition. An occasional contemporary philosopher sides with what seems to be the intent of the new California penal code, and thus *defines* punishment so as to make it morally justified at least in part by its being some sort of retribution.[3] Any such definition has the effect, among others, of making it conceptually impossible to ask if retribution is perhaps no part of the justification of punishment. The given definition thus impedes inquiry, and of course can settle no real moral question. No actual moral practice becomes right or

[1] See 'Symposium: The New Retributivism', *Journal of Philosophy* **LXXV,** No. 11 (1978), containing articles by Hugo Adam Bedau, Richard Wasserstrom and Andrew von Hirsch; D. J. Galligan, 'The Return to Retribution in Penal Theory', in *Crime, Proof and Punishment,* C. Tapper (ed.) (London: Butterworth, 1981); articles discussed below, notably those by Davis, Finnis, Goldman, Morris, Murphy and Nino; Jean Floud and Warren Young, *Dangerousness and Criminal Justice* (London: Heinemann, 1981); Hyman Gross, 'Culpability and Desert', in *Philosophy and the Criminal Law* R. A. Duff and N. E. Simmonds (eds.) (Weisbaden: Franz Steiner, 1984). The later two are not discussed here but in my 'On Justifying Protective Punishment', *British Journal of Criminology* **22,** No. 3 (1982) and 'Culpability and Mystery', in Duff and Simmonds, op. cit.

[2] I am most grateful to Nicola Lacey for criticism of an earlier draft of this paper, and also to Peter Morriss, and to critics who heard it at the Royal Institute of Philosophy, and at Birkbeck College, the City University, and the Universities of Aberystwyth and Edinburgh. My thanks to John Finnis and Carlos Nino, with whom my disagreement persists.

[3] With respect to the code, see Galligan, op. cit., 144.

wrong by act of definition. Anyone who supposes, to speak quickly, that retribution is rot, can accept such a definition and persist in his own moral view by maintaining that no actual practice, even in California, falls under the given definition.

Let us without further ado define punishment as *that practice whereby a social authority visits penalties on offenders, one of its deliberate aims being to do so.* Offenders are those found in good faith to have broken laws. Much more might be said of this conception of an offender, and of the conceptions of an authority and of penalties. To say but a word of penalties, they are measures that cause distress. A penalty is not well conceived *as an alteration in an individual's rights*, in the way of some elevated jurisprudential writing. A year's solitary confinement is not well described by a description which also covers a period of home ownership.

Philosophers and jurisprudents who have recently offered justifications of punishment clear the ground by getting rid of classical Utilitarianism, for good reason. The classical Utilitarian proposition is that punishment is justified since or when, compared with any alternative, it makes for a greater total balance of satisfaction over dissatisfaction, or a lesser total balance of dissatisfaction over satisfaction. There is the arguable idea, implicit in this view as in others, that punishment *prevents* offences, through incapacitation, deterrence, perhaps something called rehabilitation, and the formation and reinforcement of unreflective obedience to law. The objection to the simple maximizing of classical Utilitarianism, which in several ways ignores individuals, is that it justifies certain punishments of offenders which stick in the throat. It is typically said in effect, rightly or wrongly, that the reason for this is that these are punishments which are greater than *deserved*. Further, what classical Utilitarianism gives as the whole justification of punishment could be had by awful official acts of prevention whose victims were not offenders—not individuals found in the requisite way to have broken laws—but rather were individuals known to be innocent. If these awful official acts are morally intolerable—again they are typically said in effect to be intolerable because *undeserved*—it must be that punishment if it is right has some recommendation other than the Utilitarian one.

It is not so easy to deal with Utilitarianisms other than the classical kind.[4] Indeed there are some doctrines occasionally *called* Utilitarian which at least come close to escaping the objections. It is also true that the latter doctrines are a very long way from those of Bentham

[4] They are discussed in Nicholas Rescher, *Distributive Justice* (Indianapolis: Bobbs-Merrill, 1966).

118

and of his true successors, say J. J. C. Smart,[5] and are only wholly misleadingly called Utilitarian. They are not in an ordinary sense maximizing.

What follows in too much recent and contemporary reflection on punishment by philosophers and jurisprudents is an unanalysed or ill-analysed claim that punishment is partly or wholly justified because or when it is *deserved, a just desert, retributive, equivalent, proportional, commensurate, reciprocal, corresponding, fitting, merited, owed, according to the offence, according to our right or the offender's right.* The terms and constructions—they may be called *desert-locutions*—cannot properly be said to be synonymous since there is no single sense which they have. They can be, and often are, used interchangeably, with whatever reason or lack of it. It is in fact an understatement to say that locutions of the given kind have no single sense. They are hardly less than paradigms of multiple ambiguity and vagueness. To philosophers, and I suppose to some members of the reading classes in Wormwood Scrubs and those California penal farms, it must come as alarming that large books on criminal justice suppose that they can proceed on the basis of the declaration that punishment is deserved or whatever, where the declaration is multiply ambiguous and vague. Lawyers, or anyway some of you—you need us! Let us start with A for offender, O for offence, and P for penalty. What can be meant by saying that if or since P is deserved by A, the visiting of P on A is right or justified—or that P's being deserved for O is an essential part of the justification?

Let us hastily put aside several answers drawn from what can be called the Old Retributivism. If P *is deserved for O* just *is* the proposition that it is right that A get P, then we have no independent reason for its being right that A get P. Here there is only circularity, the futility of *Circular Retributivism.*[6] Does it never happen that P *is deserved for O* is so used? On the contrary, a little attention to judicial pronouncements will establish that sometimes it is. More often P *is deserved for O* has as one part of its meaning that it is right that P be imposed.

---

[5] J. J. C. Smart and Bernard Williams, *Utilitarianism: For and Against* (Cambridge: University Press, 1973).

[6] See Anthony Kenny, *Freewill and Responsibility* (London: Routledge, 1978), 69–76, and Hugo Adam Bedau, 'Retribution and the Theory of Punishment', *Journal of Philosophy* **LXXV**, No. 11 (1978), 611–615. Joel Feinberg, in an admissible analysis of the several settings in which we use desert-locutions, takes of as generally time that to say someone deserves something is to say he satisfies certain conditions of worthiness. *Doing and Deserving* (Princeton: University Press, 1970), Ch. 4.

Ted Honderich

Secondly, *P is deserved for O* has been taken as giving a certain independent factual reason for the rightness of imposing *P*. The proposition has been taken to be that there exists an equality of fact between *A*'s culpability in his offence and the distress to be caused to him by *P*. This is *Culpability–Distress Retributivism*. One thing to be said of it, as it certainly has been before now, is that we need to have it explained how there can be such a fact, there seeming to be no *commensurability* in any factual sense with respect to culpability and distress. If there are common units of measurement, what are they?[7]

These two understandings of *P is deserved for O* will have to suffice as representative of the Old Retributivism.[8] Before turning to the New, it is necessary to try to clarify some usages. The term 'retributivism' can be used to refer to *theories*—certain views on punishment advanced by philosophers, jurisprudents and the like which involve desert-locutions. A bit more will be said of the character of these views later (reference 34). Retributivism in this sense has as its two parts the Old Retributivism and the New Retributivism. The New Retributivism can be said, very loosely, to consist in attempts made to justify punishment since about 1970, bravely assumed to be new, and involving desert-locutions. The six arguments at which we shall look do have the virtue of attempting to make their use of desert-locutions clear.

So much for retributivism where it consists in arguments and doctrines of philosophers, jurisprudents and the like. In another sense of the word, retributivism is a practice and tradition. A bit

[7] The difficulty is not escaped, as some may suppose, by the idea that we can find *rough* or *broad* equivalences or correspondences or whatever. If there are no common units for quantifying tunes and buns, then a tune isn't equal or not equal to two buns—and it isn't roughly equal or not roughly equal to two buns either. Nor is the difficulty escaped by changing the subject: by supposing that we can *decide* or *judge* or *determine* that a particular penalty should go with a particular offence, as against *discover* or *perceive* a factual relation. This is a common form of lightly disguised Circular Retributivism. Galligan, op. cit., 166f, and Andrew von Hirsch, 'Proportionality and Desert: a Reply to Bedau', *Journal of Philosophy* **LXXV**, No. 11 (1978), 622–624, may illustrate these futile hopes. For a good brief discussion of Circular Retributivism, see Feinberg, op. cit., 116f.

[8] Other understandings are considered in my *Punishment, the Supposed Justifications* (Harmondsworth: Penguin, 1976), 26–33 *et seq.* I do not there take it, incidentally, as might be thought from a reading of J. G. Cottingham, 'Varieties of Retribution', *Philosophical Quarterly* **29**, No. 116 (1978), that retributivism can be *analysed* as the claim that offenders 'deserve' punishment. Nor, as might be thought, do I overlook the 'varieties of retribution' he distinguishes.

more precisely, it is a kind of punishment and a tradition of, and having to do with, such punishment. Retributivism in this sense consists in part in present and past punishment of a certain character—as distinct, say, from deterrent punishment or reformative punishment. It also consists in attitudes and ordinary talk, including the talk of judges, or judges when they are on their benches. The hallmark of the tradition, again, is desert-locutions.

The distinction between these two retributivisms—one consisting in philosophical and jurisprudential theory and the other in punishment of a certain kind and what goes with it—is perhaps clear enough for our purposes. It will be of importance. Very roughly, one of my claims will be that philosophical and jurisprudential retributivism, whatever else is to be said of it, is not a correct account of the practice and tradition of retributivism. That practice and tradition is informed by a quite different argument.

Intrinsic Retributivism

If we are after a reason for *It is right to impose P on A* it is well and truly pointless, as noticed already, to contemplate *A deserves P* if that is understood as *It is right to impose P on A*, or *There is good reason for imposing P on A*, or any relevantly like claim. One philosopher objects that this cautionary little thought involves error and confusion.[9] He further supposes, I take it, that what is standardly meant by those who use desert-locutions in connection with punishment is only this: that there is intrinsic good in precisely the suffering of the guilty—as distinct from what causes it, the penalty.

---

[9]Lawrence H. Davis, in 'They Deserve to Suffer', *Analysis* **32,** No. 4 (1972), referring to my *Punishment, The Supposed Justifications*, says I am in error and confusion because I say, as above, that sometimes people use (1) *He deserves the penalty* to mean (2) *It's right that he get the penalty*, and hence that they cannot give (1) as a reason for (2). The main presumed error, although Davis is not sufficiently explicit, must be the failure to see what is presumed to be true, and discussed below, that (1) and like claims are standardly used only to mean (3) *there is intrinsic good in his suffering, he being guilty*. The second presumed error is thus supposing that (1) does not provide a reason for (2). The presumed confusion, also owed to failing to see that (1) is equivalent to (3), is running together (1) and (2). My reply is that there is no error and no confusion since it is not true, but false, that (1) and like claims are standardly used to mean only (3). Rather, there is a use of (1) which makes it equivalent to (2), commoner than its use as equivalent to (3). What I say depends only on the use of (1) as equivalent to (2).

5

More generally, when people talk of deserved penalties or punishment, they are to be taken as really not talking of gaol sentences and the like, but of suffering itself, and they are saying that there is intrinsic good in the suffering of the guilty. The resulting view can be called *Intrinsic Retributivism*.

It is plainly false that desert-locutions in connection with punishment never have to do with the penalty, as distinct from the resulting distress. More often than not, they do. Nevertheless, let us grant that people sometimes have in mind what is suggested, having to do with only the distress or suffering. In this case, as can certainly be granted, they do escape circularity. To support the rightness of a punishment, they say something about desert, and mean nothing about punishment itself, but that there is intrinsic good in its effect, the suffering of the guilty.

It is said that there is no good argument against the judgment that the suffering of the guilty is intrinsically good or good in itself, and that there is a widespread inclination to believe it 'among the people whose moral intuitions constitute the main data we have for settling questions of value'. Hence it is 'very likely' that the judgment is 'true'.[10] Still, it is allowed that this reason for punishment might be outweighed by others, that it is consistent with the judgment that we never ought to punish.

Intrinsic Retributivism raises several very general issues in moral philosophy. If these are not to be settled here, it is possible to come to a view of the doctrine. First, it needs remembering that even if all mankind minus none were morally in favour of the suffering of the guilty, it would not follow that all or even any of them judged it to be good in itself, good without reference to anything else whatever, including what may come most quickly to mind, some consequential change in the minds, hearts, souls or whatever of the guilty. Secondly, it is mere bluff to announce the existence of a strong argument based on the claim that most or many of some group of people, a group whose intuitions somehow settle questions of value for us, have intuitions that the suffering of the guilty is good in itself. Supposing that the group can be conceived in any tolerable way, and of course in a way so as not to beg the question, it will undoubtedly include many who are morally opposed to or reluctant about the suffering of the guilty in itself, which they properly characterize as pointless or useless or irrational. How, they traditionally ask, can two bads make a good, two wrongs a right? Those who reject Intrinsic Retributivism include even retributivists.[11]

[10] Davis, op. cit., 139.
[11] Jeffrie G. Murphy and John Finnis, discussed below.

Punishment, the New Retributivism, and Political Philosophy

To put aside this head-counting, and the hard questions of its relevance, we evidently can consider directly the question of whether the judgment that there is intrinsic good in the suffering of the guilty is 'true'. Or rather, to avoid the wholly unexplained assumption of, as it seems, the objectivity of moral judgments—their having truth-values in the sense in which ordinary factual claims have them—we can consider whether the judgment is acceptable or what weight it has.

It will be useful to compare the judgment to two other judgments of intrinsic value. One is that there is intrinsic badness in suffering. If I contemplate the possibility of a person's suffering in itself, without introducing *any* further fact, I cannot but judge that it would be a bad thing, something I ought not to bring about. Consider someone who believes otherwise. He believes that if he presses a button in front of him, that will cause another to suffer. He has *no* further beliefs about the suffering. He has no beliefs as to the victim's previous actions, any deterrent effects of his suffering, any supposed repentance of his or any purifying or elevating effects, any relation of his suffering to the suffering of others, and so on. None the less, he judges that he ought to press the button. He appears to understand what he maintains, is inclined to act on it, and shows the ordinary moral emotions in connection with it. It comes to mind to say, if we suppose that he is not somehow dissembling, that he is *mad*. The judgment that there is intrinsic badness in suffering, then, is one whose denial carries such a corollary.

The second judgment as to intrinsic value, chosen more or less at random, is that there is intrinsic good in arranging straight lines of Norwegians. As with the judgment that there is intrinsic good in the suffering of the guilty, and the other judgment of intrinsic value at which we have just glanced, this judgment has to do with no further facts. Arranging Norwegians in straight lines is good in itself. To deny this judgment of intrinsic value is certainly not to be open to judgment oneself, or in danger of official action. It is the maker of the judgment of intrinsic good who is, at least, puzzling.

One point, then, is that while it may be open to anyone to judge anything whatever to have intrinsic value, it is only certain of these judgments that have weight. A second point is that if one actually succeeds in contemplating no more than *precisely* the suffering of the guilty, a judgment of its intrinsic value is perhaps *more* of the weight of the judgment about lining up Norwegians than the judgment about the badness of suffering itself. Certainly it is not much like the latter judgment. The latter judgment evidently enters into resistance to the supposed intrinsic goodness of the suffering of the guilty.

Intrinsic Retributivism in its assertion of its peculiar intrinsic good is strongly reminiscent of what seemed to have been put to rest, the doctrine of Moral Intuitionism, to the effect that there are moral properties which are open to some kind of moral perception. It remains possible or anyway conceivable that it will be maintained that anyone who does not somehow see the intrinsic goodness of the suffering of the guilty is failing in moral perception, is a victim of moral blindness. (Presumably it will also be maintained that some other people who claim the existence of different intrinsic goods are in the grips of moral hallucination.) It will be necessary to maintain, incidentally, that those of us who are blind in the given way are not blind to one thing, but to a host of them. Intrinsic Retributivism does not discover only one intrinsic good, but very many. It does not suppose, I trust, that there is intrinsic good in the rapist having just the suffering of a fine of £10, or having his driver's licence endorsed. It does not suppose there is intrinsic good in the young bicycle thief having the distress of being imprisoned for life. This retributivism, presumably, discovers as many intrinsic goods, each involving a certain guilt and a certain suffering, as there are different guilts.

What is to be said briefly in reply to any supposition of the moral blindness of many of us is that there are great difficulties in any theory or account of moral perception or intuition, and hence of moral blindness, hallucination and so on.[12] It is important, of course, that one feels no need of any such theory with respect to the judgment that suffering in itself is bad. Its foundation, whatever it is, does not bring in a curious faculty and its peculiar successes and failures.

Let us finish here, however, by retreating from what are areas of some difficulty in moral philosophy generally. Let us come to firmer ground. The best that can be said of Intrinsic Retributivism, to my mind, is that it might as a result of further thought come to provide an *insubstantial and obscure* reason for punishment. To come to a point to which I shall return several times, there surely is something solid in the retributivist tradition, something which can be made clear. It has in it an actual reason for action, one which moves ordinary men, men with an ordinary lack of what can be called moral sensitivity. It must be an axiom of inquiry, surely, that anything so persistent and effectual as talk and feeling about desert, and above all anything with such a history as the retributivist practice of punishment, has sense, clear sense, at its bottom. We may not find a

[12] Cf. P. F. Strawson, 'Ethical Intuitionism', *Philosophy* **XXIV**, No. 94 (1949). For discussions and defences of what may seem in some respects a successor to Moral Intuitionism—Moral Realism—see Honderich (ed.), *Morality and Objectivity: A Tribute to John Mackie* (London, Routledge, 1985).

justification of punishment at the bottom of the retributivist tradition, but it cannot be that there is nothing substantial and clarifiable there. The view we have been considering, about the intrinsic goodness of the suffering of the guilty, is therefore not the truth about retributivism.

Rights Retributivism, Indifference Retributivism

The next doctrine at which we shall look[13] partly consists in certain claims of a kind increasingly common in contemporary moral and political philosophy, claims as to *rights*. All of us, it is said, have rights—rights not to be injured, to keep possession of our property, and so on. A condition of our having such rights is that we respect the rights of others. In general, rights of mine entail duties of mine to respect rights of others. When an offender violates rights of someone else, he forfeits some of his own. As a consequence, if his punishment were also to have a certain recommendation having to do with the prevention of offences, his punishment would be justified.[14] We can call this the argument of *Rights Retributivism*.

It does not assert that an offender loses all his rights. He keeps all the rights which he has respected in others. He loses just those of his rights which are the counterparts of the rights of another which he has violated. Or rather, since it is said to be impracticable to deprive him of exactly those rights—certainly it would be so, say, in the case of the right not to be defrauded—the offender loses a set of rights equivalent to those he has violated. Or, again, there is not a prohibition on inflicting a harm on him equivalent to that involved in his violation of the rights of another. Here we have the long-running problem noticed above, of giving sense to talk of equivalence. It is certainly a recommendation of this doctrine, owed to Alan H. Goldman, that it provides a solution, which we can call *Indifference Retributivism*. It gives us a third argument. That is not to say that it discovers commensurability, a method of common quantifying of culpability and distress. However, it can be said to achieve much the same end as would be achieved by commensurability.

The solution draws on the idea of preference scales, essentially on the theoretically discoverable preferences of average or normal

[13] Alan H. Goldman, 'The Paradox of Punishment', *Philosophy and Public Affairs* **9,** No. 1 (1979).

[14] It is the burden of Goldman's essay that while his proposition about rights does indeed give one of the necessary reasons for punishment, a part of a justification, it is in conflict with the other part, concerning prevention. Hence the paradox of his title.

persons, and above all on the theoretical discoverability of such persons being *indifferent* between certain options. We have on the one hand the loss or harm—say L_o—caused to the victim of an offence by violation of certain of his rights. On the other hand we have various losses or harms that may be caused to the offender by deprivation of certain of his rights, through punishment. One of these losses or harms—say L_p—is such that an average person would be indifferent between L_o and L_p, preferring neither to the other. We thus have a clear idea of equivalent rights, or equivalent harms or losses, or, as we can as well say, a penalty equivalent to an offence. Certainly there are difficulties of several kinds about this procedure, some of them in effect about the specification of an average person. As is said, however, they are difficulties common to all uses of preference scales. Let us take them as superable difficulties.

That is not to say that what we now have is persuasive. What it comes to is the proposition that there is a reason for punishment, a denial of rights, in the proposition that an offender has violated certain rights of another. There are two objections, the first having to do with what is meant by saying that the offender has violated certain rights of another. For several reasons, one being the conclusion that is drawn, it is clear that *moral* rights are in question. To repeat, then, what is meant by saying that the offender has violated certain moral rights of another? It should be a matter of notoriety that so little attention is given to this question in a good deal of contemporary philosophy given over to talk and indeed declaration of rights.

To consider the matter by way of something else, the Old Retributivism includes something not mentioned above, the simple claim that the punishment of an offender is justified because of his culpability in his offence—at bottom, because he did what he ought not to have done, because he failed in an obligation. The simple claim has satisfied hardly any reflective person, whether or not of retributivist inclination. *Why* is the claim that a man has done what he ought not to have done in itself a reason for making him suffer? Why does it give us a permission or whatever? The question has taken several forms, and no satisfactory answer has ever been given.

What, exactly, is the difference between the claim that a man has done what he ought not to have done to another, failed in an obligation to another, and the claim that he has violated moral rights of another? The doctrine we are considering, like others, offers no explanation. Certainly there is a difference between the two claims, and there are several views as to what it is. One persuasive one is that the rights-claim, as against the ought-claim, makes reference to a supposedly established moral principle or to the supposed existence of support of another kind. Given some such analysis or another, there remains the question of how the rights-claim can serve as an effective reason for punishment when the ought-claim cannot. That it is wholly unlikely to do so becomes clear, as it seems to me, as soon as the rights-claim is demystified by even the beginning of an analysis.

The second objection has to do with what needs to be allowed, as it has, the existence of what can be called an equivalence of fact between offence and punishment. Here too we have a question which needs answering. There is the fact, we are supposing, that an average preference scale would show indifference between being a victim of a certain offence and being an offender subjected to a certain punishment. Why is that fact in itself any reason for subjecting such an offender to such a punishment?

It needs to be granted, in line with what has been said already of the tradition of retributivism, that there is force in citing some sort of equivalence in defence of punishment. But how is the equivalence we have before us a reason? We can find *innumerable* equivalences of the given sort, between experiences of diverse kinds. There may be indifference between not getting a job and not getting married, or getting a job as a result of a fair selection procedure and being married pretty unhappily. Such a fact supports no such claim as that my failing to give a man a job is a reason for getting in the way of my marriage. Critics of retributivism in the past have objected to the want of clear sense in talk of equivalence, and failed to note what they might have, that the producing of certain factual equivalences would not in itself give a reason for action.

Consensual Retributivism

A very recent attempt to justify punishment[15] begins from what is presented as a single objection to classical Utilitarianism. In fact it is best regarded as two objections. One is that if the Utilitarian defence were the true justification of punishment, then all or a very great deal of punishment would be unjustified because it would involve an *unfair or inequitable or inegalitarian distribution of burdens* in a society. The rational aim of punishment is indeed the prevention or reduction of offences, or more precisely burdens of a certain kind, those borne by the victims of offences. The aim is pursued by imposing penalties, burdens of another kind, on offenders. The resulting distribution of burdens would on balance have to be judged

[15] C. S. Nino, 'A Consensual Theory of Punishment', *Philosophy and Public Affairs* **12,** No. 4 (1983).

unfair or the like to offenders if no more could be offered than the Utilitarian defence of punishment. 'Why them?' is a serious question.

The other objection is that if only the Utilitarian defence could be given, then all of punishment would be unjustified, because it would involve treating all offenders merely as means and not also as ends. The Kantian maxim, I take it, is used in this objection in a commendably clear if not wholly explicit way. That is, not to treat men *as ends* is not to *recognize their own ends*.[16] Punishment considered merely as preventive does not consider the ends of offenders, presumably at least including their desires not to be punished. It treats them only as means to the end of the prevention of offences. It regards them only from the point of view of others' desires.

It transpires, if all goes well, that the view of punishment which meets the second objection also meets the first. If we satisfy the Kantian maxim, we also deal with the problem of distributive justice. What is required for a justification of punishment is an addition to a proposition about its preventing offences. What is required is Consensual Retributivism, which is the truth behind the historical absurdity that offenders want to be punished. It has to do essentially with what is called *fairness owed to consent*. Punishment must be fair in that it is among other things a product of the will of the person who suffers it, something which respects his own autonomy.

The matter is approached and clarified by way of five propositions about ordinary contracts in law. (i) Consent here can be shown or given by any voluntary act done with the knowledge that the act has as a consequence a certain duty or responsibility. I consent to pay the cab-driver merely by getting into his cab and giving an address. I do not need to say that I agree to pay. (ii) Giving my consent, in so far as the law of contract is concerned, is not dependent on my attitudes then to what it is that I consent to do, or certain of my beliefs about it. I have consented even if I dislike the prospect of paying up, or am against it all things considered, or intend not to pay up, or believe that any obligation to do so can be avoided or will not be enforced. Nor is it true that I did not consent if, when the time comes to pay up, I do not want to do so, and so on. (iii) However, in all cases of contractual consent, there is the requirement that the relevant laws be in some sense just: 'the justification of particular distributions based on the free choice of the parties presupposes the fairness of the legal framework within which those choices are made'.[17] (iv) If I do give my consent, thereby entering into a

[16]Op. cit., 306.
[17]Op. cit., 302.

contract, this gives others at least a *prima facie* moral justification for enforcing it. (v) Finally, if doing what I have consented to do will issue in an unfair or inequitable or inegalitarian distribution of burdens, it does not follow that I have not consented. It does not matter if the cab-driver is a secret millionaire, etc. Nor does it follow, therefore, that there cannot be the mentioned moral justification for enforcing the contract, despite the resulting distribution. This is the fairness owed to consent.

To come round to punishment, *an offence itself* constitutes a certain consent on the part of the offender. It is a consent *to give up his immunity to punishment,* which is to say to the gaining of a power by officers of the society. It is to consent to be used as a means to the prevention of offences. Here we have five counterpart propositions.

(i) The consent is owed to the fact that an offence is a voluntary act done with the knowledge that it has a certain *legal* consequence, the loss of the offender's immunity to punishment (ii) The consent is unaffected by certain attitudes and beliefs of the offender. It does not matter that he is against his punishment and intends not to be punished. Moreover, his consent does not depend on any explicit or implicit acceptance by him of the criminal law to which his punishment is attached. (iii) However, the law to which a punishment is attached, even if the offender need not accept it, must in fact *be* in some sense just—'it should not be, for instance, discriminatory and should not proscribe actions that people have the moral right to do'.[18] Again, it must be that if keeping the law involves a burden, liability or obligation, these things are somehow justified. (iv) Given the fact of the offender's consent, the authorities have at least a *prima facie* moral justification for exercising their legal power to punish him. (v) Finally, none of the foregoing propositions is put into question by the offender's punishment issuing in an unfair or inequitable or inegalitarian distribution of burdens in the society. There *is* fairness owed to consent.[19]

Consensual Retributivism, for the good reason that it could not, does not rest on the proposition that an offender consents to his *punishment.* The general idea of consent in question is the idea that a person, whatever his mixed feelings and disinclinations, is to be taken to consent to all the necessary consequences of his action of which he knows. In this sense he could not be said to consent to his

[18] Op. cit., 302–303.

[19] There is a related retributivist argument for punishment, essentially simply that an offender chose between two options open to him: keeping and breaking the law. This, distinct from Consensual Retributivism, is considered in my *Punishment, The Supposed Justifications,* 33 et seq. Cf. Goldmand, op. cit., 54–56.

punishment, since his punishment, unlike the loss of his legal liability to punishment, is not necessarily a consequence of his offence. There is no necessity about it. The fact of the matter may well be that he will not be punished. Moreover, if the theory did require its kind of consent to punishment itself, it could provide *no* reason for punishment where an offender actually does believe that he will not be punished. What the offender is said to consent to, then, is no more than the loss of his legal immunity. More precisely, what he consents to can be expressed as a certain conditional proposition: if he is caught, and if the authorities make no mistakes, he will not be regarded as having a legal immunity to punishment.

That leaves us with something further that it is essential to keep clearly in mind, the fact about virtually all offenders that they do *not* consent to being punished. They do not consent to it in the sense of believing it to be a necessary consequence of their action, and moreover they do not consent to it in a more standard sense. They do not consent to it in a sense, difficult to specify fully, where they can be said to desire all or more of what it is that they are said to consent to. On the contrary, they are wholly against their punishment, struggle to evade it, and so on. Rather than consent, they *refuse* or *dissent*.

But then the situation, to keep all of it in mind, includes the offender's consenting in the Consensual Theory's sense to a certain legal consequence, his losing his immunity to punishment, and his dissenting in every sense to his punishment. There is not much to be gained by asking if the first consent is 'really consent'. Let us rather ask what conclusions follow, given that the situation is as described.

First, to remember the two objections to Utilitarianism from which we began, does it follow from what we have, whatever else may be said for punishing the offender, that the resulting distribution of burdens in the society cannot be resisted as unfair, inequitable, or inegalitarian? Secondly, does it follow from what we have that his own end is being recognized if he is punished? Is his moral autonomy respected? Does it follow in turn, thirdly, that the authorities have *prima facie* moral justification for punishing him?

It seems to me impossible to accept the first two inferences, on which the third rests. It is not at all persuasive to say that the resulting distribution of burdens cannot be open to objections of the given kind since, to speak differently, we have on hand fairness owed to consent. What we have is the offender consenting in a secondary sense to a necessary condition of his punishment, and not consenting, in any sense, to his punishment. As for the second inference, how *can* it be said with any force that the offender's own end is being recognized? What we *do*, and what raises the entire problem, which is to say our punishing of him, is what he does not consent to, despite the fact that he has in a sense consented to a necessary condition of it. It is, with respect to what is important, quite false to say that the agent has 'consciously acquiesced'.[20]

As it seems to me, one can be much moved by this doctrine only by having something other than it before the mind's eye. If one is in fact supposing that all offenders consent to their punishments, or their situations, in some fuller way than specified, it is possible to think one has a strong reason for punishment. But such a proposition is not being maintained, and is in fact false.

It may be objected, against this, that consent in the specified sense is sufficient for an ordinary contract in law, and that there it gives rise to a moral justification for enforcing the contract. If such consent will work there, why will it not work with punishment? Much might be replied here, about the nature of the law in general and its safeguards, and in particular its safeguards with respect to persons who will lie about their past acceptances. Let me make only a remark on something else.

Suppose I get into a taxi-cab and give an address. I also tell the driver that I intend *not* to pay for the ride, and in the end succeed in overcoming his incredulity. He believes me. Still, for whatever reason, he delivers, me to the right number in darkest Ritson Road. We need not take legal advice before concluding that it is far from certain that a contract was made. It is far from certain, too, whatever else is said, that *what happened at the beginning of the ride* issues in a moral justification for my paying a fare.

This suggests that while consent with respect to the law's contracts does not require proof of a certain intention, it is also true that a statement of the wrong intention, so to speak, gets in the way of consent and contract. What is of most relevance, however, is this: the commission of an offence is in closer analogy to this very odd taxi case than to the ordinary case where the passenger does not say he intends not to pay. The Consensual Retributivist points to a certain act, the offence, and claims it to be analogous to giving a cab-driver an address. But the offender will also give every evidence of not intending the upshot having to do with punishment. It follows that if we begin with an offence, and find a close analogy of it that might turn up in civil law, we do not find anything remotely like a clear case of consent and contract.

There are three other things to be remarked quickly about Consensual Retributivism. First, there is a certain amount of tension between parts of it. One of its propositions is that an offence is a

---

[20] Nino, op. cit., 293.

certain consent to a punishment only if the law in question is somehow just, or if the burden of keeping to the law is a justified one. Another of its propositions, put one way, is that consent in the special sense can justify a distribution of burdens that is in a sense unfair or whatever. These two propositions, if they are not clear enough to be inconsistent, do not come together easily. Secondly, the view does indeed depend on the first proposition—the law's being just, its burdens being justified. Since this requirement is not clarified, and since it is not shown that it is met, the view is at least incomplete.[21] Thirdly, although it needs to be admitted, in line with a necessary realism about what can be done in moral and political philosophy, that Consensual Retributivism has not been *refuted* by me, it clearly does not provide a substantial and clear reason for punishment. It is unclear with respect to the requirement of justice just mentioned. The retributive tradition, above all its practices and institutions, has more in it. The consensual theory is not the truth about retributivism.

Contractarian Retributivism

A fifth and related line of thought about justifying punishment, Contractarian Retributivism,[22] begins rather as do the others. The Utilitarians, we may be told, are committed to using men as means to a social good, not treating them in accord with their dignity as persons, not recognizing that as persons they have rights. More particularly, the Utilitarians do not show what is necessary, that punishment treats a man as an end and in accord with his dignity and rights, where that is *respecting his own will or decision, having his own consent*. This is just as necessary with perfectly ordinary punishment as it would be with awful acts of victimization taken to have some preventive value. While the prevention of offences must evidently be a part of the justification of punishment, there is also something else that is absolutely essential.

[21] Nino does write that following out his suggestion as to the justification of punishment 'would lead to a discussion of the extent to which the consent of the person affected can justify measures and political arrangements which may imply inequitable burdens upon him. I shall not develop this theme here; but I venture to say that the discussion of the justification of punishment could be considerably expanded and illuminated if it embraced this topic' (op. cit., 305).

[22] This is one of several lines of thought in Jeffrie G. Murphy, 'Marxism and Retribution', *Philosophy and Public Affairs* **2,** No. 3 (1973). For clarity, I treat it separately. Cf. John Rawls, *A Theory of Justice* (Oxford: Clarendon, 1972).

One typical way in which others coerce us without infringing our rights, we are told, is by our own ordinary consent. If I consent to my neighbour's suggestion that he should keep the key to my wine store over the weekend, then he does not violate a right of mine later when I want it, but only thwart a desire. To come to the rights of offenders, it may be that they are not violated by punishment. This is so, we are told, despite the fact that they have not in the same ordinary way consented to be punished. They *have* in another way consented. It is not the way of Consensual Retributivism.

In considering this view, as becomes apparent even in its original presentation, there is no need to have things obscured by the several kinds of rhetoric, notably the rhetoric of *rights*. The essential claim is quite independent of it. It is that that justification of a punishment requires that the offender in some way consents to it, and offenders do in fact do this.

To continue, we can get some help in understanding how they do it from Kant, who writes that when a debtor is forced to pay up, 'this is entirely in accord with everyone's freedom, including the freedom of the debtor, in accordance with universal laws'.[23] What does this mean? Well, that in a certain conceivable but not actual situation the debtor 'would have been rational to adopt a Rule of Law'.[24] Kant is not much less explicit than his successors, notably Rawls, in asserting that this is not the idea of any *actual* social contract, past or present, explicit or implicit. He writes that 'the contract is a mere idea of reason which has undoubted practical reality; namely to oblige every legislator to give us laws in such a manner that the laws *could* have originated from the united will of the entire people. . . .'[25] To assert in the given way that an offender consents to his punishment is to assert that *if* he had been in a certain conceivable situation in which a social agreement was being made, and *if* he had been in a sense rational, he would have agreed to social arrangements which have the consequence that as an actual offender he is to be punished.

It is worthwhile distinguishing this claim about consent *by an offender* from something else, with which it is likely to be confused. That is the argument that a certain actual social arrangement, an actual

[23] Immanuel Kant, *The Metaphysical Elements of Justice* (1797), trans. John Ladd (Indianapolis: Bobbs-Merrill, 1965), 55ff. Cited by Murphy, op. cit., 225.

[24] Murphy, op. cit., 225.

[25] 'Concerning the Common Saying: This May be True in Theory but Does Not Apply in Practice' (1773), in *The Philosophy of Kant*, trans. Carl J. Friedrich (New York: Modern Library, 1949), 421–422. Cited by Murphy, op. cit., 226.

133

Ted Honderich

society in accordance with some conception of justice, is right or justified because it would have been agreed upon *by certain imaginable contractors,* or by contractors in an imaginable situation. The situation, because it would exclude certain influences on the contractors' choices, would confer a recommendation on what was chosen. It is *not* part of this argument that the actual members of the actual society, influenced as they are, have ever made such an agreement, or indeed that they have in any diminished sense consented to anything. The actual members are not in any way identified with the contractors. Their obligation to support their society has to do with its goodness, which goodness is established by the proposition about imaginable contractors. Here too we have an argument for the rightness of punishment in a society, but not one that has to do with consent of actual members. Having had my say elsewhere[26] about what seems to me the particular futility of this form of hypothetical contract theory as a method of establishing substantive conclusions, I shall say nothing here.

The different claim we are considering is yet weaker. It is, to repeat, that an offender's punishment is justified, at least in part, by *his* consenting to it, in a special sense, which is to say in short that if he had earlier considered the matter of punishment, and if he had been rational he would have agreed to the social arrangements under which he is now being punished. What is it to say that he would have made a contract *if he had been rational?* The short answer is this: he would have agreed if he had had the approving view of some given social arrangements had by a philosopher engaged in defending the institution of punishment.

Once Contractarian Retributivism is made clear, it is not easy to think of a weaker moral reason for imprisoning a man. The reason given is that he would, *if* he had had certain views, views which no doubt he does not now have, and may never have had, and may always have disagreed with or hated—*if* he had had such views, he would have consented to something. It is exactly as true that if he had had *other* views he would not have consented to the thing, and hence could *not* be said to consent to his punishment in the special sense. His punishment is being credited *to him* by way of an arbitrarily chosen counter-factual statement about him.

The difference between what is given as a reason for an offender's punishment, and my actual consent as a reason for my neighbour's keeping the key to my wine store, is immense. It is important not to drift into considering the supposition that the offender *did* have

[26]'The Use of the Basic Proposition of a Theory of Justice', *Mind* **LXXXIV,** No. 333 (1975).

134

views of the requisite kind. If this were the supposition in question, Contractarian Retributivism could not hope to offer a satisfactorily *general* justification of punishment. It would leave quite unjustified the punishment of offenders without the requisite views.

Let me end here with the same remark as before. Retributivism as practice and tradition has not persisted because it has been this ineffectual line of thought. This is not the truth of retributivism.

Restorative Retributivism

Finally, Restorative Retributivism, which is run together with consensual, contractarian and like ideas, but clearly can be separated from them, and, in my view, thereby improved.[27] We begin again with classical Utilitarianism. It is not only that it may issue in awful acts of victimization, but that it leaves out a consideration which is essential to the justification of ordinary punishment. Admittedly it is part of the justification of punishment that it is preventive, but it is also or as much a part that it involves a certain *equality, fairness, justice, rationality, equilibrium, balance, reciprocity, debt-repayment, or order.*

To try to become clearer about this, we are invited to consider the nature or function of the law. It legitimates certain activities for an individual and proscribes other activities. I am permitted to inherit a car, but not to drive it while drunk; I can in general forbid entry to my house, but not a policeman with a search warrant; I can buy food or medicines, but not steal them. The law, then, as well as allowing me to do things, to indulge myself in certain ways, places a vast array of what are called burdens on me, burdens of self-denial. It forbids to me certain choices, certain self-indulgences, certain exercises of my will, certain followings of my own inclinations. Each member of my society is subject to an array of burdens of self-denial. The general result is a distribution of the burdens of self-denial that is equal, fair, just, balanced, ordered or whatever.

What an offender does is put down one of his burdens. As he should not, he chooses for himself, indulges himself, exercises his will, follows his inclination. This constitutes a departure or a further

[27] Restorative Retributivism of a kind is defended, although not clearly separated from other things, in Herbert Morris, 'Persons and Punishment', *The Monist* **52**, No. 4 (1968). The same is true of Murphy, op. cit., and also Murphy, 'Three Mistakes About Retributivism', *Analysis* **31**, No. 5 (1971). See also John Finnis, 'The Restoration of Retribution', *Analysis* **32**, No. 4 (1972), and *Natural Law and Natural Rights* (Oxford: Clarendon, 1980), 260–266.

Ted Honderich

departure from the society's distribution of these burdens, a distribution that is equal, fair or the like. The essential recommendation of punishment, over and above its preventive recommendation, is that it *restores* equality, fairness or whatever, or is a move in that restorative direction. It does this, essentially, by *enforcing* a burden. The man who is punished is essentially a man whose desires, will or inclinations are restrained, not by himself but by others. The result is that the maldistribution of burdens which he has produced is corrected. Things are in a specific way put back to what they were. The punishment also encourages others to stick to the legitimate distribution.

It is important to be clear about the goods involved in the original distribution, in the ensuing maldistribution produced by offences, and in the distribution reasserted through punishment. Despite an uncertainty in some statements of Restorative Retributivism, these are not material goods, say cars, houses, food, or medicine. It is persistently asserted by one defender of Restorative Retributivism[28] that they are not, and of course they cannot be such. If the goods in question were material goods, we would be offered nothing like a *general* reason for punishment. We would have no reason for punishing attempted crimes which produce no material gain for offenders, because of failure or because no material gain was attempted, as in many offences of violence. Also, if the goods in question were material goods, it would be absurd to say the law produces an *equal* distribution of them, and any description of the distribution as *just* or the like would require further argument. Finally, it cannot be that material goods are what is in question since the unfairness of an offence is specifically said not to be an unfairness only to the victim—say the man who loses his car—but an unfairness to *all* the law-abiding members of the society.

Material goods, as I have been speaking of them, are certain things in the world. There are other things closely related to them which also cannot be the goods that are in question with Restorative Retributivism. I mean the satisfactions got from material goods. There are the same reasons for saying these are not the goods of Restorative Retributivism. It can be added that these goods also do not include the satisfactions of which one thinks in connection with offences not aimed at material gain, say certain offences of violence. The satisfactions of vengeance got by a murderer are not goods in the right class, it seems, since one can think of murders where they are missing but to which Restorative Retributivism must apply.

It becomes clear that the goods or benefits in question can perhaps

[28] Finnis makes the point clearly.

136

be described as *satisfactions-in-acting.* They are the goods of indulging one's will, or to speak informally, of *letting go,* whether legally or illegally. They are those goods which one does not have, precisely and only, as the product of obeying or forbearing, of denying or restraining oneself or reigning oneself in. Instead, here, one may have the burden of *dissatisfactions-in-not-acting.* The car thief presumably enjoys satisfaction-in-acting above all at the moment when he breaks the quarter-light, although it makes sense to say he also enjoys it later, when he self-indulgently doesn't submit to the idea of returning the car or turning himself in. In sum, then, for present purposes, the law legitimates certain satisfactions-in-acting and it proscribes others, which is to say it enjoins certain dissatisfactions-in-not-acting. Offenders put down a burden, take a proscribed satisfaction-in-acting. Punishment put such a burden on them, thereby reasserting a distribution of such burdens and benefits.

Various questions arise about the very nature of these burdens and benefits, and their relation to other dissatisfactions and satisfactions. These we must pass by. The first of two questions not to be passed by is this one: are the burdens which we now have more or less in view anything like *equally* distributed in our societies? That they are is suggested by a good deal of what is said in Restorative Retributivism. (It is perhaps suggested by that early New Retributivist, St Thomas Aquinas.[29] As implied earlier, the New Retributivism is not all absolutely novel.) To repeat, are the given burdens equally distributed? Well, one cannot avoid the thought that the burdens of self-restraint or dissatisfaction-in-not-acting, defined by law, are lighter for the man who has everything as against the man who has nothing. I refer to the having or not having of material goods and their satisfactions.

If the burdens of self-restraint are heavier for the man who has nothing, or—say instead—those in the bottom decile of income as against those in the highest decile, then if they offend, they are moving the distribution *towards* equality, rather than away from it. Their punishment is moving the distribution *away from,* rather than towards, equality. Punishment lacks *exactly* the recommendation that is being claimed for it.

As I have already indicated, it is notable that one gets a veritable welter of descriptions of the distribution that is fundamental to Restorative Retributivism. If it is said to be or to involve equality, it is also said to be *just, balanced, reciprocal,* and so on. However, we are not much helped by abandoning equality for this justice, since this justice goes unexplained. The particular distribution in question

---

[29] See Finnis, 'The Restoration of Retribution?', 134.

goes undefended. It evidently needs to be defended if Restorative Retributivism is to be complete. The doctrine, if it is not taken as involving an *equal* distribution, is essentially vague. To glance back at the interpretation in terms of equality, incidentally, we would also need to know why *that* is a good thing. Is *any* equal distribution, at whatever level, a good thing, and better than any unequal distribution?

One final thought in connection with the nature of the distribution. What some Restorative Retributivists take the law to produce is perhaps not an ordering or order of burdens which has some *further* recommendation—equality or justice or some such. What the law is taken to produce, and what the offender disturbs, is order *simpliciter*: that is, a situation in which self-denials and self-indulgences are *subject to rule,* whether the rule is good, bad or indifferent. It is a popular idea among those who benefit from rules, as distinct from those who do not, that there is a great recommendation in any old rules. That needs arguing, and any argument this is produced will be a small one.

A second question about Restorative Retributivism has to do with the relative importance of specifically the goods with which it is concerned, and with the fact that the commitment of the doctrine is to distributive justice somehow conceived. To speak quickly, surely money or food, and the satisfactions got from them, are of greater importance than specifically the benefits we have in view, satisfactions-in-acting. Surely *not having* money or food, and the ensuing dissatisfactions, are of greater importance than the burdens of self-denial with respect to them, dissatisfactions-in-not-acting. Thus, if one sets out to justify punishment by considerations of distributive justice, it is bizarre to leave out the former benefits and burdens—benefits of possession and burdens of lack or deprivation. It might well be, from the point of view of distribution, that a gain secured by punishment in terms of the distribution of self-indulgence and self-denial was outweighed by a loss secured by punishment in terms of what we can call the benefits and burdens of possession.

Restorative Retributivism, in my view, does little to justify punishment in our societies. It is necessary to say that this is a conclusion in a way shared and strongly defended by one Restorative Retributivist, Jeffrie G. Murphy.[30] He takes it that the injustice of

[30] He develops his conclusion most fully in 'Marxism and Retribution'. There is also a related concession, to my mind given insufficient attention, in Morris, op. cit. Finnis touches on the question and appears to want to have it both ways: that the theory does and does not apply to other than 'an imaginary "well-ordered" society' (*Natural Law and Natural Rights,* 264–265).

our societies makes the doctrine inapplicable to them. He also maintains, to my mind mistakenly, that Restorative Retributivism, at least with Contractarian ideas added, is the best of doctrines of the justification of punishment, and that it would justify punishment in a just society. On the contrary, punishment there could not be justified simply by reference to burdens of the specified kind, with or without the addition of Contractarianism.

Of what else can be said against Restorative Retributivism, let me say only that at best it provides only an insubstantial and obscure ground for punishment. This sixth argument, like its predecessors, is not the truth of the tradition of retributivism.

The Truth of Retributivism

Most of these arguments, in one form or another, were also considered by the acute John Mackie. The particular verdicts we have reached differ somewhat from his, but there is no mistaking a similarity in general upshot. He concluded that no retributive principle of punishment can be 'explained or developed within a reasonable system of moral thought', that all the main lines of retributivist thought are signal failures, that we cannot make moral sense of them.[31] He also had another conviction, however. It was that a retributive principle 'cannot be eliminated from our moral thinking', that retributive ideas which in one way or another are unsatisfactory, from what can be called the point of view of reason, are deeply ingrained, a part of our lives.[32] The proposition that retributivism cannot be made decent sense of, and the proposition that it is inescapable—these comprise what Mackie called the *paradox of retributivism*.

He offers what he calls a resolution of it, of which the first step is the Humean proposition that moral distinctions, such as the distinction between the deserved and the undeserved, are founded not on reason but on feeling or sentiment. What is in question with retributivism, fundamentally, is what he calls retributive emotion. Of this, Mackie offers a persuasive biological explanation, in terms of standard evolutionary theory. It begins with the advantage to species and individuals of retaliatory behaviour and feeling, and hence their natural selection; it proceeds by way of the socialization or moralizing of retributive emotion, it ends with such items as the con-

[31] J. L. Mackie, 'Morality and the Retributive Emotions', *Criminal Justice Ethics* **1**, No. 1 (1982), 3, 6. Kenny (op. cit., 69f) has the related view that retributivism is incoherent.

[32] Mackie, op. cit., 3.

Ted Honderich

sensual theory of punishment. I have no doubt that the explanation is at least in principle correct.

Nevertheless, this view of the tradition of retributivism seems to me not to deal with a main problem. It is not enough to grant that retributivism is entrenched. What must also be granted, as I have already argued, is the fact that somehow it makes sense. On reflection, surely, it is a remarkable supposition that a *tide* of ordinary moral thought and language over centuries, and, much more than that, a *tide* of institutions, should rest, as Mackie supposes, in so far as rational rather than causal grounds are concerned, on incoherence or on what is in fact without rational content. Certainly there are immense questions here, but it is surely impossible to suppose that in establishing, defending and developing retributivist institutions, punishment above all, men have not aimed at and secured something which is substantial and which is capable of clear description. There has been some profit in it all, profit which can be discerned and put into an argument. Further, it seems impossible that *no* decent argument attaches to a basic fact of this unremitting sequence of institutions: they rest on an array of connections between particular offences and particular penalties, and give these connections as an essential part of the justification of the penalties. It cannot be that all that can be said of the law's 'deserved' or 'fitting' penalties is that they derive from a confused image of factual equivalence between things that in fact are incommensurable, or from some other equally unacceptable notion, or that they derive from a clear notion of equivalence, but one which has no argumentative force.

It may be that there is no sufficient moral argument for punishment in the tradition of retributivism, and that what is said of equivalence in it does not provide one. To repeat, it cannot be that there is nothing that comes up to the level of argument, and that there is *no* force in talk of equivalence.

The truth of retributivism, as it still seems to me,[33] and in absolute brevity, is as follows. First, harmful actions give rise to what can be labelled grievances, which is to say certain desires for the distress of the agents, desires whose only and full satisfaction is in the belief that the agents are being distressed or made to suffer.

---

[33] The view was defended in my *Punishment: The Supposed Justifications*. It is evidently distinct from the view that punishment has an *expressive* function, although some things said in that theory move in my direction, e.g. that 'punishment generally expresses more than judgments of disapproval; it is also a symbolic way of getting back at the criminal, of expressing a kind of vindictive resentment' (Feinberg, 'The Expressive Function of Punishment', op. cit., 100).

Whatever else is to be said of grievances, one certainty is that they exist. A second proposition, no doubt disagreeable, is that the existence of these desires is an argument for their satisfaction. It cannot, as it seems to me, be left out. There cannot be an argument for dismissing certain desires from consideration which is nearly so overwhelming as the argument that their existence is reason for their satisfaction. There is a fundamental inconsistency in counting them as nothing. That is not to say, certainly, that the argument for their satisfaction cannot be outweighed by others, Thirdly, such desires can be *less than satisfied, more than satisfied, or just satisfied.* This again is a fact of life.

The truth of the retributivist tradition, more precisely, is that it seeks to justify punishment partly or wholly by the clear reason that it satisfies the grievances created by offences, through causing distress to offenders, and that it takes penalties to be unsatisfactory if they do less than satisfy grievances or do more than that, and satisfactory if they just satisfy it. Here, the sense of saying that penalty P is deserved for A's offence O is that P will *just satisfy* the grievance to which A has given rise by O. The requirement of an equivalent penalty, in this sense, is a direct consequence of the fundamental contention: that punishment is justified partly or wholly by grievance-satisfaction. To do less than satisfy it would simply conflict with the fundamental contention. To do more would be to cause distress which would fail to have the given justification.

Mackie had a view of the retributivist tradition which excluded the possibility that this is its sense. Essentially, he took it to consist in institutions such that we cannot look, for whatever value they have, to the effects of the distress of penalties. There is no reason to go along with this. The reason for doing so is essentially a respect for what most apologists for the tradition, notably moral philosophers and jurisprudents, have said of it.[34] What they have said is that it

[34] All of the views of the justification of punishment considered in this essay are retributivist in the sense defined earlier. That is, they all involve desert-locutions. Further, they have a common character in that they can be said to be directed *at* the offender, rather than *to* something else, and they do at least tacitly purport to give the justification of punishment inherent in the retributivist tradition. However, despite Mackie's view to the contrary, (op. cit., 4f), not all are attempts to justify punishment without reference to its effects. Restorative Retributivism, at any rate, can in a sense be said to justify punishment by an effect: the restoration of a distribution of burdens and benefits. The view is in a sense forward–looking and consequentialist. The difference between this and the other views considered suggests an alternative categorization of views of punishment, involving a different definition of retributivism. Here, *retributivism* includes only views which

depends on a reason for punishment that does not mention the effects of the distress of offenders, notably the satisfaction it gives. There would be more call for respect if they were successful in providing the supposed reason.

It is notable that what is said for punishment by those who are engaged in it, the judiciary, is often of a very different character. It is plain that when judges declare in one way and another that the coming distress of offenders is *deserved*, they are not excluding the satisfaction it gives to others. Consider the most entrenched of judicial utterances, that offenders must *pay their debt*. What is to pay a debt? Does somebody not *get* something? How very odd it would be if no one did. Necessarily, someone does.

Various related objections have been made to this view. One is that it is obviously false because it reduces to this: 'that a judge ought to sentence because the people outside in the street are baying for blood'.[35] It reduces to nothing of the sort. The fact of punishment's being informed and defended by grievance-satisfactions is a fact shaped by considerations of consistency, precedent, the law's fundamental ideas of the reasonable, and so on. (James Fitzjames Stephen, the Victorian judge, made the often-quoted remark that 'The criminal law stands to the passion of revenge in much the same relation as marriage to the sexual appetite'.[36] The remark, I take it, expresses my view of the truth of retributivism, and the consistent fact that retributive punishment is other than ungoverned vengeance.) It may be objected, again, that the view reduces the retributivist tradition to 'just a primitive bit of intuitive vindictiveness'.[37] Part of what can be said in reply is along the same lines: that the view in no way conflicts with the fact that the criminal law and punishment constitute a developed institution—authoritative and rule-governed. That the view finds a basis for punishment that can be characterized mistakenly as 'primitive' seems to me a recommendation of it. That it finds a basis which is

---

do not justify punishment by any effect. It includes the two Old Retributivist views considered above, and all the New ones except for Restorative Retributivism. The other two categories of views would be those of a *Utilitarian* kind and those informed by a principle of *distributive justice*. The later category would include Restorative Retributivism and my own view, set out below.

[35] Nigel Walker, in 'Symposium: Predicting Dangerousness', *Criminal Justice Ethics* **2**, No. 1 (1983), 15.

[36] *General View of the Criminal Law of England* (London: Macmillan, 1863), 99. Cf. Henry Sidgwick, *The Methods of Ethics* (London: Macmillan, 1963), Bk III, Ch. 5.

[37] Murphy, 'Three Mistakes About Retributivism', op. cit., 169.

'intuitive', in one pejorative use of that word, which suggests want of clarity, is false.

To repeat, then, the sort of defence for punishment that is suggested by and indeed embodied in the retributivist tradition, at least in its more recent part, is that punishment is morally justified because it prevents offences and just satisfies grievance. That, at any rate, is the foundation of the defence. In the second part of that foundation we have what we have failed to find elsewhere, a retributive reason for punishment which is neither insubstantial nor obscure.

It is necessary to say, however, that what the retributivist tradition suggests is in fact a family of arguments based on prevention and grievance. They will differ, for example, in regarding prevention or grievance or both as giving rise to a moral permission to punish or to an obligation. Some of these arguments will have internal difficulties. For example, one cannot marry the grievance proposition in certain ways with the prevention proposition if the latter is construed in a classical Utilitarian way. It is so construed if, for example, it carries the Utilitarian idea that one must always choose the particular means to a given end which is least costly in terms of the distress it causes. There may be *no* penalty for a murder, say, which both satisfies the Utilitarian requirement having to do with the minimal effective distress to the offender, *and* the requirement of satisfying grievance.[38] Still, let us suppose that we can find members of this family of arguments that do not have such internal troubles.

On some of these views, we are both permitted and obliged to punish offenders when their punishments just satisfy grievance and also are in some defined sense preventive. If prevention seems an undeniable consideration with respect to the justification of punishment, and if the retributive part of these views is as it should be—clear and such as to specify an actual gain—that is not to say that any such view is defensible, that it *does* provide a moral justification of punishment. There are clear objections, of which I shall quickly mention but two.

Any such view gives weight to, and argues from, the existence of grievance-desires in a society. It gives weight to, and argues from, the possibility of certain satisfactions, satisfactions of grievances. As I have already said, it appears to me impossible to disregard the existence of such desires and their possible satisfaction. To do so is high-minded, certainly, but also confused. That is not the end of the story, however.

[38] Cf. Goldman, op. cit., on conflicting parts of 'mixed' theories of punishment.

Consider an analogy. A man wants a whisky, and will be unhappy without it. That this is so is *a* reason for giving it to him. But of course there may be reasons against. They may be overwhelming reasons against his having a drop, or another drop. They may be such as to make it a good idea that he have only a well-watered whisky. They may be such as to make it a good idea to give him what he wants, but with an admonition. So with grievance-desires for the punishment of offenders. Clearly they cannot be taken just as they are, unreflectively, as automatic justifiers, or automatic part-justifiers.

How then do we judge them? Many things might be said, but in the end, we shall come to one basis, which is a conception of the good or the fair or the right society. We shall necessarily regard the satisfaction of grievance-desires from the point of view of what we take to be the fundamental moral principle for the ordering of our lives together in society. Clearly it is impossible to embrace such a view of punishment as we are considering if it does not do this, and instead unreflectively takes grievance-desires as *given*.

A second objection to such a view, which takes us in the same direction, has been in a way anticipated.[39] Such a view takes only or mainly into account two categories of satisfactions. One is satisfactions of grievance-desires. The second is satisfactions of all our desires not to be victims of offences. But of course these are but *some* of the categories of desire which must and do often enter into our reflection on the good, just or right society. There are others. There are the ongoing dissatisfactions of offenders in being punished. There are also the dissatisfactions owed to a lack or deprivation of material and other goods, which dissatisfactions are not owed to offences but to the legal distribution of these goods within a society.

To make the point in question by way of an extreme example, suppose we consider the justification of punishment within a truly racist society. There is an absurd incompleteness in supposing we can consider the justification of the society's punishments only in terms of the two categories of desire mentioned above. A view of the kind we are considering, then, is wholly inadequate because, at least, it is strikingly incomplete.

Political Philosophy and an Answer

Both the objections to such a view then brings us to the conclusion that it is necessarily bound up with political philosophy. More

[39] See above, pp. 136–139. Cf. Goldman, op. cit., 44.

precisely, it is bound up with the question of the fundamental principle or principles for the judgment and guidance of societies. Views of punishment derived from the retributivist tradition are by no means unique in this respect. The same is true of all the theories of punishment which comprise the New Retributivism. The fact, far from being in the background, was forced upon us in consideration of Consensual, Contract and Restorative Retributivisms, as was noticed when we considered them. It is a fact too about the classical and other Utilitarian theories of punishment. Here, of course, the fact is also not in the background. The Utilitarian theories of punishment are presented, in the first instance, as deductions from a general principle, which principle is in fact a response to the fundamental question of political philosophy, that of how the various benefits and burdens are to be distributed.

It is one of my conclusions, then, that the question of the justification of punishment is immovably located within political philosophy, and, more precisely, that any answer to the question requires a prior answer to the fundamental question in political philosophy. Philosophical and jurisprudential reflection on punishment has in fact led a life of its own, for whatever reasons, and continues to do so. It cannot properly do so. For example, there is not the slightest possibility of dealing adequately or even pertinently with the question of justification by attending only to the supposed intrinsic good of the suffering of the guilty, without reference to the rest of their lives and the lives around them.

This general conclusion is not, I think, a philosophical proposition of a certain somewhat boring kind. I have in mind propositions to the effect that solutions to certain problems presuppose solutions to others. The largest of these propositions are to the effect that moral philosophy depends on the philosophy of mind, ontology on epistemology, and so on. Consistently with that, one can respectably spend one's philosophical life concerned only with moral philosophy, or only with ontology.

The conclusion to which we have come is not that the problem of the justification of punishment is something which, although it presupposes or depends on something else, *can be considered independently*. The problem of the justification of punishment does not just presuppose in this way an answer to the fundamental question in political philosophy, essentially a question about the distribution of burdens and benefits in a wide sense. It is more proper to say, rather, since the satisfactions and dissatisfactions of punishment are *a part* of those burdens and benefits, *a part* of the very subject-matter of the distributive question, that to address the question of punishment necessarily *is* to address the distributive question. Further it is simply *irrational* to address *part of* a single distributive question, where that is to ignore a part of what can be or in fact is distributed. No doubt punishment raises many questions, but there is nothing that can be called the question of its moral justification which is left to be considered if one puts aside the great question of the distribution of goods in society.

My second conclusion, already drawn, is that the New Retributivism is no success story. None of the views we have considered is effective, and no consistent combination of them is much better. The third, also already drawn, is that the clearer and *more* arguable justification of punishment which actually comes out of retributivist institutions is clearly inadequate.

What remains to be given, my fourth conclusion, can in some respects be anticipated. It is an answer to the question of whether punishment in our societies is right or wrong. My answer must be a part of a conclusion drawn from what I take to be the fundamental principle, certainly of a moral kind, by which societies are to be judged, and by which societies ought to be guided. Further, it can be anticipated that my answer to the question about our punishments must go undefended here, for the reason that the fundamental principle must go undefended. That is not something to be done quickly. It is not that punishment is a very large question, but that something else is.

The problem of classical Utilitarianism, in a word, is unfairness. This is so, as we know, with respect to punishment. The most common response to this, in connection with punishment, has been to go over to or attempt to add a principle of retributive justice. That is, philosophers and jurisprudents have advanced such doctrines as those we have considered: Culpability–Distress Retributivism, Intrinsic Retributivism, Rights Retributivism, Indifference Retributivism, and the Consensual, Contractarian and Restorative varieties. It is a small virtue of some of the latter of these that they take a small step in the right direction—towards questions of distributive justice. They do not reach the subject, but give us a plethora of unexamined predicates instead: *equal, just, fair,* and so on. The correct response to the shortcoming of classical Utilitarianism, in my view, is not retributivism, but a clear principle of *distributive* justice, an answer to the question of how all benefits and burdens in society are to be distributed.

My own general answer is the Principle of Equality. It is not to the effect that we should have as our *main* aim the securing of an equality of anything. It is not a principle whose main aim is just some *relationship* between the well-being of individuals or classes. It is not fundamentally about getting everybody on a level. To see the mistake of such an aim, by way of one example of importance, suppose we are concerned not with wealth or a number of other things, but with *human satisfactions generally,* and in particular with all such satisfactions of two classes of people over their whole lifetimes. It must be mistaken to prefer an equality of satisfactions at a low level to an inequality at higher levels. The Principle of Equality, which can be argued actually to be the principle which has informed the tradition of egalitarianism, does *not* have the consequence that we should prefer the low-level equality.

The Principle of Equality is to the effect that our fundamental aim should be to make well-off those who are badly-off, and that we should use effective means. Its fuller statement, which has been attempted elsewhere,[40] does of course require adequate definitions of what it is to be badly-off and to be well-off. Further, its fuller statement requires a specification of the effective means to its end, particular policies which we should follow. Many of these, consistently with what was said above, *will be* policies having to do with the *equal* distribution of something, say political power.

A good, just or right society, then, is one directed by the Principle of Equality. Its institutions are in accord with it. Are our contemporary societies directed by the Principle of Equality? Is our punishment in accord with it? The answer is no, more so in this time than it has recently been. Does it follow that punishment in our societies lacks moral justification? That it is wrong? The short answer is yes.

The longer answer takes into account that our punishment is part of one of a certain set of possible alternatives. One is the alternative of our societies as they are but without punishment. One is the alternative of our societies just as they are, with punishment. A third is the alternative of societies in accord with the Principle of Equality and with punishment. A fourth is the alternative, to which there is no obstacle but ourselves, of such societies without punishment, or with very little of it. Our punishments now in our societies are wrong at least in the sense that they enter into what is at least the second worst alternatives.

[40]'The Question of Well-being and the Principle of Equality', *Mind* **XC**, No. 360 (1981).

Philosophy, Language and the Reform of Public Worship

MARTIN WARNER

> When I studied the Scriptures then I did not feel as I am writing
> about them now. They seemed to me unworthy of comparison
> with the grand style of Cicero (Augustine, III, 5).

> As for the absurdities which used to offend me in Scripture, ... I
> now looked for their meanings in the depth of mystery (*sac-
> ramentorum*) (Augustine, VI, 5).

I. Philosophy and Practice

The form of this lecture is in large part dictated by my understanding of the requirements of the context within which it is set. The
overall series title is 'Philosophy and Practice', and the sequence of
lectures is arranged in association with the recently launched Society
for Applied Philosophy. So it may be as well to begin with a few
brief remarks about this setting.

A difficulty common to the titles both of the Society and the
lecture series is that they appear to presuppose a conception of
philosophy as uncontaminated by the world of human activity, so
that philosophy can be juxtaposed with, and even applied to, that
world. The obvious analogue is mathematics, where the contrast
between pure and applied has its most usual home, but whether
philosophy should be construed in purely formal terms—as involved
essentially in analysis on the mathematical model—is itself a
philosophical issue. Further, philosophy, like mathematics itself, is
something which is practised—a human activity—and one of its main
branches, that of ethics, may take that very practice as part of its subject
matter, as in Aristotle's discussion of the value of the contemplative life.
The contrast 'Philosophy and Practice' is therefore not without its
problems.

These considerations should not be taken as constituting a
significant objection to either title. They rather bring out the
difficulty of framing, in a non-question-begging way, any title which
relates philosophy to what lies beyond itself, for one of the few
widely agreed features of philosophy is that it is self-reflexive—it
takes itself as one of its own topics. The best that can be done, and
this is achieved admirably by both titles, is to gesture to features of

human concern which are recognizably different from the activity of philosophy but towards which that activity might profitably be directed.

The features suggested by 'Practice' in the series title are those to do with action as distinct from those practices—often called 'theoretical'—which have at best a somewhat indirect impact on how men live their lives and comport themselves outside study, library and lecture room. Thus the attention given in this series to issues in politics, the law, medicine and family life—and in the case of this lecture to an aspect of that whole process of *aggiornamento* which has taken hold of the Churches.

Differing conceptions of philosophy will dictate divergent treatments of varying types of practice, so understood, but in the present case there is sufficient distance between the somewhat abstract subdivision of philosophy I want to consider—the philosophy of language—understood in its own terms, and the practice of liturgical reform for the notion of 'application' to gain a better than usual grip. Indeed, in this context—though not in all—there may even be scope for some of the traditional—and today often rejected—ways of construing the 'application' of philosophy; if 'handmaid to theology' is perhaps carrying this thought a little far, the less highly charged notion of the philosopher as 'under-labourer . . . clearing the ground a little' (Locke, *Epistle to the Reader*) may still have a role to play.

The ground to be cleared I intend to circumscribe fairly narrowly. First, the aspect of *aggiornamento* in question is the linguistic dimension of public worship. Second, I shall construe 'linguistic' primarily in verbal terms; I am well aware that the language of ritual goes beyond the verbal level, but the most important philosophical work on language uses words, sentences and/or speech as providing at least its starting points and benchmarks; some of my remarks, however, will have a bearing on the non-verbal context in which the language of worship operates. Third, my focus will be on liturgical worship, for it is over reform in this area that much of the recent controversy has concentrated. And fourth, although for reasons I shall shortly give, I make substantial reference to recent Biblical translation which is an ecumenical activity, my more strictly liturgical references will be, for the sake of economy, to recent changes in the Church of England; the problems facing those of the Roman obedience are interestingly and importantly different, though some of my more general remarks have application here too.

Further, in accordance with my rubric of 'under-labourer', the bearing which the philosophy of language has on this narrowly conceived area is itself restricted. There are a wide variety of considerations which bear on the proper language and ordering of the liturgical worship of the Church of England: theological, historical, pastoral, evangelical, psychological, linguistic, literary, practical, and even legal. Any of these can provide direct guidance to the revisers. The role of philosophy I am considering is different, operating more at a second-order level in two, interconnected, ways. First, the advice tendered on behalf of the first-order considerations may involve presuppositions which are themselves in need of philosophical scrutiny. Thus analysis may reveal that a given set of such considerations may only have the significance for action their proponents conceive them to have given, say, a specific position in the philosophy of language which itself has implications for other first-order considerations; given a different understanding of language it may well remain open for would-be revisers to make the same decisions as they might otherwise have done, but not always for exactly the same reasons. Second, the weight given to a particular consideration may well turn on its type; thus in recent practice it would appear that issues concerning scholarly accuracy with regard to translation (the 'linguistic' considerations) often weighed more heavily than 'literary' ones, and it is at least arguable that theological ones should take priority over both, where distinguishable. But philosophy may have a bearing on the degree to which they are distinguishable, and how one should classify such matters; if meaning can be tied to truth conditions and abstracted from context such distinctions look firmer than if it cannot.

But although second-order, these somewhat abstract considerations have a direct relevance to contemporary controversy. In the late sixties and early seventies the revisers made most of the running, with Prefaces and Commentaries accompanying their work and the book-length discussion of *The Eucharist Today* by members of the Church of England Liturgical Commission of 1974 (Jasper). Articulate dissentient voices were to be heard (e.g. Robinson) but no serious attempt was made in print to meet the objections in detail (Ian Robinson's name does not appear in the index of *The Eucharist Today*); reliance seems to have been placed on the debating capacity of the various Synods. Since then the groundswell of opposition to the new forms of liturgy and Biblical translations has increased, with the foundation of the Prayer Book Society and its two journals in 1976, through the articles in *Theology* starting in 1977 with those of David Cockerell and Stephen Prickett, and the 1979 issue of the *PN Review* which was associated with petitions on the matter to the General Synod, up to the more recent collections of essays (Morris, and Martin and Mullen); the list could be considerably extended, but it is noteworthy that there has been very little intellectually serious response from those criticized. Indeed, although a few

151

exceptions can be instanced, the debate appears increasingly to resemble a dialogue of the deaf, with the objectors to the innovations paying decreasing heed to the detail of the arguments with which the new forms were originally presented and defended, and the supporters of the current revisions even more obviously repaying the compliment. It is symptomatic that the most recent attempt to assess the present state of affairs by the revisers and their associates, *Liturgy Reshaped* (Stevenson), refers to the objectors as constituting a 'lobby' with ill-concealed distaste (177), and ignores their arguments.

In part this unedifying spectacle can be traced to the way that controversy has tended to polarize, in ways that hardly aid clarity, between defenders of the ancient forms and advocates of the modern, with all the political and social overtones that ancient versus modern debates tend to produce. But beyond this, though in various ways contributing to it, is a sense that the arguments mounted by the opposing sides fail to meet each other; from a conviction that an opponent's arguments fail to engage with one's own to the despising of those arguments is a dangerously short step. But this failure to engage often turns on different and incompatible presuppositions being involved in the arguments in question, and some of these are philosophical in nature. What are the mutual relations between meaning, translation and style? How far can the truth of an utterance be considered in isolation from its context, both linguistic and other? Are considerations about the imaginative dimension of certain forms of language theological or merely literary? The presupposing of divergent answers to such questions as these can powerfully aid mutual incomprehension in the polemical arena.

These are hardly original considerations. It may well be that an increasing awareness of the importance of such matters has played a role in the recent reconstitution of the Liturgical Commission under new leadership, having correspondingly less intellectual and emotional capital locked up in *The Alternative Service Book 1980*, with the brief that, in monitoring current practice, issues of meaning should be its chief concern. The conjunction of this new development with the inception of the Society for Applied Philosophy seems an opportunity too good to miss.

It is not the part of an under-labourer to take sides in first-order controversies. I have thus chosen examples which provide room for manoeuvre by opposing parties, hoping in this way to generate light rather than heat. Further, my concern has been to provide a schematic survey of possibilities rather than to work out in detail the implications of any one preferred position in the philosophy of language. To give some concreteness to the discussion, I do indeed close the lecture with an indication of how I suspect relevant analysis should develop, but the bulk of my remarks should be of relevance even to those who do not share my suspicions—providing they are nevertheless also concerned to assist in 'clearing the ground a little'.

II. Liturgical Revision and Biblical Translation

(i) Practice

'Following old liturgical practice, our new material is a tissue of scriptural allusion' [Frost (I), 11]; this comment by one of the more linguistically self-conscious members of the old Liturgical Commission indicates one main reason why liturgical revision and Biblical translation cannot be kept entirely separate. Another is that the public reading of the Scriptures in regular sequence is an integral part of both the old and new services; indeed, some parts of the Bible itself appear to have been written, at least in part, for liturgical contexts. Thus I shall draw my examples from Biblical translations as well as service books; all should be familiar even to the merely occasional church-goer.

My aim in using these examples is not to score debating points for or against the new versions, but to introduce in specific settings two concepts that will have theoretical work to do later on—the concepts of 'imaginative demand' and of 'context'.

The first example is drawn from the traditional Gospel for Christmas Day, still permitted as such—optionally—by the 1980 liturgy, the Prologue to St John's Gospel. The Gospel opens with the pre-existent Λόγος, of which more shortly, and then moves on to the sphere of human history; at the point of intersection of timeless with time, marked as such by an abrupt shift in the tense structure, we have a verse which presents a central theme of the fourth evangelist, the conflict of light with darkness. The first edition of the *New English Bible* translation renders it thus: 'The light shines on in the dark, and the darkness has never quenched it'. It is difficult to see how darkness can be expected to quench light, but the Greek is more subtle; the word καταλαμβάνειν can mean both 'take under control' and 'take into the mind'. Modern as well as more traditional commentators are agreed that both senses are operative here (e.g. Marsh, 104; Temple, 7–8), and if they are then significant demands are being made on the imagination of the reader or hearer. On the first interpretation, a thick mist-laden darkness can muffle a light so that it sheds little illumination, though it can hardly quench it, and on the second the darkness is personified; the old '*Authorised Version*' uses a word which alerts the mind to the second interpretation but allows scope to the first, 'the darkness comprehended it not'. The point is, presumably, that in no sense, physical or mental, did the darkness absorb or 'receive' the light, and thus we find seven verses later that those who do receive the light are not of the darkness at all, but rather 'sons of God'. In short, the ambiguities of καταλαμβάνειν provide a context in which to interpret the later verse and, through it, the whole account of how the Λόγος 'dwelt among us'. This whole complex web of imagery and associations is cut through in the modern rendering, and in its place we are faced with the curious spectacle of darkness failing to quench light.

But it should be admitted that the translators had a difficult task. The physical dimension of the old 'comprehend' is hardly in current use and a modern equivalent for καταλαμβάνειν is hard to find. The *Revised Version* took advantage of its margin (useless, of course, for public reading) to give two renderings, one physical the other mental, and the *Revised Standard Version*—usually by far the most accurate of the conservative revisions—here stumbled badly with 'overcome'. The most idiomatic equivalent is no doubt 'grasp', but the 'mental' uses of this term verge on slang; Archbishop Temple's suggestion 'absorb' has similar problems. In the face of such difficulties one needs some confidence that the imaginative demand made by the ambiguities of καταλαμβάνειν really matters, is not a mere literary flourish of no cognitive significance, in order to continue the struggle to find *le mot juste*. True to its aim of avoiding ambiguity, another recent version—that of the *Good News Bible*— gives a further disambiguated rendering: 'The light shines in the darkness, and the darkness has never put it out'. The *New English Bible* revisers, however, were plainly unhappy with cutting the Gordian knot in the manner of their first edition, and in the second find an impressive resolution to the problem: 'the darkness has never mastered it'. The *Good News* revisers and the *New English* revisers, to judge by this example alone, would appear to attach different degrees of importance to the imaginative demands made by the original and the interconnections of overall context.

My second example is the opening of the same Gospel. For centuries the Christmas Gospel has begun 'In the beginning'. The Greek is Ἐναρχῆ, which is identical with the Septuagint's opening of *Genesis*, a cross reference preserved both in the Vulgate and in the traditional English versions but lost in the *New English Bible*, whose *Genesis* starts 'In the beginning of Creation' but whose Fourth Gospel opens 'When all things began, the Word already was'. In the Greek the echo of *Genesis*, the tenses, and the later verse three together ensure that the temporal reference is dominant here, but the word ἀρχή is itself ambiguous, with the meanings of 'source' and 'fundamental principle' as well as the temporal one. The Vulgate's *In principio* captures these nuances rather well; in English it is more difficult, but the traditional unspecific and evocative 'In the beginning' goes some little way towards doing so. On the other hand the *New English Bible*'s 'When all things began' makes no attempt to capture anything of the sort. The only element on which the imagination can fasten apart from the temporal reference is the comparatively banal neuter plural of 'all' imported from verse three, which in both the original and the traditional versions is held back until a rich theological context has been firmly established.

Here once again ambiguity makes, in the original, imaginative demands. But the potential relevance of context is even more extensive. The issue of whether it matters whether 'all things' are introduced as a subject of reference before or after a theological context is established may reasonably be regarded as a somewhat local matter; but whether the opening words of *Genesis*, therefore of the Torah, and hence of the whole Old Testament, are to be read as the context of the opening of the Fourth Gospel is arguably of rather wider significance for reading the latter. But here the translators appear to have had no second thoughts; a fairly strong doctrine of the cognitive irrelevance of extra-textural allusion appears to be operating, whatever the ambiguities of the translators' assumptions about the significance of textually local contexts. Nevertheless, it would be wrong to ascribe the translators' assumptions here to all our revisers; *The Alternative Service Book 1980*, after more than a decade in which parishes had experimented with a variety of translations, prints as its preferred rendering of St John's *Prologue* that of the more traditional *Revised Standard Version*.

My third and final example is drawn from *The Alternative Service Book* itself, from what to the ordinary communicant is psychologically the high point of the Holy Communion service—his reception of the consecrated bread and wine. The reception is much less obviously central to the priest or 'president' for whom the focus is on the act of consecration, and the fact that the Liturgical Commission has been dominated by priests may have a bearing on how it has handled this part of the service; this suggestion is not simply gratuitous, for the point of the example is the role of non-verbal contexts for the utterance of and response to speech acts, and these are importantly different for celebrant and people.

In the 1662 Order the words of distribution preserve a careful balance between doctrines of the Real Presence ('The Body of our Lord Jesus Christ') and more Zwinglian approaches in terms of a memorial meal ('eat this in remembrance that Christ died for thee'). Originally this represented a compromise generally acceptable because both sets of phrases are grounded in Scripture, but as with many such compromises the Anglican tradition has claimed to discern spiritual value in the very fact that no one party has been able to impose its own preferred theology on the formularies to the exclusion of others, so that the requirements of comprehensiveness have left room for the mystery of God. In this instance it is not so much ambiguity as incipient paradox that provides the materials of imaginative demand, for at the spiritually crucial moment of the reception of the Elements, all communicants are made aware of the central mystery of Christianity—the identity between the Jesus of past history and the Christ of present faith. How to weight the two sets of phrases is left to the individual; some are more at home with the notion of a memorial than that of a Real Presence, others with the belief that the Christ of their faith is really present to them in the eucharist than with the identification of that Christ with any historical figure. But what each holds of most value is endorsed by the words of distribution, and that which is at present dark is presented as also part of the faith—a mystery to be treasured and explored. In Rite A of the new order one pole of the tension is relegated to the psychologically secondary position of the invitation to communion; 'The body of Christ' the communicant is somewhat brusquely told, or alternatively 'The body of Christ keep you in eternal life'—and the Dominical saying about doing 'this in remembrance of me' are removed from the words accompanying the reception of the Elements as if they had less weight.

It is the context of these words on which I wish to focus. In the old Rite the words of distribution were far too many to be said to each communicant at a normal service. As he knelt at the altar-rail a communicant heard the words being said several times as the priest or his assistant approached and passed on, while only a phrase or clause was directly said to him; there was thus a strong communal element at this point in what is often stigmatized as an over-individualistic service, and at this communal moment both sides of the faith were presented together. In the new order the rest of the service is made more communal (the Creed, for example, opens with 'We believe' rather than 'I believe') but here alone the balance swings the other way; the words of distribution are short enough to be repeated in their entirety to each individual, and what that individual is told as he receives is just one side of the old paradox. Of course, both poles of the tension are still maintained in the invitation, said to the whole congregation before its members go up to receive, and it may be protested that this safeguards the traditional balance—for the same thing is still said. But such a protest presupposes that changes of context leave meaning invariant, and this presupposition deserves scrutiny.

156

(ii) Theory

When we look for articulations of the linguistic assumptions lying behind the new versions and forms we find surprisingly little systematic discussion, and not all of what there is pointing in the same direction. But it is perhaps revealing that the *New English Bible* was prepared not only by panels concerned with 'the actual work of translation' but also by one made up of 'literary advisers' supposed to represent 'a delicate sense of English style' (1970 Preface). This framework need not carry much in the way of theoretical commitment; it might merely represent making the best of a bad job in the absence of fully competent translators. But it seems clear that the embodied distinction between style and content was widely accepted at the theoretical level; not only did the *NEB* translators betray no serious unease with it in their various Prefaces and Introductions, but it was upheld in no uncertain terms by the chairman of the Liturgical Commission in his Introduction to *The Eucharist Today*: 'in addition to questions of meaning and translation, there are also questions of style' (3).

Further aspects of what appears to be something of a revisers' consensus emerge from this Introduction, perhaps the most surprising element of which is that clarity appears not to be a stylistic matter. 'It is the duty of the Church', we are told, 'to ensure that translations are correct and that meanings are clear'; these matters are primary, and objections to formulations on such stylistic grounds as that they lack 'richness' may properly be overridden with such revealing remarks as 'at least the new text expresses clearly what the original ... (was) trying to say'. We have here a clue to what is intended by the now less than clear word 'clarity'; it is a property of meaning which, in turn, is conceived of as something other than a mere function of the text which may only approximate to—'try to say'—the meaning. Meaning thus appears to be something construable in terms of a set of co-ordinates independent of style, perhaps a matrix of some kind, and presumably possesses 'clarity' when it can be precisely specified by such a matrix; a linguistic form 'expresses' this meaning 'clearly' when it stands in a specific relation (which need not be one of 'richness') to this meaning. A philosopher attempting to make sense of Dr Jasper's Introduction to his team's defence of their work soon notices familiar and controversial positions such as these embedded in the subtext.

How seriously they are intended is unclear, for all the invocation of the authority of a linguistics textbook in the immediately succeeding paragraph. But whether fully recognized or not these assumptions appear to have had an influence far beyond the

Liturgical Commission. They render intelligible the *NEB* translators' belief that pursuit of their 'aim of making the meaning as clear as it could be made' frequently 'compelled us to make decisions' rather than allow 'a comfortable ambiguity'; in such places they have conceived it as their duty 'to take the risk rather than remain on the fence' (*NEB*, 1970, Introduction to the New Testament). Recourse to some such assumptions as those embedded in Dr Jasper's essay is even more obviously required to make sense of the Preface to the *Good News Bible*:

> After ascertaining as accurately as possible the meaning of the original, the translators' next task was to express that meaning in a manner and form easily understood by the readers.... Every effort has been made to use language that is natural, clear, simple and unambiguous.

With such a brief it is little wonder that their Christmas Gospel has the darkness failing, with respect to the light, to 'put it out' rather than master it. But it is difficult to see how any adequate response to Dr Prickett's trenchant objection that 'religion is *not about* things that are natural, clear, simple, and unambiguous' (Prickett, 407) could be mounted without exploring the theological viability of the revisers' linguistic assumptions.

For it is against these assumptions that we must read those apparently concessive remarks by the revisers which recognize the importance of stylistic 'richness'. The official *Commentary* on the so-called 'Series 3' Holy Communion service declares that 'there is a need for richness of association and beauty of sound.... Ideas and emotions must often be expressed through metaphor and image'; and 'we have therefore tried to use language and techniques such as a modern poet might use' (8). Such considerations are spelt out in greater detail in papers by Dr Frost (Frost (I), (II)) invoked by Dr Jasper's Introduction; liturgy, Dr Frost remarks, 'needs to be clear and many-layered', a difficult juxtaposition which is apparently intended to be read in terms of the later 'complexity beneath simplicity', 'richness of implication' and 'pregnant ambiguity' (Frost (II), 162–163). In a companion essay these characteristics are seen as representative of 'the language of poetry' ((I), 25) where 'surface simplicity must conceal further depths' (21), for 'Christians are faced with the task of teaching modern man to think and feel again *through metaphor*' (9). These very strong claims, which on the face of it appear to point away from Dr Jasper's separation of style from meaning, nevertheless need to be read in the light of Dr Frost's conclusion that 'What most people will value is the new *clarity*' (27). Here we have at least verbal agreement between member and chairman of the Liturgical Commission, but whether it is more than this depends on adequate elucidation of what counts as clarity. One suspects that different linguistic assumptions may lie behind Dr Frost's essay from those behind Dr Jasper's, but the need to provide a (comparatively) united front is masking the fact. Often, in reading the writings of the revisers, the impression is given that extraneous considerations dictate the necessity to use certain code words and phrases ('clarity', 'generally understood', 'richness' and so on) but that different writers have access to variant code books. If this is so, then it seems likely that the actual revisions are the outcome of practical compromises between theoretically incompatible assumptions, hence the desirability of taking specific examples of the product of such compromises rather than relying entirely on the revisers' theoretical reflections.

Now much contemporary theology is thoroughly traditional in leaning more towards Dr Frost's integration of thought with imagery and metaphor than to Dr Jasper's separation of meaning from style. Unlike the recent chairman of the Church of England's Liturgical Commission, the chairman of its Doctrine Commission explicitly (if partially) endorses Dr Prickett's critique of the *Good News Bible* translators with their underlying linguistic assumptions (Wiles, 18, 132). If, as a form of somewhat misleading shorthand, we may see the one Commission as representing practice and the other theory, it may be that theory and practice are significantly out of line beneath a veneer of verbal agreement and, in a sense rather different from that of Dr Frost, 'surface simplicity conceals further depths'. For Professor Wiles, the 'theoretical' chairman, 'religious language may appropriately be described as a form of "imaginative construction"' analogous to those of 'literature or poetry', involving 'symbols of that which cannot be directly spoken' (18–19). In support he invokes that seminal Oxford theologian, the late Austin Farrer, who long ago argued that

> Poetry and divine inspiration have this in common, that both are projected in images which cannot be decoded, but must be allowed to signify what they signify of the reality beyond them (Farrer (I), 148; see also Farrer (II), 24–38).

And in the essay cited by Professor Wiles Farrer argued both 'that metaphor, the poet's chosen instrument, is not the language of emotion, but the language of description' and also that metaphor is 'the best means of description' ((II), 29). Such claims, of course, were grounded in his reading of Scripture for, as Farrer was at pains to insist, 'the thought of Christ Himself was expressed in certain dominant images' ((I), 42). With this background it is not surprising to find Professor Wiles upholding a strongly cognitive view of imagination and metaphor.

To support it he looks to the philosophers. Dame Mary Warnock's claim that 'the imagination is the source... of *truth*' (Warnock, 408) is grist to his mill, as is Professor Max Black's 'strong creativity thesis' with regard to metaphor according to which

> some metaphors are what might be called 'cognitive instruments', indispensable for perceiving connections that, once perceived, are *then* truly present (Black (II)).

Professor Black's work, indeed, is a traditional hunting ground for theologians. The late Bishop Ramsey, from whose position Professor Wiles is careful to distinguish his own (Wiles, 26, 134) despite its obvious affinities, made extensive use of some of Black's earlier work on models and metaphors in probably his most sophisticated defence of his 'models and qualifiers' approach to theology (Ramsey, Lecture I). Black's underlying thesis is that certain metaphors cannot be paraphrased into literal language without loss of 'cognitive content', because they operate by means of a type of 'interaction' between 'focus' and 'frame' (in which extra-textual 'associated commonplaces' play an important role) to generate insight that 'plain language' cannot give (Black (I)). Now if 'focus' and 'frame' both represent 'systems' rather than individuals (291) and unique cognitive insight may be generated by holding the two ranges of concepts and related associations together in the imagination, and if—further—the desired interaction is properly affected by the wider context both linguistic and extra-linguistic (287), then it would appear that where the language of imaginative demand with sophisticated contextual cues is operative in an original text—as in my two Biblical examples—then genuine cognitive content is lost in any translation that seeks to be 'clear, simple and unambiguous', or is insensitive to context. It falls under the same codemnation which Black pronounces on any literal paraphrase of an 'interaction' metaphor:

> the relevant weakness... is not that it may be... deficient in qualities of style; it fails to be a translation because it fails to give the *insight* that the metaphor did (293).

III. Philosophy of Language

(i) Strawson's 'Homeric Struggle'

It would be too easy, however, to rest here, for we need to ask what conception of language lies behind Professor Black's position and, indeed, whether it is acceptable. To do this it will be useful to introduce a little, somewhat traditional, terminology. In the general area of the theory of language or semiotics it is conventional to make a threefold division between syntax (the study of formal relations between expressions—such as grammar), semantics (in the narrower sense of that word, which is the study of the relations between linguistic items and the non-linguistic items to which they typically apply), and pragmatics (the study of the relations between linguistic expressions and the use or users of these expressions).

Now one very powerful strand in contemporary philosophy of language sees matters concerning meaning and truth—and hence such notions as 'cognitive content'—as analysable in terms of the first two categories without any essential reference to linguistic use or users. To cite a few familiar oppositions, Saussure's *parole* is parasitic on *langue*, Chomsky's 'performance' on 'competence', Frege's 'associated idea' on his 'sense and reference', and Austin's 'illocutionary force' on his 'locution'. In opposition to this tendency is Black's thesis, which associates certain forms of meaning and cognitive content indissolubly with pragmatic considerations. It would be remarkable if attention to one particular type of one use of language—the metaphorical—were by itself sufficient to overthrow such a general and massively defended position, and of course it does not. I have argued elsewhere (Warner) that the evidence Black adduces in his earlier article can all be accommodated in terms of theories of illocutionary force and that in default of independent demonstration that such pragmatic matters can constitute 'cognitive content' his thesis collapses; Black's work is not the place to look for such a demonstration.

Others, however, have attempted it. Indeed, Professor Sir Peter Strawson sees this debate as lying at the centre of current philosophy. He terms it

the conflict between the theorists of communication-intention and the theorists of formal semantics. According to the former, it is impossible to give an adequate account of the concept of meaning without reference to the possession by speakers of audience-directed intentions of a certain complex kind.... The opposed view...is that....the system of semantic and syntactical rules ...which determine the meanings of sentences is not a system of rules *for* communicating at all. The rules can be exploited for this purpose; but this is incidental to their essential character....

A struggle on what seems to be such a central issue in philosophy should have something of a Homeric quality; and a Homeric struggle calls for Gods and heroes. I can at least, though tentatively, name some living captains and benevolent shades: on the one side, say, Grice, Austin, and the later Wittgenstein; on the other, Chomsky, Frege, and the earlier Wittgenstein (Strawson, 171–172).

Strawson himself sides with the communication-intention theorists who insist that concepts drawn from pragmatics have an irreducible role to play in the theory of meaning. The contemporary research programme he not unreasonably takes as representing formal semantics is that of Professor Donald Davidson. For the latter we understand an indicative sentence if and only if we understand its truth conditions, it is in principle possible recursively to ascribe truth conditions to each of the indicative sentences of a given language L by means of logical machinery adapted from that developed by Tarski, and a theory which does this is a theory of meaning for L; elements of the language which are not indicative sentences are to be construed on the pattern established by those that are (Davidson (I)). This is probably the most influential contemporary variant of the old doctrine that the sense of a sentence is determined by is truth-conditions, a doctrine which—when truth-conditions were construed in terms of verification conditions grounded in sense-experience (an input here derived from pragmatics)—formed the pivot of logical positivism.

Professor Davidson's programme has implications both for the theory of translation and for that of metaphor. So far as translation is concerned, at least in its most radical variety, it is grounded in a truth theory for the target language L supported by stringent specifications of what is to count as empirical evidence and the so-called 'Principle of Charity' to the effect that we should construct our hypotheses in a way that maximizes agreement (Davidson (II)). On such an account cognitive content is carried by the truth theory, thus it is little wonder that he gives Black's account of interaction metaphors short shrift:

> No theory of metaphorical meaning or metaphorical truth can help explain how metaphor works. Metaphor runs on the same familiar linguistic tracks that the plainest sentences do.... What distinguishes metaphor is not meaning but use....
>
> What I deny is that metaphor does its work by having a special meaning, a specific cognitive content (Davidson (III), 43, 46).

On this account style is clearly to be construed as a function of use, meaning is independent of it, and translation is concerned with meaning. Meaning is to be construed in terms of recursively ascribable truth conditions and where an expression fails properly to fit any coherent set we may nevertheless (by virtue of one version of the Principle of Charity) be able to discern what it is 'trying to say' and in our translation reasonably decide not to 'remain on the fence' but rather express that meaning 'clearly'. Here we have substantial intellectual backing for what I earlier, perhaps tendentiously, characterized as the 'revisers' consensus'. If it reinforces the leading assumptions of the old Liturgical Commission (with Dr Frost perhaps dissenting) it is, however, inimical to the programme of the chairman of the Doctrine Commission. Reinforcement here, it would appear, must come from the opposing captains in Strawson's 'Homeric struggle'.

Sir Peter himself attempts to carry the war into the enemy camp. Rather than merely insisting that considerations drawn from pragmatics have an essential role to play in an adequate theory of meaning, in the paper cited earlier he argues that the notion of a truth condition itself depends on such ideas. The concept of truth, when analysed, leads to 'the notion of the *content* of such speech acts as stating'; but this requires us to pay attention to the notions of those speech acts with their audience-directed intentions, thus the theory that meaning is to be elucidated in terms of truth conditions, 'far from being an alternative to a communication theory of meaning, leads us straight in to such a theory of meaning' (Strawson, 180–182). But heroic sorties of this sort do not always achieve their objects. Professor Holdcroft has elegantly demonstrated that the most this kind of move can show is that there is an internal relation between the concept of truth and that of an assertive act, not that the former can be 'explained in terms of' the latter (Holdcroft (I), 6–13). However, even this is some gain, for if there is such an internal relation then a breach appears in the middle wall of partition separating semantics from pragmatics.

The communication-intention theorists Professor Strawson has in mind are probaby best represented by the research programmes emanating from Austin's account of illocutionary force, especially as developed by Professor Searle, and that arising out of Professor Grice's analyses of audience-directed intentions and principles of conversation. For present purposes it will be sufficient to focus on the implications of these programmes for the analysis of metaphor. For Searle, whereas sentence meaning and utterer's meaning are the same in literal discourse in metaphor they come apart, and metaphor represents one subclass of speech acts in which we 'say one thing and mean something else'. There is indeed such a thing as 'metaphorical meaning', but it is located not at the level of sentence meaning but of utterer's meaning (Searle, 76–77). For Davidson, of course, there is only sentence meaning; it is part of the Searlean programme to integrate such elements as utterer's meaning into general semantics.

On Searle's account, in order to understand a metaphorical utterance a hearer requires knowledge of the truth conditions of the sentence—literally construed—some awareness of the conditions of utterance, certain background assumptions shared with the utterer, and a set of shared strategies and principles (in principle specifiable) for relating Black's focus and frame. These considerations, taken together, explain how it is that metaphors are not adequately paraphrasable into literal language; such a paraphrase 'will not reproduce the semantic content which occurred in the hearer's comprehension of the utterance' (Searle, 84–85, 112, 114). On this account, much of the significance for liturgical revision and Biblical translation we noticed with respect to Black's account still has force.

Analogous considerations apply in the case of the Gricean programme. Here analysis of the ways in which intentions interact in communicative discourse has brought into the open a whole set of quasi-logical relationships we had no machinery for handling before, usually called 'implicatures', which are governed by the so-called 'principles of conversation'. Metaphor is analysed in terms of a certain type of flouting of these principles (Grice, 53). Such flouting involves a distinct set of implicatures, so metaphor has clear cognitive significance, and adequate response to the imaginative demands required in any given instance to establish the relevant subset requires attention to context—both linguistic and extra-linguistic. Similar features are to be found in intended cases of ambiguity (54–55).

If the available options in the philosophy of language are to be construed in terms of Strawson's 'Homeric struggle', then it seems clear to me—for reasons admirably set out by Professor Holdcroft ((I), (II))—that the most exposed positions on both sides will have to be given up. The recursive ascription of truth conditions or some analogue appears to be an essential element in any adequately developed semantic theory and, for the sort of considerations outlined earlier, it seems improbable that any such conditions can be fully explicated by communication-intention theory. On the other hand, such pragmatic matters as illocutionary force, intention, principles of conversation and non-verbal context appear to be needed to complete any truth-conditional analysis even at the semantic level. The latter claim is probably even more controversial than the former, so I shall just sketch one line of argument that points in that direction in the context of radical translation or, to use Davidson's preferred term, 'radical interpretation'. As Holdcroft puts it,

Without any theory of communication at all, one is in no position to have a theory about the communicative behaviour of speakers of another language. And without a theory of their communicative behaviour, one is in no position to interpet their utterances by ascribing truth conditions to them. . . .

Radical interpretation always takes place in a context which is assumed to be highly structured, in that a complicated network of connections between the belief expressed by the speaker's utterance, his beliefs about the context, his beliefs about the 'place' of his utterance in a talk-exchange, and the audience's beliefs, are assumed (Holdcroft (II), 195–196).

Davidson's version of the 'Principle of Charity' only appears to do its work of necessary supplementation to truth-conditional analysis by trading on ambiguities that cannot in principle be eliminated within the scope of formal semanticist theory (189–203).

It may be questioned whether the full significance of all this 'complicated network' is adequately catered for by that 'revisers' consensus' I outlined earlier.

(ii) On Avoiding the Sacrifice of Iphigenia

Aeschylus tells us that it was in deciding to sacrifice Iphigenia that Agamemnon put on the harness of necessity which led to the struggle sung by Homer and all that flowed from it (Aeschylus, 218). I have argued that if the philosophy of language is to be construed in Strawson's terms of 'Homeric struggle' then a negotiated settlement seems required. But I confess to a radical unease with the very terms in which much of the current discussion is conducted—which certainly is much as Sir Peter indicates even now, despite the fact that his paper is more than a decade old. My suspicion is that we should refuse the harness of necessity the frameworks I have outlined place upon us, avoid the sacrifice of Iphigenia, and decline to go to Troy at all.

This unease does not arise primarily from the fact that there are certain influential research programmes that need some shoving and hauling to fit into the Strawsonian framework; Professor Dummett's harnessing of broadly verificationalist considerations to an intuitionist logic being the most obvious example. It is rather that the framework of problems in which these debates are fought out has such a dubious provenance yet such extensive influence. It extends, indeed, across the Channel, where Professor Ricoeur's insistence on 'discontinuity between speculative discourse and poetic discourse' (Ricoeur, 258) meets, and in turn is met by, Professor Derrida's attempt to 'substitute another articulation for the . . . classical opposition of metaphor and concept (Derrida (I), 263; see also (II),

11–16). Put at its simplest, this provenance is that of the Enlightenment, with—more specifically—what has been called its 'dissociation of sensibility' (Eliot, 288; for a contemporary discussion of the theological implications of this notion, see Louth). In its linguistic dimension this dissociation had much to do with the language reforms associated with the Royal Society and the project of a universal language or 'character' in which each word would relate to a different idea and the syntax be transparent—and hence controversies expressible in it in principle capable of being settled (cf. Cohen (I) and Slaughter). Leibniz's logical work was in part intended as a contribution to the syntax of the universal character, and although the semantics proved intractable, the logical positivist movement with post-Leibnizian logical syntax providing the framework within which the verification principle did its semantic work is its lineal descendant. It is difficult not to see the whole truth-condition approach to meaning, with its dissociation of imaginative demand from cognitive content or 'literal meaningfulness', as closely associated with this tradition; the use positivism was able to make of it is hardly an accident. And of course, ever since the later work of Wittgenstein, upholders of such 'pragmatic' notions as use, intention, force and communication as essential to semantics have defined their position by reference to the opposed one; without Wittgenstein's *Tractatus* there could hardly have been a *Philosophical Investigations*.

It may, therefore, be wise to look beyond the horizon of the fashionable disputes, and here the work of historians of philosophy can be suggestive. Contemporary Classical scholarship has drawn to our attention linguistic features which fit but uneasily into contemporary categories. In particular, the influential work of the late Professor Owen on the Aristotelian corpus has made the phenomenon of what he called 'focal meaning' of pressing significance; the phenomenon whereby an expression 'has a primary sense by reference to which its other senses can be explained' (Owen (I), 31–32; see also Owen (II)), a subclass of those widespread yet puzzling linguistic phenomena whereby the same expression often has different yet related meanings. From Aristotle to Aquinas, and beyond, the theories philosophers developed to deal with these matters were seen as having decisive implications for the whole of philosophy; Aristotle used his solution to combat Plato's theory of Forms and, under the general rubric of 'analogy', Aquinas rooted his understanding of theological discourse in his variant of the Aristotelian account. But with the Cartesian revolution this set of problems drops out of sight in favour of the mirage of a 'universal character'—though in this century an incipient awareness of something lacking has resurfaced with such concepts as the Rylean 'systematically misleading expressions' and the Wittgensteinean 'family resemblance'. The old Aristotelian solutions are clearly inadequate for a number of reasons, but one may suspect that a renewed and systematic attention to the problems might have significant implications for the philosophy of language.

These suspicions are strengthened by a recent pioneering work that attempts to fulfil just this function. Professor Ross's *Portraying Analogy* argues that the analogy phenomenon applies to all words and thereby throws doubt on the doctrine that sentences have truth conditions that are their senses. The networks of analogy that allow us, for example, to drop stitches, friends, and hints without merely equivocating over the word 'drop' put in serious doubt the possibility of constructing a lexicon, with all the ramifications of meaning each word may have, that would fit into a classical truth-conditional theory for a language L. This is not the place or time critically to assess these claims. But the central intuition looks plausible, so I shall close by outlining how Ross's account bears on the problems with which I have been concerned, in the hope that—to use the Platonic tag (Plato, 114d)—'this or something like it' is the truth.

A key concept in Professor Ross's account is that of a 'benchmark sentence', together with its close cousin a 'benchmark situation'. The former is 'a sentence whose environment fixes the meaning as far as the analysis will require'; the latter is

> an experience or observation or story that provides a stereotype, a paradigmatic case, that fixes the ... linguistic meaning of a predicate ... used to construe it. The facts of the case in law, clinical observations in medicine, a bible story, are examples (Ross, 212).

A further concept is that of 'craftbound discourse', applicable where skill in action is necessary for a full grasp of the discourse (158); it is argued that religious discourse is so 'craftbound', for 'religion is taught in order to modulate living' and 'living in God ... is the object of the craft of Christian doing' (167). Analogy phenomena are a function of linguistic meaning rather than utterer's meaning (11), and operate by means of an interaction between linguistic inertia and linguistic force (3); in craftbound discourse the basic vocabulary is anchored to benchmark situations such as 'Scripture stories' that 'structure and stabilize the central meaning relationships' (158), and the destabilizing 'force' is provided by the way that 'words resist concatenating into unacceptable expressions by making step-wise meaning-adaptations, comparatively to other occurrences, to avoid doing so' (3), thereby generating 'potentially infinite polysemy' (49). On this account truth-conditional analysis is relegated to the status of

167

'an articulation device, instrumental to encompassing strategies
...that determine the units of appropriate logical and conceptual
decomposition' (179); its role in semantics, though important, is not
the pivot on which meaning turns, for 'sentence meaning, antecedent
linguistic meaning, affects truth-conditional analysis. For it is
through the sentence, rather than the statement expressed, that
equivocation and analogy affect expressive capacity' (180). Meaning
is a function of being 'a well-formed and acceptable sentence', and
the criteria of acceptability are provided, at least in part, by
benchmark considerations and related aspects of the analogy phenomena (182). Metaphor is analysed in terms of analogy (109–119)
and thus the well-known problems attendant on locating metaphorical meaning at the level of utterer's meaning rather than sentence
meaning (Cohen (II), 65–66) are avoided; to this extent Ross sides
with Davidson. But by distancing sentence meaning from truth-
conditional analysis in the way he does the semantic door is opened
to considerations which on the old, and by now somewhat myth-
eaten trichotomy, would be counted as belonging to the province of
pragmatics. Indeed, all the old landmarks of Strawson's 'Homeric
struggle' look markedly different in this sort of perspective. Is there
another Troy, one wonders, for us to burn?

At the level of Biblical translation and liturgical revision the
implications of such an account of language could be far-reaching.
The *Good News Bible*'s assault on ambiguity may be seen as showing
a marked preference for 'linguistic inertia' over 'linguistic force', and
talk about 'imaginative demand' construed in terms of the latter
concept. Dropping echoes of the opening of *Genesis* from St John's
Prologue may be construed as representing a decision to weaken the
role of a certain set of Old Testament benchmark sentences in the
Fourth Gospel. And the significance of benchmark situations may
enable my remarks about the non-linguistic context of the words of
distribution to be given linguistic significance.

No such considerations can of themselves be determinative for
revision; but when under-labourers have 'cleared the ground a little'
that ground may look rather different from how it looked before—
and the lie of the land thereby revealed not unreasonably influence
the proceedings of our 'master-builders'.

References

Bibliographical references to the traditional liturgical forms and
Biblical versions have been omitted as otiose; the modern work cited,
however, is listed below.

Aeschylus: 'ΑΓΑΜΕΜΝΩΝ', in *Aeschyli: Septem Quae Supersunt Tragoedias*, Denys Page (ed.) (Oxford: Clarendon Press, 1972).

ASB: *The Alternative Service Book 1980* (Clowes, SPCK and Cambridge University Press, 1980).

Augustine: *The Confessions of St Augustine*, trans. Rex Warner (New York: Mentor Books, 1963).

Barnes: *Articles on Aristotle*, Jonathan Barnes, Malcolm Schofield and Richard Sorabji (eds), 4 vols (London: Duckworth, 1975–1979).

Black (I): Max Black, 'Metaphor', *Aristotelian Society Proceedings* **lv** (1954–55); reprinted in his *Models and Metaphors* (Ithaca, New York: Cornell University Press, 1962).

Black (II): Max Black, 'More about Metaphor', in Ortony.

Buchanan: Colin Buchanan, 'Liturgical Revision in the Church of England in Retrospect', in Stevenson.

Cockerell: David Cockerell, 'Liturgical Language, Dead and Alive', *Theology* **lxxx** (1977).

Cohen (I): Jonathan Cohen, 'On the Project of a Universal Character', *Mind* **lxiii** (1954).

Cohen (II): L. Jonathan Cohen, 'The Semantics of Metaphor', in Ortony.

Commentary: Church of England Liturgical Commission, *A Commentary on Holy Communion Series 3* (London: SPCK, 1971).

Davidson (I) Donald Davidson, 'Truth and Meaning', *Synthese* **xvii** (1967).

Davidson (II): Donald Davidson, 'Radical Interpretation', *Dialectica* **xxvii** (1973).

Davidson (III): Donald Davidson, 'What Metaphors Mean', *Critical Inquiry* **v** (1978).

Derrida (I): Jacques Derrida, 'White Mythology: Metaphor in the Text of Philosophy', in his *Margins of Philosophy*, trans. Alan Bass (Brighton: Harvester, 1982).

Derrida (II): Jacques Derrida, 'The *Retrait* of Metaphor'. Trans. editors. *Enclitic,* **ii** (1978).

Dummett (I): M. A. E. Dummett, 'What is a Theory of Meaning?', in *Mind and Language*, Samuel Guttenplan (ed.) (Oxford: Clarendon Press, 1975).

Dummett (II): Michael Dummett 'What is a Theory of Meaning? (II)', in *Truth and Meaning: Essays in Semantics*, Gareth Evans and John McDowell (eds) (Oxford: Clarendon Press, 1976).

Dummett (III): Michael Dummett, *Truth and Other Enigmas* (London: Duckworth, 1978).

Eliot: T. S. Eliot, 'The Metaphysical Poets', in his *Selected Essays* (London: Faber and Faber, 1951).

Farrer (I): Austin Farrer, *The Glass of Vision* (London: Dacre, 1948).

Farrer (II): Austin Farrer, 'Poetic Truth', in his *Reflective Faith* (London: SPCK, 1972).

Frost (I): David L. Frost, *The Language of Series 3* (Bramcote: Grove Books, 1973).

Frost (II): David L. Frost, 'Liturgical Language from Cranmer to Series 3', in Jasper.

GNB: *Good News Bible* (London: The Bible Societies/Collins/Fontana, 1976).

Grice: H. P. Grice, 'Logic and Conversation', in *Syntax and Semantics.* Vol. 3: *Speech Acts*, P. Cole and J. L. Morgan (eds) (New York: Academic Press, 1975).

Holdcroft (I): David Holdcroft, *Words and Deeds: Problems in the Theory of Speech Acts* (Oxford: Clarendon Press, 1978).

Holdcroft (II): David Holdcroft, 'Principles of Conversation, Speech Acts, and Radical Interpretation', in *Meaning and Understanding*, Herman Parret and Jacques Bouveresse (eds) (Berlin and New York: Walter de Gruyter, 1981).

Jasper: *The Eucharist Today: Studies on Series 3*, R. C. D. Jasper (ed.) (London: SPCK, 1974).

Locke: John Locke, *An Essay Concerning Human Understanding*, A. C. Fraser (ed.), 2 vols (New York: Dover, 1959).

Louth: Andrew Louth, *Discerning the Mystery: An Essay on the Nature of Theology* (Oxford: Clarendon Press, 1983).

Marsh: John Marsh, *The Gospel of St John* (London: Pelican New Testament Commentaries, 1968).

Martin: *No Alternative: The Prayer Book Controversy*, David Martin and Peter Mullen (eds) (Oxford: Blackwell, 1981).

Morris: *Ritual Murder*, Brian Morris (ed.) (Manchester: Carcanet, 1980).

NEB: *The New English Bible* (Oxford and Cambridge: Oxford University Press and Cambridge University Press, 1st edn (New Testament only) 1961; 2nd edn 1970).

Ortony: *Metaphor and Thought*, Andrew Ortony (ed.) (Cambridge: Cambridge University Press, 1979).

Owen (I): G. E. L. Owen, 'The Platonism of Aristotle', in Barnes, Vol. 1.

Owen (II): G. E. L. Owen, 'Logic and Metaphysics in Some Earlier Works of Aristotle', in Barnes, Vol. 3.

Plato: *Plato's Phaedo*, John Burnet (ed.) (Oxford: Clarendon Press, 1911).

P.N. Review: *P.N. Review*, **xiii** (Manchester: Carcanet, 1979).

Prickett: Stephen Prickett, 'What do the Translators Think They are Up To?', *Theology* **lxxx** (1977).

Ramsey: Ian T. Ramsey, *Models and Mystery* (London: Oxford University Press, 1964).

Ricoeur: Paul Ricoeur, *The Rule of Metaphor: Multi-disciplinary Studies of the Creation of Meaning in Language*, trans. Robert Czerny (Toronto, Buffalo and London: University of Toronto Press, 1977).

Robinson: Ian Robinson, 'Religious English', in his *The Survival of English: Essays in Criticism of Language* (Cambridge: Cambridge University Press, 1973; a revised version of a paper first appearing under the same title in *The Oxford Review* for 1968).

Ross: J. F. Ross, *Portraying Analogy* (Cambridge: Cambridge University Press, 1981).

RSV: *The Holy Bible: Revised Standard Version* (London, etc.: Nelson, 1952).

Ryle: G. Ryle, 'Systematically Misleading Expressions', *Aristotelian Society Proceedings* **xxxii,** 1931–32).

Searle: John R. Searle, 'Metaphor', in his *Expression and Meaning: Studies in the Theory of Speech Acts* (Cambridge: Cambridge University Press, 1979; also in Ortony).

Slaughter: M. M. Slaughter, *Universal Languages and Scientific Taxonomy in the Seventeenth Century* (Cambridge: Cambridge University Press, 1982).

Stevenson: *Liturgy Reshaped*, Kenneth Stevenson (ed.) (London: SPCK, 1982).

Strawson: P. F. Strawson, 'Meaning and Truth', in his *Logico-Linguistic Papers* (London: Methuen, 1971).

Temple: William Temple, *Readings in St John's Gospel: First and Second Series* (London: Macmillan, 1945).

Warner: Martin Warner, 'Black's Metaphors', *British Journal of Aesthetics* **xiii** (1973).

Warnock: Mary Warnock, 'Imagination: Aesthetic and Religious', *Theology* **lxxxiii** (1980).

Wiles: Maurice Wiles, *Faith and the Mystery of God* (London: SCM, 1982).

Wittgenstein (I): Ludwig Wittgenstein, *Tractatus Logico-Philosophicus*, trans. C. K. Ogden (London: Routledge & Kegan Paul, 1922).

Wittgenstein (II): Ludwig Wittgenstein, *Philosophical Investigations*, trans. G. E. M. Anscombe (Oxford: Blackwell, 1953).

The Right to Strike

DON LOCKE

I

Only a fool would attempt to discuss the morality of strikes in twenty-five pages or less, and even he will fail. For one thing he can be sure in advance that whatever conclusions he might come to will be ridiculed as outrageous, prejudiced or self-serving by one party or the other. There is, in particular, the accusation that the attempt to discuss in moral terms what is essentially a political issue, is itself an exercise in bourgeois politics disguised as morals, their morals but not ours. But there is also, and more worrying to my mind, the sheer complexity of the issues. This complexity is, however, simply unmanageable in the space available, and I have gone instead for the simple story, in the hope that the essentials will stand out that much more clearly. Whether I have got the right essentials, whether the elegance of the picture compensates for its lack of realism, is something that will have to emerge.

But even at this level of over-simplification, the topic will have to be restricted. So let me point out first of all that I am concerned only with the moral right to strike, whatever that might be, and not with legal rights. That is, I am concerned with whether and when people are morally entitled to strike, or morally justified in striking, not with what their legal rights in striking are, or even ought to be. No doubt moral rights and wrongs should have some effect on the law, but they are not the only factor when it comes to making a political or legislative decision, and I shall leave such questions strictly alone. This means that I will have little if anything to say about some issues which currently bulk large in discussions of the right to strike, such as immunity from damages arising from strike action, or the law of picketing.

Next, the moral issues might be divided into three. There is first the question of the morality of striking as such, the question of how far and in what circumstances people are justified in doing or are entitled to do those things which a strike inevitably involves. After all any strike is a deliberate attempt to inflict harm on others. As such a

This paper has benefited enormously from discussions at the University of Warwick Political Theory Workshop and the University of Birmingham Philosophical Society. I am grateful to all those, too many to mention by name, who took part.

strike, any strike, must be bad, an evil, and needs justification. This is not of course to say that strikes cannot be justified, only that, unlike drinking beer from a wineglass (or vice versa), they need to be.

Then, secondly, there are questions about the conduct of strikes, the question, for example, of how far strikers are entitled to go in attempting to boycott or blockade their place of work. I imagine that for most of us peaceful picketing and passive protest fall on one side of a dividing line, and force and violence against persons and property fall on the other. But what about verbal abuse, threats and intimidation? What about physical intervention that stops short of violence, e.g. blocking a roadway, or interfering with the supply of needed goods and services?

Third, there are questions about the effects of strikes, especially on third parties, both individuals and the community at large. Any strike worth the calling will presumably have an effect not only on those against whom the strike is directed, but also on others, innocent third parties, whose responsibility for or control over the point at issue may be precisely nil. Sometimes, as with strikes of police or the armed forces, the community as a whole may be at risk; sometimes, as with strikes of firemen or ambulance drivers, individual lives may be in danger; sometimes, as with strikes of sewage or power workers, it may be both. And sometimes it may be part of the strikers' explicit intention to cause maximum public inconvenience, so as to produce maximum public pressure on the other side. Can such things be justified, and how?

As it happens it was the last of these issues which originally attracted me to this topic, but as it turns out I shall have time to discuss only the first: what we might call the nature of strikes, as opposed to their conduct and their effects. Obviously what we have to say about this issue should have implications for what we say about the others, and I shall not always be able to resist pointing these implications out. But a more detailed treatment will have to wait till another occasion.

Finally, a strike is not the only weapon in an employee's armoury. There are also go-slows and work-to-rules, boycotts and refusals to do this or that without, however, refusing to work at all. I remember hearing somewhere of a transport workers' dispute where the 'strikers' continued to work as normal, but neglected to collect any fares. That, presumably, was one form of industrial inaction which commanded public support. But for simplicity I am going to concentrate on the strike proper, and on what I take to be the simplest, central case, the 'terms of employment' strike as I shall call it, i.e. the strike where what is at issue is the employee's terms of employment, including their conditions of work as well as their wages. Obviously strikes can be and often are of other sorts. Thus, strikes may involve people who are reasonably content with their own terms of employment, but strike in support of colleagues who are discontented with theirs; and strikes can extend in this way not only to other employees but to other employers and even, as in the case of a general strike, to other employments. And from these sympathy strikes it is only a short step to protest strikes, where the strikers' objection is not to their terms of employment but to their employers' policies, for example their trading with or investing in various businesses or countries, or expanding or contracting in various places or directions. From here again it may be only a short step to political strikes, directed not at the employer as such but against some government policy, whether it be nuclear deterrence, immigration controls, the legalization of abortion or anything else. The boundaries between these different types of strike may sometimes be hard to draw, but that need not detain us. My main concern is with strikes over the terms of employment; and I shall deal with sympathy, protest and political strikes only in passing.

II

Having said something about strikes I should now say something about rights. I confess, however, that I have no theory of rights to offer: I do not really know what a right is, or where it comes from; I find the voluminous literature on the topic almost wholly unrewarding, and the manifold distinctions and divisions of rights, into natural and acquired, positive and negative, active and passive, special and general, claims and liberties, privileges and powers, permissions and entitlements, almost wholly unilluminating. It is the fashion in moral philosophy these days to appeal to rights as some sort of trumps, a court of last resort, a point at which the argument must stop: if something is your right, or infringes a right, then there is apparently not much else to be said about it. But if rights are to be invoked in this way then we need to be told what they are and where they come from, how they are to be justified and explained. Without that, it seems to me, the appeal to rights is mere rhetoric, at best a shorthand for what can be said more plainly in other terms. In particular, to say that people ought to retain or be given something because it is their right, is not really to explain why they ought to have it, but merely to repeat, in more resounding terms, the claim that they ought to have it. In fact, personally, this seems to have it the wrong way round: the right depends on the 'ought', not the other way about; it is their right because they ought to have it, not 'They ought to have it because it is their right'.

There are, however, two important features of rights, as I dimly understand them, which I intend to invoke by using this terminology, despite my qualms. The first is that you can be within your rights and still be wrong, factually or morally. To put it enigmatically, any right must be a right of doing wrong; or more epigrammatically, the function of a right is to make all right what otherwise might not be right at all. If something is already right, either permitted or required, then you need no right to justify your doing it. We claim a right as a justification for doing something only if what we are doing would be morally questionable in the absence of that right. So if, for example, parents have the right to bring up their children in whatever way they think fit, this means that they should be allowed to bring up their children as they please, even if what they do is mistaken or misguided.

This does not of course mean that anything they might propose to do, however wrong, can be justified by that right. For that the right in question would have to be absolute or unlimited. More typically rights have to be weighed against other rights, and against other values more generally; and sometimes other wrongs can outweigh a right: parents' rights may have to be overridden, to prevent a greater wrong. Nevertheless, if a right is to be overriden or infringed in this way, that needs to be justified, and justified not simply by the wrong that is prevented, but by the wrong that is prevented outweighing the wrong of infringing or overriding the right. That is, the infringing of a right has to be justified as the lesser of two evils. And where, conversely, it is the infringing of the right that is the greater evil, then the right in question has to be a right of doing wrong.

Thus a right is best thought of as an entitlement, a permission to do what might otherwise be wrong. But—and this is the second feature of rights I wish to emphasize—a right is also more than a permission: it is what I will call, with due apologies, an 'obligated permission'. That is, to claim a right is, as I see it, to claim that you *ought* to be allowed to do or have something, should you want it: if you have a right to something then others should not attempt to prevent you from doing or having it; and if they do, they are at the very least in the wrong. Indeed the point of an appeal to rights is typically that those who try to prevent you should be prevented in their turn: there is a requirement on others to let you do or have that to which you have a right; and this in turn may involve a requirement on others to prevent anyone who is trying to prevent you from doing or having it. The right to free speech, for example, does not merely mean that you may say whatever you like. It also means that others should not try to stop you saying whatever you like; and if they do, it is they who should be stopped, not you.

This, then, is what I mean by an 'obligated permission'. I apologize for the barbarism, but it seems to me to imply—what 'obligatory permission' does not—that the obligation is not on the person who has the right, but on others, to see that he is allowed to retain or acquire that to which he has the right. No doubt some will object that this is true only of rights in the stronger sense of 'protected' rights, or privileges, not in the weaker sense of rights as permissions or liberties. The idea here seems to be that anything which is permissible or allowed is something to which we have a right, on the grounds, apparently, that if something is morally neutral or indifferent then we need no further authority or permission to do it. Thus we have a right to do anything which is not explicitly forbidden: all behaviour is innocent until declared guilty, not the other way around. But it seems clear to me that a right must be more than a mere permission. It may, for example, be permissible for me to join a certain club or organization, in the sense that I do no wrong if I do, without my having the right to belong. This is because if other people, e.g. the existing members, wish to prevent my joining, they may. If instead, I were to claim that they ought to let me join, and therefore should not be blackballing me, I would be claiming not merely that it is permissible for me to join, but the right to belong. Similarly any student is permitted to get First Class Honours, in the sense that they do no wrong if they do, but they none of them have the right to a first class degree, not even those who do get one. All that they have—and it should enough—is the right to be awarded First Class Honours if their work is of the appropriate standard. And that is not just a permission, it is their right.

One reason for confusing rights with permissions may be that a difference in the content of various rights is mistaken for a difference in the nature of those rights. Imagine a university, unfortunately not my own, where a number of car-parking spaces are available to all, on a first-come first-served basis, but where each professor has his own designated place. The sense in which I would then have the right to park in this particular place, which has my name on it, seems obviously stronger than the sense in which you, poor mortal, have the right to park wherever else you can find room. Indeed the latter, it seems, is not a right in my sense at all, i.e. not an 'obligated permission', since there is no requirement on others not to prevent you from parking in this place or that, for example by getting there before you. Your right, it seems, is merely a permission or a liberty, not a protected right or privilege like mine. But the difference lies not in the nature of our two rights, but in their content: yours is a right to park there, provided you get there first; mine is a right to park here, whenever I arrive (perhaps not such a good idea after all, as it tends to make absences conspicuous). Apart from that the two rights and their implications are the same. In particular, if you do have a right to park in any undesignated space, provided you get there first, then others ought to allow you to do so: they ought not prevent you, and if they do they should be prevented in their turn, provided, that is, that you did get there first. Your right, no less than mine, is an obligated permission. It is just more limited than mine.

Thus the right to strike, if such there be, should consist in the fact that people ought to be allowed to go on strike. That is, they should not be prevented from going on strike, if that is what they want to do; and if others do try to prevent them, e.g. by restrictive legislation, then it is those others, not they, who are in the wrong. Moreover, and more crucially, they ought to be allowed to go on strike even if they are in the wrong, whether mistaken or misguided, at least up to the point where the wrong that they do by going on strike is greater than the wrong involved in infringing or overriding that right to strike. This, as I understand it, is what is claimed by the moral, as opposed to the legal, right to strike.

But where does this right come from, how is it to be explained or justified? And what, more exactly, is it a right to do? The right to strike is, of course, a right to *strike*. But what, more exactly, is a strike, and a terms of employment strike in particular?

III

One swallow does not make a summer, nor does one non-worker make a strike. Even if any number of employees get fed up, give up, get up and go home, that need not be a strike. They may merely be abandoning this job for another, or for no job at all. Even if they then attempt to persuade others not to take that job in their place, even if they put pressure on others so as to prevent that job from being done at all, even that is not necessarily a strike. Workers in a medical laboratory who, sickened by what they are asked to do, join the Anti-Vivisection League and picket their former place of employment in the hope of preventing such experiments from being carried out in future are not, strictly, on strike. It would be a strike only if they claimed that the jobs in question were still theirs, so that anyone else who did that job in their place would be taking their job from them. What the striker objects to, apparently, is not the job as such, but the conditions under which it is done or the reward that it brings, what I am calling 'the terms of employment'. This distinction between the job itself and its terms of employment may not always be clear, but in going on strike as opposed to resigning in protest, the striker in effect draws it: he accepts, indeed retains, the job as such, but he rejects the terms of employment.

Now what, in this, requires justification? The mere withdrawal of labour, the refusal to continue working on the terms currently on offer, I take it does not: particular contracts and special agreements aside, there seems no general requirement that people work on terms they find unacceptable, or for that matter that they work at all. Admittedly there is in the meagre philosophical and moral literature on this topic a double argument, 'perhaps too slender to be pushed unduly', that no man can lay claim to the right to refuse work at all times and on any grounds, however, trivial. Stating this largely in the author's own words (Kirk, 1927, pp. 355–356), one argument is that inasmuch as an artist or statesman is not justified in depriving the community of his talents by withdrawing into a life of cultured or selfish ease before his period of active work could reasonably be thought to have ended, the same requirement should also apply to the less talented artisan. The other argument starts from the assumption that those who withhold their labour have no right of being supported in voluntary idleness except from private means (!) or savings previously accumulated, and then argues that since society tolerates, approves and in some small measure legislates that each man should have an income in excess of his immediate needs in order to provide for sickness, old age and the requirements of family life, the use of these savings to enable him to cease work on insufficient grounds or before his normal time of retirement therefore constitutes an abuse—though not perhaps, in an ordinary and isolated case a serious abuse—of the tolerance and approval which society has conferred upon his opportunities for saving. These arguments date, significantly, from the time of the General Strike. They are, I take it, the sort of thing which gives casuistry (see the book's sub-title) a bad name.

But a strike is not simply a refusal to do some job yourself. Typically it also involves the withdrawal of labour by a body of employees acting in consort. So in the traditional terminology a strike is a combination, perhaps even a conspiracy. But combinations, similarly, do not seem to need justifying, at least not in principle: surely people are entitled to combine, even conspire, together in all sorts of ways, whether it be to throw a party or play Beethoven's Fifth? What will need justification, if anything does, is what they combined to do, not the fact of combination itself.

So the objection has to be not that strikes are combinations, but that they are combinations in restraint of trade, monopolistic interferences with the free market economy. One obvious reply to this is that the free market economy is not necessarily, in and by itself, a good thing, nor are cartels and monopolies necessarily bad: the free market economy is good only because of the benefits it brings, and interferences with it can easily be justified, either because they avoid the disadvantages or harms which free markets also produce, or because they bring even greater benefit. But to argue in this way, that some combinations in restraint of trade can be justified, is of course to concede the main point at issue, that combinations in restraint of trade do need to be justified. The more radical objection would be that the free market is not, even in general, a good thing, so that what need to be justified are the occasions on which it is allowed to operate, not those on which it is prevented from operating. Such an argument is of course possible, indeed familiar, but I will not pursue it here. After all it seems perfectly possible for one man to go on strike all by himself, either because he is a firm's only employee, or because he is the only employee who objects to his terms of employment. If that is so then the objection to combinations must be an objection to the way strikes are conducted, in particular to unionization, and not to strikes as such. In other words these issues of combinations, monopolies and cartels in the supply of labour, seem to relate more directly to the question of unions, and especially the closed shop, than to the question of strikes as such. Not that the two are entirely distinct: strikes and unions ultimately depend on each other for their power and effectiveness. But the issues now being raised are becoming too complex and too general to be dealt with here, and I pass by, hurriedly, on the other side.

In any case it seems to me that the relevant objection is not that strikes are a combination or conspiracy, but that they are a boycott. Boycotts, like cartels, may be good and they may be bad, though with boycotts it is, as we shall see, a matter more of causes than effects. But at least it seems clear that boycotts need to be justified, not because they interfere with the free market economy, but because they involve the deliberate infliction of harm and suffering on their object, and perhaps others as well. And that is not all.

What is boycotted in a strike is not goods or services, but a job, or set of jobs. Typically the strikers attempt to see to it that a particular job is not done, perhaps by persuading others not to do it, perhaps by preventing it from being done at all. Hence the familiar apparatus and ideology of strikes, the picket line and the appeal to union solidarity, the attempt to prevent not only blacklegs but essential goods and services from going into the place of employment, and the attempt to ensure that those not directly involved in the dispute at least do nothing in their own employment to enable the disputed job to be carried on. In practice a strike is often not so much a boycott as a blockade.

But this is not strictly necessary to a strike. For one thing, the strikers may be positively relieved to find that essential and emergency services, in particular, do continue in their absence, provided that the arrangement is explicitly understood to be temporary, for the duration of the dispute only, and preferably conducted only at great inconvenience—and, even better, cost—to their employers. For another, they may be positively delighted to discover that the jobs which they object to have to be done in their absence by the management, who for these purposes get cast in the role of bosses. What the strikers insist on, rather, is that even if the job has still to be done, even if they are prepared to permit it to be carried on in their absence, it nevertheless should not be taken from them, because it is still their job. Thus strikers may or may not attempt to prevent that job from being done at all, but what they must certainly object to, what they must certainly attempt to prevent, if they are to count as striking in the first place, is others taking that job from them, whether it be by employing other people in their stead, or by moving the work, and therefore the job, to another place, or even, as in the case of multinationals, another country.

So what is distinctive about a strike is, as I suggested before, the refusal to do a particular job, combined with the insistence that that job is none the less still yours. Now this in itself seems curious enough to require some explanation: how can someone be entitled to claim a job as his, when he isn't willing to do it? Surely if he doesn't want to do it and others do, then it should be their job, not his? But what seems to require justification is the apparent consequence of this, the attempt to prevent others from taking that job, even though they might be willing, even eager, to do it in the striker's place. Surely this is an unjust restriction of liberty, the liberty of employers to employ, the liberty of workers to work? If there is, as many claim, a right to work, how can there be a right to strike, a right, that is, to prevent others working, when they are both willing and able?

Thus a strike is not just a boycott, it is an enforced boycott, an attempt to force others to join in the boycott, even though they might be perfectly willing to take that job on the terms which the striker rejects. Of course, if it were simply a matter of persuading others not to take that job, that would hardly need justification. Presumably one man may attempt to persuade another of just about, but not quite, anything he pleases. Indeed, if strikers succeed in persuading someone not to take a job, they are not in any obvious sense preventing them from taking it. What needs justifying, rather is the attempt to prevent someone from taking a job, after you have failed to persuade him not to. Much depends, of course, on the form which the prevention takes: for most of us there will be some limit somewhere, beyond which we think strikers should not go; and I have already said that I will not attempt the perhaps impossible task of determining where that limit should be. But what does seem clear to me is that, of necessity, a strike goes beyond merely attempting to persuade people not to break the strike; to use a suitably vague phrase, it involves putting pressure on those who would break the strike, to make it difficult or unpleasant for them to do so. That, surely is what the apparatus and ideology of strikes is for: not just to persuade non-strikers so that they willingly accept whatever restrictions the strikers seek to impose; but to put pressure on them so that unwillingly, if needs be, they decline to break the strike, for fear of public criticism and condemnation, of calumny and obloquy, to put it no higher.

There are of course those who think that a strike should be restricted to the attempt to persuade. But if I am right this attempt to restrict strikers to friendly persuasion is an attempt to prevent a strike from being a strike, and therefore an infringement on the right to strike as such, if such there be. Indeed, since the right to persuade seems, like the right to withdraw your labour and the right to combine, at least in some things, a right which we surely have whether there is a right to strike or not, it is only this right to prevent which provides a distinctive, substantive component to the right to strike as such. (More accurately, it is a right to attempt to prevent. The right to persuade, similarly, is a right to attempt to persuade, or else those who are not persuaded have infringed your rights!) So this is the right which needs to be explained and justified: not just the boycott, but the enforced boycott.

IV

What I have said so far will seem to many unnecessarily vague and theoretical. Whatever it might be in theory, a strike is in practice a war, or at any rate a battle, between opposing forces, with each side using whatever means it can to inflict maximum damage on the other, in the hope of bringing it to its knees or at least to the negotiating table. More exactly, each side hopes to gain more in the long term, and not necessarily for itself alone, than it stands to lose in the short run. But to achieve this, each side hopes to inflict more damage on the other than it does on itself. Thus strikes are bad not only in their effect, which is the infliction of harm on both parties, but also in their intention, the intention being precisely that: the infliction of harm. Moreover, those who suffer this harm need not be restricted to the other party to the dispute; and as we have seen even this may be part of the strikers' explicit intention. This, surely, is what needs to be justified, not simply the attempt to prevent some few people from taking a job that they want?

Not surprising, therefore, that the most popular justification of strikes, in the meagre moral literature on the topic, is by analogy with a just war: the 'just war' justification, as I shall call it (cf. Manning, 1891; Kirk, 1927). Traditionally this doctrine of a just war has two parts: the *jus ad bellum* or justice of waging a war, and the *jus in bello* or justice in waging a war. We are here concerned only with the first of these, which is in turn traditionally divided into three components: a just cause, a good intention, and proper authority. Let us, for simplicity, take the second and third of these for granted; so a war, or a strike, will be justified if the cause is just. But what, exactly, constitutes a just cause?

Traditionally there is no general answer to this question. What happens instead is that particular causes are specified as just, case by case. The most familiar of these is self-defence, but there are others: provocation which stops short of actual aggression, the breaking of treaties, the protection of nationals in foreign territories. If we had to provide some general characterization I suppose it would involve something like the right of each nation to protect its vital national interests. But this does not by itself necessarily justify war: the interests at stake also have to be sufficiently important, the breach of them sufficiently grave, to justify so extreme a measure as war.

Notice too that the just cause justification appears to allow that both sides can be justified in fighting. It at first seems that if one side is in the right, the other must be in the wrong. But there is of course the possibility that both sides are in the wrong; and even the possibility, explicitly allowed by some just war theorists, that both causes might be just. Typically, of course, both sides will claim that their cause is just, and it may be difficult for an impartial outsider to decide between them. But since vital national interests can and do conflict, will there not be cases where both sides can claim, quite correctly, to be defending vital national interests? Or if one side is provoked into invading the other, is not the other justified in fighting back? Or if the claim to some piece of territory is obscure, and arguable on both sides, might not both sides be justified in waging war over it, in defence of their sovereignty? You might think, perhaps, of certain windswept islands in the South Atlantic.

The important point, however, is that a just cause justification has to be distinguished from what I will call a 'lesser evil' justification. That is, the mere fact that war would involve less evil than the failure to fight does not by itself provide a just cause. In particular, one country is not justified in interfering in the internal affairs of another, not even to right a wrong: one country is not, for example, justified in invading another to protect the latter's citizens against an unjust and despotic government (think of Russia under Stalin, Germany under Hitler, Uganda under Amin). Even today, when a small Caribbean island is invaded by the most powerful nation on earth, the official justification, at least initially, has to be that it was necessary to protect the citizens of the larger power who happened to be on that island.

Moreover, the appeal to the lesser of two evils is not only not sufficient to provide a just cause justification, it is not even necessary. That is, provided that a nation has a just cause then, by the just war doctrine, it is entitled to go to war even if the result is to produce more harm, not less, i.e. even if less harm would be done, all things considered, by peacefully submitting. In particular, if a war is to be justified as the lesser of two evils then it must first and foremost be successful: a war which failed to secure the good or right outcome would merely compound the evil. But this too is no part of the just war doctrine: a war is justified not by its results, nor even its success, but by the justice of the cause. This means explicitly that a nation can be justified in going to war, in self-defence or in defence of some vital interest, even when it stands no chance of winning. Thus the British invasion of the Falklands, if justified by a just cause, would still have been justified even if the results had been much more disastrous than, thank God, they were; and would have been no less justified if it had failed, or even if—as at one time seemed likely—it was bound to fail.

Turning now from wars to strikes, the most obvious justification, once again, seems to be self-defence. It may not be the only one: exploitation, victimization, unfair dismissal, the non-recognition of unions, and so on, might all be seen as providing a just cause, and hence as justifying strike action. And if the just war analogy can thus justify protest strikes, it seems that it can also justify sympathy strikes, provided that common interests are at stake, just as one nation may ally itself with another even if it is not itself attacked, or even provoked (I think of New Zealand in both world wars). Even so there will be limits. To adapt what was said in the case of wars: a just cause seems to involve something like the right of employees to protect their legitimate interests, but the breach of this right does not by itself constitute a just cause: the interests at stake have to be sufficiently important, the breach of them sufficiently grave, to justify so extreme a measure as a strike. Moreover some protest strikes, having to do for example with the employers' trading with or investing in various countries, would seem not to be justified, as not involving matters which directly affect the employee's interests, as opposed, perhaps, to their desires. Nor would purely political strikes be justified, not only because the point at issue is not strictly an issue between employees and employers, but also—to invoke a feature of the traditional *jus ad bellum* which I earlier put to one side—because it is not clear that either side has proper authority in the matter.

But I am now trespassing into areas I promised not to invade, so let us concentrate on the most obvious and for our purposes most relevant just cause, self-defence. A man's wages 'must be sufficient to enable him to maintain his wife and children in reasonable comfort', said Pope Leo XIII in 1891, and seemed to imply that if they are not, then he is entitled to strike. But this seems to apply only to those whose terms of employment do not allow them even an adequate standard of living. It is not clear that anyone who already enjoys a reasonable standard of living could justify a strike in the name of self-defence, no matter how unjustly he might regard himself as treated by comparison with others: unfair treatment does not in itself constitute an infringement of vital interests, nor justify a response in the name of self-defence. So it might seem that in a welfare state, which guarantees for everyone whatever is currently regarded as the minimum acceptable standard of living, no one could have this justification for striking. Certainly Kenneth Kirk, Bishop of Oxford, writing before the welfare state but after a general strike, comes explicitly to the conclusion that

> We may indeed doubt whether, under modern conditions, the worst grievances of any existent body of workmen approximate even remotely to such a degree of gravity as would justify 'war' on the scale of a general strike (1927, p. 361),

and if no existing grievances could justify a general strike then, it is not clear that any current grievances could justify so much as a local strike now.

However, Cardinal Manning, interpreting Leo XIII, is prepared to be more generous:

> A man has a right and an absolute liberty to work for such wages as he thinks just, and to refuse to work for less. Men have both the right and liberty to unite with others of the same trade or craft and to demand a just wage for their labour. If this just wage is refused, he has both right and liberty to refuse to work—that is to strike.

185

7

> Leo XIII fully recognizes this liberty. So long as the cause is just, the right to strike is undeniable. He 'is free to work or not' (1891/1901, p. 14).

Unfortunately Manning here fails to distinguish between the right to refuse to work and the right to strike: does the fact that you have a right not to work for wages you consider unjust mean that you have a right to go on strike if you think your wages unjust, or only if they actually are unjust? He also greatly exaggerates Leo's position: *pace* Manning (1891/1901, p. 15), 'On the liberty of strike, Leo XIII is equally explicit', it might be more accurate to say that, on such matters, the encyclical is explicitly inexplicit. Leo does insist that because of the necessity for, and the natural law of, self-preservation, workers are entitled to a basic subsistence wage ('remuneration ought to be sufficient to support a frugal and well-behaved working man' (1891/1928, p. 40)), and that 'all may justly strive to better their condition' (1891/1928, p. 35). But rather than drawing the conclusion that workers are therefore entitled to strike if these conditions are not satisfied, Leo says instead that 'the law should be beforehand and prevent these troubles from arising' (1891/1928, p. 36). Moreover, and one gets the impression more importantly, as well as intervening and so taking away the need for strikes, the law should also intervene to prevent strikes getting out of hand ('neither justice nor the common good allows any individual to seize upon that which belongs to another, or, under the futile and shallow pretext of equality, to lay violent hand on other people's possessions...' (1891/1928, pp. 35–36)). So for Leo, evidently, industrial disputes should be settled by legislation, not strike action: 'If by a strike, or other combination of workmen, there should be imminent danger of disturbance to public peace; ... or if employers laid burdens upon their workmen which were unjust, or degraded them in conditions repugnant to their dignity as human beings'—or for that matter in any number of other conditions, including 'if in workshops or factories there were danger to morals through the mixture of the sexes or from other harmful occasions of evil'—then 'in such cases there can be no question but that, within certain limits, it would be right to invoke the aid and authority of law' (1891/1928, pp. 34–35).

Nevertheless it is clear that Manning believes—and believes that Leo XIII believes—that if your wages are unjust you have a just cause, and are therefore justified in striking. But what constitutes a just wage? Here too Manning believes that

> The Encyclical has given a very explicit and definite answer. It is impossible to define the maximum. It is only necessary to define the minimum ... It must be sufficient to maintain a man and his

home ... Beyond this it is impossible to go. Every kind of industry and labour, skilled and unskilled, in all the diversities of toil and danger, will have its special claims; but the lowest line is the worker and his home (1891/1901, pp. 14–15).

Manning glosses this, however, as meaning that the minimum just wage must therefore be the same for all: 'This does not mean a variable measure, or a sliding scale according to the number of children, but a fixed average sum' (1891/1901, p. 14). He notices one consequence of this: 'It follows, therefore, that an employer who would take single men without homes at a lower wage would commit a social injustice, full of immoral and dangerous consequences to society' (1891/1901, p. 15); but seems not to notice, or at any rate does not discuss, another more obvious consequence, that by this reckoning the minimum just wage will inevitably be below the level needed to support any family which is larger than average. There is of course an argument that larger than average families deserve to be penalized, but this is not an argument you would expect to occur to someone in 1891, and to a Cardinal least of all.

More curiously still, Leo XIII accepts that a minimum wage should permit a man to save, and even acquire property; but instead of seeing this as a reason for fixing the minimum somewhere above what is necessary for subsistence, he insists instead that it should be possible for 'a sensible man to study economy' even within a subsistence income: 'he will not fail, by cutting down expenses, to put by some little savings and thus secure a small income' (1891/1928, p. 40)! But it would be unfair to poke too much fun for scorn at these thinkers from another era. Although Leo XIII is much less explicit than Cardinal Manning, both on the right to strike and on what Manning calls 'the despotism of capital', the concern of both men for the condition of the working classes as they saw it is real and manifest, especially in their rejection and condemnation of the idea that a just wage might be determined by the 'free' but binding consent of both parties, in accordance with the laws of supply and demand. This argument, says Leo, is 'by no means convincing' (1891/1928, p. 39). Manning, typically, is much more outspoken (1891/1901, pp. 15–16).

But what hardly needs emphasizing in all this is that the concern seems to be with the bare minimum necessary for survival: not so much self-defence as self-preservation, or what the lawyers call necessity. Admittedly Manning explicitly allows that a just wage may be greater in some employments than in others, but he gives no indication how to determine a just wage in these other cases, and the implication still seems to be that it is only when your terms of employment are just about as bad as they can possibly be, that you are justified in striking.

This brings me to a second, more general difficulty with the just war justification, as applied to strikes. According to this analogy a strike is justified when its cause is just, and the means adopted no more than is justified by the justice of that cause. But there is first the difficulty, and often the impossibility, of deciding whether the cause is just, let alone sufficiently just to justify the strike. This is particularly obvious in the case favoured by Manning, the demand for a just, or fair, wage. Whether a particular rate for the job is or is not fair, of course, something on which people may legitimately differ: in most actual cases, a wage which seems manifestly unjust by comparison with others more favoured, can also be made to seem manifestly more than just, by comparison with others even less favoured still. It says something for society's view both of women and the caring professions that the one clear exception to this general rule, the profession whose claim to be under-rewarded seems invariably to be indisputable, having regard either to its social importance or the terms of its employment, is the profession of nursing.

More typically, however, it is by no means clear whether a wage is unjust, and a strike therefore justified. This might not seem to matter: is it not just a fact of life that people do disagree, radically and sometimes violently, about whether a particular strike is justified? Is this not just the sort of thing which is, and has to be, ultimately a matter of opinion? But the question is not whether a particular group of strikers is in the right—that, assuredly, is something over which there can be radical, irresoluble disagreement—but what they are entitled to do. It is no help to society or the law to say that they are entitled to strike if their wage is unjust, but not if the wage they reject is a fair rate for the job, if there is then no agreed method for determining what a just or a fair wage might be. Indeed, if there were some agreed method for determining a just or fair wage, e.g. an appeal to some wages or incomes authority, then surely the appeal to that authority ought to take the place of strike action, since no strike could be justified which contravened its decisions!

Behind this difficulty lies a more fundamental one: that this just war or just cause justification does not, in fact, provide a right to strike at all. 'So long as the cause is just', said Cardinal Manning, 'the right to strike is undeniable' (1891/1901, p. 114); and implies thereby that where the cause is not just, there is no right to strike. But in that case it is not, strictly, a right at all: if something is already right, you need no right to justify doing it; you need a right to justify what you do only if what you do would otherwise, in the absence of that right, be wrong. As I put it earlier, a right is a right of doing wrong, and the right to strike therefore means that people are entitled to strike even if they are not in the right, even if they are mistaken or misguided. And this is precisely what the just cause justification does not provide: people are justified in striking if, but only if, their cause is just.

Now there is a way (suggested to me by Barrie Falk) of solving both these difficulties together, by trading them off one against the other. It is, it may be said, precisely because it is a matter of opinion about which people may legitimately disagree, whether or not a particular cause is just, that individuals are entitled to act on the belief that their cause is just, even if they happen to have got it wrong, at least in our opinion. In the absence of a suitable authority, individual opinion must reign supreme, and people are therefore entitled to act on their own opinion, right or wrong. But this seems to me a rather weak justification of the right to strike, a justification out of ignorance as it were. It may be significant that there seems no corresponding right to war. Various people may or may not have the right to declare a war, just as various peole may or may not have the right to declare a strike. This is presumably the requirement of proper authority, referred to above. But there seems to be no right to war as such: nations are not entitled to go to war, right or wrong, or just because they think they have a just cause, whether they really have one or not; in going to war over some issue a nation can be doing what it has no right to do, not because it infringes other rights, but because it had no right to fight over that issue in the first case. But I admit I am not clear about this, and there are other justifications of the right to strike to consider.

V

In the previous section I distinguish a 'just war' justification from a 'lesser evil' justification of strikes and wars. The traditional just war doctrine would not regard a war, or a strike, as justified merely because it is necessary to avert a greater evil; and conversely, you might be justified in waging a war, or a strike, even though there would be less harm or suffering if you did not. In particular, the justification for fighting a war or a strike does not depend on the likelihood of success: if your cause is just you are entitled to fight, even if it seems certain that you will fail. But having distinguished the two, we should now consider a lesser evil justification of strikes: the claim that bad though they may be, strikes can nevertheless be justified as the lesser of two evils, in that the effect of not striking would be even worse. Note that this means that a strike can be justified only if it seems likely to succeed, or at least likely to result in better terms than could be achieved without strike action, though it also means that those terms must be sufficiently better to outweigh any damage caused by the strike itself.

This might at least seem to have the advantage of realism. Surely no one is going to fight a strike which they seem bound to lose; surely neither side will embark on a strike unless they feel sufficiently confident of gaining more than they stand to lose. But there is a crucial difference here. What actually motivates a strike may be some calculation, on both sides, of the likely costs and benefits, if not to themselves alone then at least to those who might broadly be construed as being on the same side, employers or employees as the case may be. But the moral justification will depend on a calculation of the costs and benefits to all affected parties, and innocent third parties as well as those directly involved in the dispute. So a strike might be sound sense, in the sense of rational self-interest, yet not be morally justified as the lesser of two evils. And, just possibly, vice versa.

Now a lesser evil justification, it seems to me, is in some respects more generous than a just war justification, but in others less so. It is more generous in that it sets no limits in principle to either the issues or the terms on which a strike may be fought, provided always that the end result is better than would otherwise have been the case. There is therefore no reason why strikes should be restricted to points at issue between employers and employees: a purely political strike could still be justified, provided that the results are good overall, where this good could consist merely in bringing some matter to public attention, and not necessarily an immediate change in the disputed policy. Similarly there seems no reason why strikers should restrict themselves to peaceful or even lawful means: since, on this justification, success is the essence, strikers will be justified in using whatever means may be necessary to ensure victory, always provided that any harm is in the end outweighed by the good that is achieved thereby. On this justification it is the results that count, and anything can be justified, provided it is necessary to achieve the best possible balance of good over bad.

But while this lesser evil justification may be more generous in principle, it may also be more restrictive in practice. Remember that no strike seems likely to succeed unless it inflicts unacceptable damage on the other side and, inevitably therefore, on third parties as well; remember too that the lesser evil justification depends on a calculation of harms and benefits to all affected parties, and not just those directly involved in the strike; and it begins to seem doubtful whether any strike, other than a purely token one, could ever be justified in this way. No doubt those who take strike action would often suffer unfairly if they did not. But if the justification of strike action is in terms of the lesser evil overall, and not the justice of the cause, it is not at all clear that the disadvantages they suffer could justify, i.e. outweigh, the disadvantages which a strike inevitably imposes on others. I do not say that it is impossible ever to justify a real, as opposed to a token, strike in this way; but I do say that it is going to be difficult. This is why it is important to distinguish the just cause from the lesser evil justification.

However, the main objection is that like the just war justification, this too fails to justify a right to strike. On this account a strike is justified when, but only when, striking produces less harm, less evil, all things considered, than the failure to strike. At first sight this too seems to be something on which different individuals will have very different opinions, with no obvious way of deciding between them. But as I have just suggested, if we lift our eyes from the details of the particular calculation and consider instead what the overall result seems likely to be, all things considered, we might find it surprisingly easy to agree that, on those grounds at any rate, no strike is justified. The objection is, rather, that if there is a right to strike then it is a right to strike even if you have got it wrong, even if you are mistaken in thinking that the harms which will result for you if you do not strike outweigh, and therefore justify, the harms that will result for others if you strike.

Where both the just war and the lesser evil accounts go wrong, it seems to me, is in failing to distinguish between the justification of particular strikes, and a justification of the right to strike; or to use the terminology which I will prefer, between justification and entitlement. The right to strike does not, of course, mean that every strike is justified. As I have insisted, the right to strike is a right to strike right or wrong. In other words, you can be entitled to strike, even when a strike is not justified. An adequate account of the right to strike must therefore be in two parts: first, a justification of what in strikes needs justifying; and second, an explanation of what entitles people to strike even when no strike is justified.

VI

Earlier we noticed two things in the very nature of strikes, as opposed to their conduct and effect, which seemed to require moral justification. The first was that strikes are a boycott, involving the deliberate infliction of harm on others, including innocent third parties. The second was that strikes are an attempt to enforce this boycott, and therefore an attempt to prevent people doing what they would otherwise be minded to do. These, apparently, are what have to be justified, if there is to be any such thing as the right to strike.

I want to suggest now that we can see both of these things as justified, or any rate justifiable, if we think of the strikers as making, in effect, a certain sort of moral or quasi-moral, claim: a strike is not simply a refusal to continue working on the terms currently on offer; it is also, in effect, a claim that those terms are unacceptable, and it is because they are unacceptable that the strikers refuse to accept them. Now if this claim were understood purely descriptively, as meaning that nobody can be expected to do that job on those terms, then it could be easily tested, by seeing whether sufficient people are prepared to do the job on the terms which the strikers reject. And this would have interesting, if somewhat unexpected, implications for the practice and conduct of strikes. On the one hand strikers would not be entitled to prevent those who are willing to accept those terms, from doing their job in their place. They could, of course, attempt to persuade others not to take that job, i.e. persuade them that those terms are, as they claim, unacceptable. But if they fail, if those others are willing to accept the job on those terms, then those others must be allowed to do so. Significantly, but unsurprisingly, many are prepared to accept this first implication, but not the next. For on the other hand the success or failure of the strike should not be allowed to depend on extraneous factors, such as the strikers' ability to hold out. It should be settled instead by whether or not sufficient people are willing to accept the disputed terms. There should therefore be some form of financial support for those who are on strike for as long as their proposition, that their terms of employment are unacceptable, is up for public testing. So perhaps employers should be required to pay strikers even during a strike, up to (but not beyond) such time as somebody else can be found to do the job instead; so that if that time does not arrive they will eventually have to concede the strikers' demands, the strikers having thus proved the truth of their proposition!

But, of course, the strikers' claim is to be understood prescriptively, not descriptively: not as meaning that nobody can be expected to do that job on those terms, which, human weakness being what it is, is unlikely to be true, however justified their claim; but as meaning that nobody should be expected to. And it is this moral or quasi-moral claim, which I shall now suggest, justifies both the boycott and the enforcement of it. On both points I will have to be brief.

Boycotts, first of all, can be of two kinds. On the one hand there are boycotts which are intended to right some wrong, or at any rate punish some evil, even if, as it sometimes turns out, the disapproval expressed is merely token. We might call these 'punitive' boycotts; examples might be the boycott of South African oranges or Californian grapes. In these cases the intention, at any rate, *is* to inflict harm, but this harm is deserved, and the justification is the hope of doing good or the justice of the cause. But on the other hand there are boycotts which consist in the refusal to do something because it would be wrong to do it. For want of a better word we might call these 'exculpatory' boycotts: examples might be a boycott, by governments, unions or individuals, on supplying arms for external use to an aggressor nation, or supplying arms for internal use to a despotic one. In these cases the intention need not be to inflict harm—quite the opposite in fact—and if harm is inflicted, intentionally or not, the justification is not the hope of doing good or the justice of the cause but simply that to do otherwise would be wrong. If the workers at Auschwitz had refused to man the gas ovens their boycott would, I suppose, have inflicted harm of sort on some, in the minimal sense that it frustrated their desires; but their boycott would have been justified not as a form of punishment, but as a refusal to do what was manifestly wrong.

Now because strikes clearly do involve the deliberate infliction of harm on the other side, it is tempting to assume that they constitute punitive boycotts, and therefore require justification of the sorts we have already considered and rejected, in terms of the lesser of two evils or a just cause. But I think we can now see that strikes are exculpatory boycotts: the claim, at any rate, is that in refusing to work on the terms currently on offer the strikers are refusing to do what nobody should be expected to do, what it would therefore be wrong for them to do and, for that matter, wrong for anyone else to do in their stead.

But although this may justify the boycott, as necessary to avoid doing what it would be wrong to do, it does not by itself justify the enforced boycott. Inasmuch as a strike is a declaration that certain terms of employment ought not to be accepted, then obviously anyone who does accept those terms is, in the strikers' opinion, mistaken and misguided, a fit object of criticism, complaint and condemnation. But criticism, complaint and condemnation are one thing, or perhaps three things; actually preventing someone from doing what *we* regard as wrong is something else again. Normally the fact that we regard what someone does as mistaken or misguided, or even immoral, does not by itself justify our stopping him from doing it. If he genuinely believes that he is right and we are wrong then, as often as not, he must be allowed to act on that belief. That is what a belief in human autonomy, liberty or freedom largely comes down to: we must each of us be allowed to go to the Devil in our own way. Once again there are limits, there are some things which we believe people should not be allowed to do, even if those people themselves genuinely believe that what they do is right. But generally, any restriction of individual liberty seems to require some further justification, beyond the fact that what that person proposes to do is, in your opinion, mistaken, misguided or immoral. And this is what we still need in the case of strikes. The right to strike, as we noted, puts a restriction on the right to work. But why should this right override the other?

The answer, I suggest, is that a strike is a Prisoners' Dilemma situation. Human weakness being what it is, the fact that something ought not to be accepted will have little or no bearing on whether or not people actually do accept it. Even if it will eventually be to the advantage of everyone that they refuse to accept this job on those terms, there will always be those who can find some personal or short-term advantage in taking a job on terms which others have rejected, especially where the alternative is no job at all. Or to put it in the familiar terms of the Prisoners' Dilemma: individuals can gain an advantage over others if they compete for what is available; but everyone will do better, collectively if not individually, if they co-operate; provided, that is, that everyone does co-operate, and that some do not seek to gain an advantage over the rest.

The equally familiar solution to a Prisoners' Dilemma is to enforce co-operation, which is precisely what a strike attempts to do. But this enforced co-operation can be justified in either of two ways. The first is by an appeal to self-interest: each individual will do better for himself if everyone co-operates, himself included, than if some compete. True, it will be better still for each individual if others co-operate and he competes, and the more who co-operate when he competes, the better he may do; but in a situation where if one competes, all compete and all do worse, it will be better for each individual if co-operation is enforced, on himself as well as on others. But this justification does not apply to the case of strikes. For one thing it is not the case that if one competes, all compete and he does worse: if he competes he gets the job, and the strikers lose it, so he does better than they. For another it is not the case that he will do better for himself provided everyone co-operates: if he co-operates the strikers keep the job, and he goes without. Rational self-interest, if that is what counts here, demands the competitive move.

The second justification of enforced co-operation in a Prisoners' Dilemma appeals to morality or the collective good: it is the group as a whole which does better if all co-operate, and the more who co-operate the better the group will do, even though particular individuals might be able to do better for themselves by competing. This means, first, that anyone who does co-operate is doing the right, morally best, thing; second, that anyone who competes at the expense of those who do co-operate is gaining an unfair advantage; and third, that those who co-operate when others compete are actually penalized, disadvantaged, for doing the correct, i.e. moral, i.e. co-operative, thing. In such a situation enforced co-operation is justified not in the name of self-interest but in the name of justice: it has been plausibly argued (Ullmann-Margalit, 1977) that moral norms emerge precisely from the need to ensure the right, morally correct outcome in a Prisoners' Dilemma situation. And this, similarly, is what justifies enforced co-operation, i.e. the enforced boycott, in the case of a strike: if the terms of employment are, as the strikers claim, unacceptable then enforcement is necessary, not merely to ensure the right or best result overall, but to avoid injustice to those individuals who rightly refused to accept employment on terms which nobody ought to accept.

This, then, is my justification of the enforced boycott. But as I am sure you have noticed, this justification depends on an assumption which I have so far avoided making explicit: that when the strikers in effect claim that their terms of employment are unacceptable, and then act on that claim, what they claim is correct, i.e. those terms are unacceptable. If this claim is correct, it justifies both the boycott, as an exculpatory boycott, i.e. as necessary to avoid doing something wrong; and the enforced boycott, as necessary to avoid a bad outcome, and in particular injustice to individuals, in a Prisoners' Dilemma situation. But if this claim is incorrect—if these terms are not such that no one ought to accept them—then neither conclusion follows, and neither the boycott nor its enforcement have been justified.

In short, we are no better off now than we were with the 'just war' and the 'lesser evil' justifications. For one thing there is liable to be every bit as much irresoluble disagreement over whether these terms of employment really are unacceptable, as the strikers in effect claim, as there is over whether a particular wage is fair or a particular cause is just, and for much the same reasons. For another this justification justifies only particular strikes, and not the right to strike as such. What still needs to be shown is how employees can be entitled to strike even when the particular strike is not justified, i.e. how they can be entitled to make that quasi-moral declaration and act on it, even when that declaration is false.

So we need another argument, to justify the right to strike as such.

The general form of this argument is familiar enough, and I will have to be briefer still. So let me remind you first, in my own self-defence, of what I said at the outset, about the inevitable simplicities of my discussion.

VII

We can begin with the familiar point that labour, like any other commodity, is subject to the laws of supply and demand. If there is a surplus of jobs over takers the terms of employment, including conditions of work as well as wages, will tend to improve, as employers compete for the scarce commodity, employees. If there is a surplus of takers over jobs the terms of employment will tend to worsen, as employees compete for the scarce commodity, jobs. Thus under full employment the terms of employment will tend to improve until they reach the point where it is not worth employers' while to employ: they may be unable or unwilling to provide the necessary terms, and so go out of business; or they may find it cheaper to install machines instead. But a surplus of jobs over people wanting them has always been the exception, limited to particular times, places and occupations. The norm throughout history and as far as the eye can see, especially at a global level, is a surplus of people over jobs: if not actually unemployment, then at any rate underemployment. Under these more familiar conditions the terms of employment will tend to worsen until they reach the point where it is not worth employees' while to accept a job on the terms currently on offer. If it really were the case that any job is better than none, that point would never be reached. But sooner or later there will come a time when there is actually no advantage, financial or otherwise, in taking a job: you might as well stay at home and starve, as go to work and starve just the same.

In practice this lower limit is set not by starvation, but by the extent to which others in the family or community are willing or able to support those who cannot find acceptable employment. In a welfare state this support is institutionalized, in the form of unemployment relief. So in Britain it will be the level of unemployment relief, and ultimately supplementary benefit, which in effect sets the lower limit to wages, by establishing a point, above or below it, where it becomes more sensible not to work at all. The mythology is that unemployment benefit is a form of compensation for those who really want to work but cannot find a job—society should not penalize those who are out of work through no fault of their own—and that anyone who actually prefers living on the dole to working for a living is a scrounger and abusing the system. Admittedly we hear much less of scroungers now than we used to, now that the potential candidates include our friends, neighbours and colleagues, to move no nearer home. But since voluntary unemployment is surely to be preferred to involuntary employment, such scrounging ought actually to be encouraged: it is positively desirable that some people would rather live at the minimum level ensured by unemployment benefit than take a job which someone else would rather have. Ideally, unemployment benefit should function not as compensation but as an incentive; and under conditions of moderate unemployment—where, curiously, complaints about scroungers tend to be loudest—this ideal was probably realizable. But as jobs become ever more scarce, and we want more and more people to prefer voluntary idleness to enforced labour, the more tempting the level of unemployment benefit will have to be—until, perhaps, we reach the point where the only ones working are those who are *not* doing it for the money! But there are obvious difficulties here, most notably the cost of all this to an already hard-pressed economy, and the danger that unemployment benefit will eventually approach the point where employers prefer not to employ at all, and I must return to my argument.

So, an upper limit to the terms of employment will be set by the point at which employers prefer not to employ, and a lower limit by the point at which employees prefer not to be employed. Under full employment the pressure will be upward; under unemployment the pressure will be downward. Now I take it that the favourite fiction of the philosophers, the impartial spectator, will agree that the former is more desirable, if less likely: if human satisfaction is our goal, then the terms of employment ought to be the best that they can be, not the worst. I am saying, notice, that a wage ought to be not just just or fair, but the best possible, the best the market can bear. I admit that this is little more than intuition on my part, for which I have no argument beyond an appeal to your own impartial spectating. So, in case you have your doubts, let me remind you that there are limits to what this best can be, a limit set by the point at which employers prefer not to employ; and so far as I can see this point will be determined, in the last analysis, by each employer for himself. I hope to be saying no more than that, ideally, the terms of employment should be the best the employer can manage, not the worst.

Now this in turn means that we need something to counteract those equally beloved market forces, something to push the terms of employment up, not down. But the most obvious devices, like a statutory minimum wage, or welfare payments for those who prefer not working at all to working on the terms currently available, merely provide a floor for the market forces to push against: they do not provide pressure in the opposite direction. What can provide this pressure, however, is people's refusal to work on terms they consider unacceptable, Moreover, what counts as unacceptable terms is, of course, a relative matter, relative to time, place and occupation. And with increasing prosperity, or the spectacle of others, or merely possible, wealth to goad you on, the trend tends to be upwards, so much so that we in the developed world have come to take virtually for granted that our terms of employment, our standard of living and our conditions of work, must inevitably improve, even annually. In that case pressure will be ever upwards, at least to be best that the market can bear, which is as much as we can reasonably demand.

There are, however, obvious difficulties. The fact that one person considers his terms of employment unacceptable, and therefore refuses to work on them, does not of course mean that others will find them unacceptable too, or refuse to work on them even if they do. And if it is merely individuals who refuse to work on those terms, then so long as there are others willing and able to take their place, the pressure will still be down, not up. It is only if everyone refuses to accept the terms which they reject, that the pressure will be up, not down. So what we need is some mechanism or device which will ensure, as best it can, that other people do not take a job whose terms those whose job it is have rejected as unacceptable. And this, as we have seen, is precisely what a terms of employment strike is.

Notice here that this involves more than merely ensuring that nobody else accepts the terms which the strikers reject. If that were all, the strikers should have no complaint if others take that job on better terms, and in particular on terms which the strikers themselves would regard as acceptable. But that would not be meeting the strikers' demands; it would only be rubbing salt in their wounds! As we have already seen a strike attempts to ensure, instead, that nobody takes that job from them, not even on better terms. This too is easily explained and justified. If those who strike can be replaced with impunity, even if it has to be on better terms, then no one will dare to strike in the first place, and people will not refuse to work on terms which they regard as unacceptable. That is why the strikers, in striking, insist that the job they refuse to do is none the less still theirs.

Thus strikes—or, preferably, the threat of strikes—can provide the desired upward pressure on the terms of employment, not just at the bottom, where the terms of employment are most obviously unacceptable, but at any point, wherever people regard their terms of employment as unacceptable and, therefore, refuse to accept them. Take away the weapon and the threat of strikes and there may be nothing beyond the benevolence and charity of individual employers to prevent the terms of employment sinking to that level, wherever it might be, that people would prefer not to work at all, with all that that involves, than do that job on those terms. This, as I see it, is the ultimate justification of the right to strike. It is, moreover, a justification of the right to strike, right or wrong: the argument does not depend on strikers being in the right when they declare their terms of employment unacceptable, and therefore refuse to accept them; on the contrary it is explicitly an argument that they should be allowed to declare their terms of employment unacceptable, and to act on that declaration, whether those terms really are unacceptable or not.

VIII

As I approach the end of this paper I am more than ever conscious that my argument sacrifices realism for simplicity, but I do not have time to complicate my story now. Instead I should like to say something about the limitations to the argument so far, and its possible development.

The gist of my argument has been that (1) employees are justified in refusing to work on unacceptable terms, this (exculpatory) boycott being justified on the grounds that it would be wrong for them to do so; that (2) they are also justified in attempting to prevent others taking that job from them, even though they are not prepared to do it themselves, this enforced boycott being justified in the name of justice, not self-interest, in what is a Prisoners' Dilemma situation; and that (3) the need to maintain some upwards pressure on the terms of employment, particularly in conditions of unemployment, means that employees ought to be allowed to declare their terms of employment unacceptable, and to act on that declaration as justified above, whether those terms really are unacceptable or not. That is, they are entitled—they ought to be allowed—to do those things, whether they are justified in the particular case or not. Or to put it in a phrase, they have the right to strike, which means a right to strike, right or wrong.

Nevertheless, this justification of the right to strike clearly has its limits. There is first the fact that the argument has explicitly been limited to the terms of employment: there is nothing here to justify sympathy strikes, protest strikes or political strikes. Again, the argument has explicitly been limited to boycotting the jobs whose terms of employment are at issue. Obviously, ensuring that the disputed jobs are not done, or are done only to the extent that the strikers are prepared to let them be done, is not the only way of putting pressure on an employer. It might well be simpler, and almost certainly more effective, to try to prevent him from functioning in any way at all. But any extension of a strike beyond boycotting, blockading or blacking the jobs in question, has not been justified by my argument.

On the other hand, to say that these, and other, things have not been justified by my argument, is not of course to say that they cannot be justified at all. For one thing, we have already seen that a justification in terms of a general right to strike is not the only justification of strike action: there are, for example, the just war and the lesser evil justifications as well. Admittedly these further justifications apply only when strikers are actually in the right; but when they do apply they may justify more than is justified by the right to strike alone. And for another thing, there is the further possibility of finding other justifications for the right to strike as such, in particular justifications for strikes of other sorts, sympathy, protest and political strikes as well as strikes over the terms of employment. There is not time to develop such arguments in detail here, but an argument for a right to political strikes, for example, could begin from the claim that parliamentary democracy is an uncertain beast at the best of times, and that it is good, right and proper that citizens be able to bring their opinions to the attention of their representatives by whatever means seem necessary to ensure that they will be taken into account. What is a political strike but one way of lobbying the legislature; and if other forms of lobbying are permissible, why not this one? This is not, of course, to say that political strikers are entitled to force their opinions on parliament, only that they are entitled to bring those opinions, and the strength with which they are held, to its attention. In other words this argument would justify only a publicity-raising token strike, not a strike based on non-negotiable demands. But even here there may be other arguments as well.

But at this point I want to concentrate on a rather different limitation to my argument. My defence of the right to strike has been based on the assumption that it is, on the whole, a good thing that the pressure on the terms of employment be up, not down. But what if it so turns out that this pressure is no longer a good thing, or is misapplied, so that it actually makes things worse, not better? What happens then to the right to strike?

Two such cases spring immediately to mind. One possibility is that the upward pressure exerted by strikes and the threat of strikes may eventually push the terms of employment up to the point where employers prefer not to employ, either because it is not worth their while, or because it is cheaper to install machines instead. At that point the upwards pressure will succeed in making things worse, not better, unless provision for the unemployed is more generous than there seem any reason to expect. At that point the right to strike seems to lose, indeed to destroy, its own justification. Another possibility is that since the effectiveness of strike action is something which will vary widely from one group of employees to another, the effects of an upwards pressure exerted by strikes and the threat of them is bound to be extremely uneven. So while it may result in improved terms for some employees, it may also produce a distribution of rewards which is excessively unfair, having regard to any criterion other than sheer industrial muscle. At this point it may no longer be so obvious to the impartial spectator that upward pressure, exerted in this particular way, is a good thing.

Both these possibilities are real enough, and both seem to me to affect the right to strike. More exactly, the mere possibility does not mean that there is no right to strike after all. But at the point where the right to strike destroys its own rationale, or produces evils which outweigh the good on which it depends, then at that point, it seems to me, there is no longer a justification of the right to strike as such, a right to strike right or wrong. Of course it will be difficult to say when that point has been reached: any such balance of competing goods and evils is a difficult matter, on which individuals may legitimately disagree. In particular, the mere fact that one particular strike may make things worse, not better, for others or even for those directly involved, does not mean that the general right to strike therefore disappears. The right to strike is an entitlement to strike even though the particular strike is not justified; and it is a right to be foolish, as well as a right to be in the wrong. But where the results of the general practice are more bad than good then the general practice, the entitlement, will lose its justification. Not that I think, for all the publicity, that we are quite at that point yet.

So I have barely scratched the surface, even of the one of the three aspects of this problem that I chose to discuss. But this is the point at which I, for one, lay down my tools. No doubt you went on strike long ago.

Postscript

This paper was written and delivered before the miners' strike of 1984, in which the conflict between the right to strike and the right to work was illustrated dramatically. If I had written it then the emphasis would no doubt be different: in particular I would probably not have chosen as my central case a terms of employment strike within a private enterprise. But although the events of that strike have caused me to think long and hard about what this paper says, I do not think that I now want to change its arguments, or even its conclusions.

References

K. E. Kirk, *Conscience and Its Problems: An Introduction to Casuistry* (London: Longmans, Green & Co., 1927).

Leo XIII, *Rerum Novarum* (1891) published as *The Condition of the Working Classes* by the Catholic Social Guild (Oxford, 1928).

H. E. Manning, 'Leo XIII on the Condition of Labour', *Dublin Review* (1891), reprinted as *Leo XIII on Labour* by the Catholic Truth Society (London, 1901).

E. Ullmann-Margalit, *The Emergence of Norms* (Oxford: Clarendon Press, 1977).

Imprisonment

ANTHONY O'HEAR

> Morals reformed—health preserved—industry invigorated—
> instruction diffused—public burthens lightened—economy seated
> as it were upon a rock—the gordian knot of the Poor Laws not cut
> but untied—all by a simple idea of Architecture.
>
> Jeremy Bentham, *Panopticon,* p. 39

It is appropriate that a lecture in a series on 'Philosophy and Practice'
should open by considering Bentham's ideas on imprisonment. For
Bentham, incontestably a philosopher, was equally incontestably a
practical reformer. This, indeed, is a received idea among philosophers; that is to say, most philosophers know that Bentham
designed 'a model prison of novel design' (Mary Warnock), but few
have actually considered the design, its implications or its effects.
Most are content, like Warnock, with observing that the panopticon
plan was formally rejected, before passing on to the abstraction of
Bentham's felicific calculus, his notion of utility, and his ideas about
the foundations of law. Yet, strange as it may seem, the underlying
idea of the panopticon has never been completely abandoned. One
aspect of the idea pervades penal thinking, even while prison practice
is still influenced by Bentham's practical proposals; moreover, the
panoptic ideal has taken root far beyond the walls of actual prisons.
Here is philosophy in practice, and yet, in many ways, practically
and intellectually a failure.

To understand the nature of the failure, we shall have to go
beyond and behind philosophical abstraction. We will have to see
why Bentham's hopes for prisons failed in practice. But, that they
and similar ideas had failed and were perhaps bound to fail has been
widely recognized since 1830 at least. Yet Benthamite ideas and
practice continue to pervade penal practice. So this leads us to ask
why such overtly inefficacious ideas should still be so influential. So
we have to go behind the ideas to the underlying social reality. And
in doing this, we shall be led to go beyond ideas about prisons,
because, as I shall argue, prisons as we have them cannot be
considered in abstraction from the criminal justice system as a whole,
and our ways of social stratification and organization generally.

Prison, as we know it today, is a recent phenomenon. It seems so
natural that talk of alternatives to imprisonment can be made to
sound quite radical. Yet prison was itself a radical alternative for
dealing with crime only 200 years ago. It was a radical alternative to

punishment by public torture and execution, by public humiliation, by transportation: in 1776 in John Howard's survey of English prisons, those prisons that did exist contained debtors rather than felons, and the felons that were incarcerated were in the main people awaiting trial or sentence of death or transportation. Anyone in a prison could bring families and friends in, or indeed prostitutes if they could afford it. Better-off prisoners could secure all sorts of privileges from the keepers who were private contractors, unsupervised by higher authority. Food and drink had to be bought from the keepers. Discipline was arbitrary and capricious. To a large extent, prisons were self-governing, with a flourishing subculture, including mock trials and punishments conducted by the inmates themselves. Disease, disorder, brutality and corruption were rife, and these were the features of prison life that shocked the reformers of the eighteenth and early nineteenth centuries. These were men like John Howard, motivated by religious ideals, or men like Bentham, shocked by the obvious and multiple inutility of contemporary institutions of punishment. Reformers from both religious and rationalistic-cum-utilitarian standpoints hoped to replace the brutal unequally applied and ineffective system of criminal justice that existed in the eighteenth century with a system of fixed and equally distributed penalties, which combined correction of the mind with correction of the body, which produced bodily health rather than disease, and which sent formerly dishonest men out honest, either through having come to terms with God and their conscience or through having been (in Bentham's phrase) 'ground honest' by the prison machine.

People often write as if there is something inconsistent with punishing somebody and hoping to reform him at the same time. Maybe there is, and maybe all that imprisonment can achieve is a system of 'humane containment', to use a characteristically weasely phrase that was current in Home Office jargon in the 1970s. But, if that is so, a re-thinking of the style of imprisonment currently practised is called for, because the types of rules and structures that currently govern penal practice are inherently panoptic in Bentham's sense and hence, in aim, reformatory. Some people may think that our present system of imprisonment is disordered and corrupt, and that there is therefore not much difference between Newgate in the 1760s and Wormwood Scrubs in the 1980s. But they would be wrong in two vital respects, respects which take us to the essence of Bentham's panopticism. In the first place, the only rules or work or timetables which obtained in an eighteenth-century prison were at the discretion of the keepers, the upshot being that they were more honoured in the breach than in the observance. But then, secondly, and more crucially, in Newgate in the 1760s, there was 'roughly one turnkey, officer or watchman for every hundred prisoners'. Hence the flourishing of inmate subculture. By 1830 panoptical reforming zeal had produced a ratio of one officer to eighteen prisoners in Coldbath Fields House of Correction. I have recently read that the current inmate/staff ratio in British prisons is 1:1·74, and there are 19,695 prison officers alone for 44,000 prisoners (*Social Trends*, 1983). At Grendon Underwood, about which I will say more later, the ratio is 1:1. 'Humane containment' surely does not require such ratios. Has panopticism then triumphed in a way unsuspected even by Bentham, who thought that one of the advantages of his plan was that the many could be surveyed by the few?

Panopticism is the principle that everyone in an institution is constantly visible to someone, although not everyone is visible to anyone. In Bentham's panopticon (which could be used as a factory or a workhouse, as much as a prison), there is an observation tower at the centre and, surrounding it, a ring-like structure divided into storeys and individual cells. The cells are backlit, while the tower's windows are covered by venetian blinds, so that all that is happening in each cell is visible from the tower, although the inmates of the cells will be unable to see what is happening in the control tower. The aim of the structure is to ensure that each prisoner or worker or intermediate guard or supervisor can be seen from the control tower and realizes that this is so, but that they should not know when or even if they are actually being observed.

Bentham was, as just suggested, well aware that the guards themselves needed supervising and guarding. In this, he was at one with Howard and the other reformers, both religious and radical, one of whose main complaints about eighteenth-century prisons had been the disorderly and corrupt lives led by prisoners and guards alike. To remedy this, and to produce the circumstances of observation and control in which rogues might be rehabilitated through the extinction of anti-social traits and the reinforcement of positive social attitudes, by a careful blending of pleasure and pain, the lives of everyone in a modern prison were to be regulated by rule and a detailed discipline, dividing the day up into segments for work, for eating, for sleeping, for solitary meditation, and so on. Staff and inmates alike were to be bound by discipline and rule, segregated from each other and from potentially disruptive influences of the outside world and would alike be overseen by the unseen eyes in the inspection tower. As Michael Ignatieff sums it up, rules

had a double meaning for the reformers. They were an enumeration of the inmates' deprivation, but also a charter of their rights.

>They bound both sides of the institutional encounter in obedience
>to an impartial codes enforced from outside. As such they
>reconciled the interests of the state, the custodians and the
>prisoners alike (1978, p. 78).

But who, it will be asked, oversaw the superior controller in his
inspection tower which is also to be his house? Bentham thought that
his inspection-machine could be operated by anyone, by the governor's family or friends, for whom the scene from their lodge would
be 'very various' and 'not altogether unamusing'. More than that, the
general public would be allowed to visit the inspection tower to
observe human behaviour in laboratory conditions. Their motivation
for these visits would not matter, whether it was out of anxiety for
the internees or out of general curiosity. The governor would still be
judged by his institution being open and visible to the public—to the
'great open committee of the tribunal of the world' as Bentham put
it—as much as it is to him. More than that, as the regulator and
observer of what goes on in his institution, and enclosed in the
middle of it he will himself be the first victim of any disaster within,
such as an epidemic or revolt, a hostage in his own hands, as
Bentham says, for the salubrity of the whole.

Modern prisons, whether their architecture be nineteenth or
twentieth century, preserve in essence many of the most significant
features of Bentham's panopticon. This is hardly surprising as,
despite the formal rejection of the panoticon project, prison
architecture and planning in the early nineteenth century followed
Bentham's ideas, except that the state prisons were not, like
Bentham's to be privately run to make a profit for the governing
entrepreneurs. To quote Ignatieff again, in both the Panopticon and
the prison regimes actually established in the nineteenth century,

>the pain of intention (was substituted) for the pain of neglect, the
>authority of rules for the authority of custom, the regimes of hard
>labour for the disorder of idleness. In both the criminal was
>separated from the outside world by a new conception of social
>distance, epitomized by uniforms, walls and bars. The ruling
>image in both was the idea of the eye of the state—impartial
>humane and vigilant—holding the 'deviant' in the thrall of its
>omniscient gaze (1978, p. 113).

It is especially relevant in this last respect that current penal practice
follows Bentham in spirit, if not in architecture. The modern
'psychiatric' prison, Grendon Underwood, may look more like a
college than Pentonville, but Bentham would surely have recognized
this 'very human and humane institution' as it has been described by

a one-time director of Prison Medical Services, as a laboratory of scrutiny and reform, just as much as his own panopticon, that manufactory of reformation, from which convicts would not be released until they had given satisfactory proof of their reform. Only the modality has changed. Tony Parker was told by one of the psychologists employed at Grendon that

> perhaps one of the things that can be said in favour of Grendon is that we do have a certain amount of freedom here, more so than one would in other prisons, to contemplate the possibilities of, and sometimes to carry out, brief experimental work (1970, p. 130).

He was also told by several of the inmates that they were simply playing the system, making the 'right' responses to the therapy and so on, so as to stay on in the pleasant surroundings of Grendon until they achieved remission or parole, in exactly the same way as nineteenth-century reports show prison chaplains constantly being deceived by hypocritical professions of reform. He was also told by one prisoner that 'I don't think I could exist for very long without someone watching over me'.

Surveillance and institutionalization, whether inspired by commercial–utilitarian ideas (Bentham), religion (Howard), or the psycho-sciences (Grendon Underwood), these are the key features of the modern penitentiary, although, in contrast to Benthamite panopticism, surveillance in contemporary prisons is strictly one way. The prison service operates under conditions of great secrecy. The public are not able to observe what goes on in prisons, except with the permission of the Home Office and under strictly regulated conditions. Journalists visiting prisons, for example, have to sign a statement agreeing not to publish any information they learn during their visit. Prisoners themselves, like the public generally, are not allowed to know the Standing Orders for prisons, although they are liable to punishment for any breach of these orders. Their rights to consult solicitors over grievances and to be legally represented when they are themselves tried on disciplinary charges are strongly restricted. Not surprisingly, there has been a crop of cases recently to the European Commission on Human Rights on such matters, and the Home Office always seems to oppose any attempt to grant prisoners the most elementary legal rights of defence, representation, and appeal to independent arbitration. It is, in fact, almost impossible for a prisoner to establish misconduct against him by prisoner officers, particularly with the apparently growing use of riot squads made up of unidentifiable officers from other prisons to quell incidents in prisons. Moreover prisoners are not allowed to check or comment on the records being compiled on them by their warders, records on which their chance of parole depends. In other words, the most elementary safeguards against the abuse of the Benthamite type of prison—foreseen by the reformers themselves—have not been implemented. In any impartial assessment of the relationship between imprisonment and the crime rate, the crimes committed in prison against the inmates will have to be included.

It is clear that the natural momentum of the institution to preserve discipline in what may be circumstances of considerable degradation to inmates and staff alike, when combined with the veil of official secrecy, makes it all too easy for a man in prison to be deprived of natural justice. The reforms, so boldly entered on in the nineteenth century have failed to produce the intended effect of dispensing with a need for guards to guard the guards, though it might be argued that this is because in this respect the reforms have never really been put into practice. However, where the reformers are more directly open to criticism is in their assumption that human nature is so malleable that a prison machine could be devised so as to grind rogues honest. Bentham's metaphor of grinding rogues is in its way more revealing than much of the talk of reformers since his time. One of the few members of the medical staff from Grendon who would speak to Tony Parker spoke of the way in which large numbers of people in prison are dangerous to themselves:

they go through life determined to find trouble and be punished; and this is a very serious state of mind for anyone to be in. Something has to be done about it . . . (1970, p. 214),

for their own good, presumably. Of course, this was Bentham's idea too, and Howard's in their own ways. The reforming trick is always to make controlling a man appear as if it is in his own best interests, and the reforming itself a favour done to him. But prison cannot be a favour. Nor can it reform, except indirectly, as perhaps in the Barlinnie special unit, by producing the conditions in which a man might discover some constructive talents or interests he was formerly unaware of. But reform is not going to be achieved by seclusion, discipline, exhortation or 'therapy', all of which will tend to alienate an individual from the controlling authority, to separate him in mind and spirit from the rest of mankind, and to instil in him a dependence on institutional structures from which he will find it hard to break out.

All the evidence points to this, and it was recognized at a very early stage of the prison reform movement, as has been documented by Michel Foucault (1977, pp. 264–268) with a host of references to and quotations from writers of the 1830s and 1840s. Among points made are that prison itself produces delinquents by throwing anti-social individuals together, by exacerbating their anti-social propensities by condemning them to 'an unnatural, useless and dangerous existence', by laying them open to assaults by warders or by other prisoners, by the use of the parole system once they leave prison, which makes it hard for them to find honest work, and which keeps them under constant surveillance, and which, by throwing their families into destitution, produces further delinquency. What we have had since the 1830s has in fact been a realization of the failure of prison as a reformatory, but this is usually attributed to internal failures of technique or of severity. Both these responses seem to me to be fundamentally dishonest. As William Godwin pointed out in 1793 in his *Enquiry Concerning Political Justice,* coercion is 'no argument: it begins with producing the sensation of pain, and the sentiment of distaste. It begins with violently alienating the mind from the truth with which we wish it to be impressed.' And penal technique and its context is bound to be coercive. On the other hand, making prison more severe will not reform convicts in any fundamental sense, and greater brutality in prisons generally brings about public disquiet, as it did with Howard and Bentham. Indeed, prison officers do not like working in 'penal dustbins', nor do governors like presiding over them, apparently. And so the movement for something useful to be done *in* prisons *to* prisoners gets further impetus, and the failure of the penitentiary to reform represented as a mere failure of technique.

But if the hope that prison might be able, by some technique or other, to reform criminals is a forlorn one, involving now a certain amount of naivety or bad faith on the part of those who advocate it, this does not mean that prisons might not be necessary to society, and justifiable on other grounds. As noted earlier, they replaced a whole range of other penalties and any society needs some way of dealing with those who break its laws. A legal system without sanctions of any sort is unlikely to be very effective; the overall social good to be gained from having an ordered and generally beneficial state will undoubtedly outweigh a certain amount of pain and loss of freedom for those who offend, if such is indeed the cost of protecting the rights and freedom of the majority. But in saying this, we still have to determine how the pain and loss of freedom is to be construed, and what form it should take.

One view of punishment that is currently quite fashionable is that the state or society has a right or even a duty to express its disapproval of law-breakers in a ritual or symbolic way causing them pain. This view has the advantage over some others in that we do not now have to justify punishment in terms of its effects: if punishment does not reform or deter, that does not matter, because that is not its point. In a way this 'expressive' view of punishment takes us back to the pre-nineteenth century theatre of public humiliations and executions, which, interestingly were, on occasion counter-productive for the authorities, in that they gave the criminal a chance to become a popular hero (as often happened in public executions). This aside, however, two awkward problems remain for the idea of punishment as expression of outrage. First, we surely cannot justify depriving someone of life or liberty simply because we disapprove of them. The onus will be on us to show that depriving them of life or liberty is either deserved on other grounds or the only means to some overriding social good. In other words, if our expression of social disapproval is to be through the pain or death of someone else, then we have to show an independent justification for inflicting pain or death on them. No doubt legal punishments do express social disapproval, but they also need some further justification. We are now beyond the stage at which the demands of ritual alone would appear to justify the killing of a goat or a cat, yet the expressive justification of punishment says in effect that men can be killed or imprisoned for purely symbolic reasons. Then, secondly, the expressive function of punishment is not well served by shutting people from public view and rendering them effectively incommunicado. Roger Scruton, an advocate of the view that punishment should 'express and propitiate outrage' is not afraid to draw this conclusion:

> The healthiest form of punishment will be immediate, intelligible, even violent, conceived by the citizen as a natural retaliation...

and he goes on to say that imprisonment is not the best way to convey to either public or criminal 'an adequate sense of punishment as a *response* to crime, in the way that a human action may constitute a response' (1980, pp. 82–84). While this is true, it is not true that an expressive response to crime, in the form, presumably of flogging, mutilation or public execution, can be justified simply in terms of the expression of natural outrage at offence. Indeed, civilized society and the law itself since the time of the Orestia can be seen as an attempt to sublimate and redirect in a more positive way the feelings that fuelled the natural and fruitlessly repetitive cycles of revenge that characterize earlier societies.

It will perhaps be said at this point that the criminal does not simply bear the brunt of our outrage. Rather, he deserves retribution for his offence. Through his own suffering he must repay his debt to society, whether in doing so any further good is achieved or not. This view is usually known as retributivism, and despite its familiarity and what I shall later suggest is a grain of truth in its implication that it would be just to punish only where offences exist, I must confess to some difficulty in understanding it as a justification for merely inflicting a surplus of pain on an offender. It is quite unclear to me how simply sending someone to prison or punishing him in some other way repays his crime, his victim or society itself. How, except by a mysterious 'moral alchemy' (to use a phrase of H. L. A. Hart) are offences repaid or cancelled out just by inflicting suffering on the perpetrator of the offence? In addition, retributivism when combined with imprisonment leads us, as Scruton points out, to engage in 'an absurd mathematics of crime, according to which it seems the robbery of a mail train is roughly four times as bad as premeditated murder—a result which is deeply repugnant to the normal conscience'. The repugnance is in some measure due to the incoherence of thinking that there could be a single currency of desert, whereby crimes of vastly different sorts all paid for in years, months and days. But this incoherence is inherent in the very idea of retributivism, and compounded by its being cashed out in terms of imprisonment. Small wonder that judges in sentencing appear to place more stress on the degree of outrage they work up for a crime, or on the supposed deterrent effect of a sentence than on anything like a strict calculus of penalty.

Expressive and retributive justifications of punishment, then, are of doubtful validity in themselves, and, in addition fit better with more overtly barbaric penalties than imprisonment. It is, however, possible to view retribution in a somewhat different light from the traditional one of the offender's pain in itself cancelling out his debt to society, and to see it as a demand that an offender repay or make reparation in some way to his victim. With this there can surely be no quarrel, nor with the idea that such compensation be organized by the state according to standard procedures of investigation and enforcement. If one of the main reasons for a state at all is to provide security for its members, it is not unreasonable to see the provision of compensation for victims as one of its duties. What is *prima facie* surprising is that neither states, nor philosophers come to that (though cf. Day, 1978), have paid much attention to the idea of victims being compensated through the efforts of their injures. A system of enforced controlled reparation as a punishment for small property crimes might well be practicable and would make far more sense from everyone's point of view, including the victim's than the costly and frequently counter-productive imprisonment of petty thieves. One-third of the prison population is apparently behind bars because of petty theft. The removal of such people from the prison system and of petty theft from the category of imprisonable crime would be a major practical improvement to our system of criminal justice. In saying this, however, I am reversing the arguments of the eighteenth- and nineteenth-century reformers who argued very strongly in favour of imprisoning petty criminals, where previously they might have gone free, and of those who nowadays advocate short sharp shocks to such people, in order to prevent them becoming bigger criminals. All the evidence, of course, points the other way, that prison itself makes one-time petty criminals into bigger and persistent ones, and that keeping them out of the prison system is the best way of preventing this downward spiral.

Of course, there are plenty of crimes which are not petty thefts or small burglaries, and where the idea of reparation to victims, or some sort of mediation between victim and offender is inappropriate. We want to deter such crimes. How should society set about doing this? Moreover, can we be sure that a system of reparation and mediation would actually deter the petty crimes which are not actually committed, but which the present system of imprisonment, it is claimed, does deter?

To deal with these questions and the whole idea of deterrent sentencing satisfactorily, we desperately need information of an empirical sort, but it is in fact extremely hard to discover the truth in assessing the deterrent effects of legal sanctions, once we get beyond the limiting cases of having no sanctions at all or of punishing every wrongdoer with some extremely severe penalty. But the latter would be impossible without total supervision of everyone all the time, which is in itself impossible and surely unacceptable anyway on ethical grounds. So, in practice, we have to consider what to do to deter crime in a world in which the vast majority of actual crimes are going to go undetected. (The Metropolitan Police are proud of a clear-up rate on reported crime of 17 per cent, which is probably nearer 5 per cent in fact if we take unreported crime into account.) Research studies have shown that well-directed blitzes on specific offences, with heavy policing and heavy penalties, can have some temporary effect on the incidence of those offences, but for normal circumstances, the conclusion of the studies on the effect of deterrence is in conclusive.

In the words of Deryck Beyleveld, in his review of the relevant studies,

> there exists no scientific basis for expecting that a general deterrence policy, which does not involve an unacceptable interference with human rights, will do anything to control the crime rate (1979, p. 136).

Beyleveld does point out that most studies in this area claim to have discovered significant correlations between probability of sanctions and offence-rates, though no correlation between severity of sanctions and offence-rates, but he is highly critical of the methodological assumptions of the studies. He thinks we are just as much in the dark on the deterrent effect on the crime rate of increasing police manpower as we are on the effect of increasing fines or sentences. What, however, is not in doubt is that at any given time in Holland 1·3 per 10,000 of the population is in prison, compared with 8 per 10,000 in Britain, while the crime rates of the two countries are roughly comparable. (The figures for Italy, France, Denmark, Luxembourg and Germany are 2·2, 3·9, 4·5, 5·9 and 6·7, respectively.) It seems likely that a lot less imprisonment and far shorter sentences will not by themselves decrease the deterrent effect of legal sanctions, which can be other than imprisonment, as I have already suggested in connection with reparations for petty crime. In view of the uncertainty surrounding the deterrent effect of sentencing policy, one is led to the conclusion that imprisonment—itself a great evil to the person imprisoned, highly costly and wasteful of all sorts of resources, and a contributing cause to further offences both inside and outside the prison—should not be used in the mere hope that it might deter people, except in the case of major offences, whose harm greatly outweighs the evils of imprisoning a man against his will. In fact, this whole area is one where far more empirical knowledge is required before sensible conclusions can be drawn.

However, even supposing we had more evidence that other people would be deterred from some major crime by your being in prison, would thus justify you being put there, as a public utility, so to speak? According to D. D. Raphael it would, if you had committed a crime:

> where however a person is guilty of having wilfully done wrong, he has thereby forfeited part of his claim to be treated as an end in himself: in acting as a non-moral being he leaves it open to his fellows to use him as such (1955, p. 71).

This is surely going too far; apart from anything else, no one could claim the right to be treated as an end on this basis. Nor can I agree with Rousseau's claim in the *Social Contract* (Bk 1, Ch. IV) that the criminal, by declaring war on the state from within, places himself outside the state and morality. Nevertheless, it might be possible in cases of crimes where direct reparation is impossible because, for example, the harm done is too great, or too personal, to be repaired to see one's enforced reparation on being convicted in terms of the deterrent effect on potential wrongdoers, thereby saving their potential victims. Imprisonment could then be seen as a sort of proxy-reparation, helping not one's own victims but other potential sufferers from similar offences.

Anthony O'Hear

In addition to possibly providing the means for some people to make reparation for wrongs that cannot be directly righted imprisonment could also be justified as a means of taking some types of dangerously anti-social people out of circulation for a time, at least. We all have our favourite examples of candidates for this role, hit men for organized crime, terrorists, drug racketeers, men who prey violently on women, and the like. Talk of dangerous crime and dangerous criminals, however, raises a number of difficulties. Would we, for example, be justified in detaining people who are merely potentially dangerous, or continuing to detain people who have been convicted of a dangerous offence, after the completion of their sentence on the grounds that they are likely to offend again? One would feel a lot happier here if dangerousness were far more clearly defined and predictable than it actually is. What evidence there is suggests that of people predicted on psychological or medical grounds to be dangerous, only one in three or one in four will actually commit a dangerous crime. In these circumstances, we could hardly be justified in detaining for an indefinite period even on strict utilitarian calculations all those whom are potentially dangerous according to the available criteria. Moreover, if we were able to predict with considerable accuracy that certain people will definitely commit a violent crime, we would hardly be justified in inflicting any surplus of pain on them beyond some sort of supervision over them, because our ability to make such predictions itself testifies to their inability to do otherwise.

I am suggesting that if imprisonment of convicted serious criminals is a way of deterring others from serious crime, and if it is the only way of stopping actually dangerous people from continuing their activities, then it will be right to punish them by means of set terms of imprisonment. My reasoning here, as in my suggestion regarding reparation is broadly utilitarian, in that the justification if institutional reparation and imprisonment, where appropriate, would be in terms of their generally beneficial effects; in the case of imprisonment, this would be in terms of any discoverable deterrence and prevention. To make these proposals for punishment by means of reparation or imprisonment consistent with our intuitions of natural justice and our beliefs about human responsibility for actions, we would also have to ensure that people should not be put in prison except when they had done wrong. This is the grain of truth at the heart of retributivism, that we should punish only when wrong has been intentionally done, and in some way proportionate to the wrong done. But this provides only the conditions in which any question of punishment can arise. It does not, I have argued, justify particular institutions of punishment or applications of it. To assess

214

these questions we need to look to further goods that punishing might plausibly secure, such as restoration of what is owing, deterrence and prevention of wrong-doing. Nevertheless our retributivist intuitions regarding just punishment rule out detaining people just because they might be dangerous. Apart from the other reasons I have given, sentencing for this reason would be far too open to abuse and would involve an unacceptable degree of surveillance over and pseudo-medical interference with people in prison and in the population as a whole. Further, the prisons that would be needed in order to deter and interrupt major crime should not attempt to treat or reform the individuals in them, for the reasons given earlier in the paper. The discipline within the prisons, then, would not need to be structured as if to reform. Indeed, in the words of Mountbatten's recommendations for maximum security prisons it should be 'as liberal and constructive as possible' inside, including opportunities to study and work for a fair wage, and the prison as secure as necessary without. Given that those inside will be let out sometime, visits and contact with the world outside should be maximized consistent with security, and prisoners should be accorded full legal rights.

What I have been suggesting in the preceding paragraph is in some ways in line with Mountbatten's proposals of 1966 for maximum security prisons, which were never put into effect for political reasons. The difference between my suggestion and the Mountbatten report is that I do not think that there should be any other prisons at all, and that given the failure of prison and our lack of knowledge in these areas, we should experiment boldly with alternatives to imprisonment. Prisons in the modern sense were introduced as an experiment in the reformation of human beings, and this experiment has failed. I point this out against the background of a current daily prison population of 44,000 compared with 10,000 in 1928 and 1938, 20,000 in 1956 and 29,000 in 1964: the population is to rise to 52,000 by 1990 when ten new prisons are ready, or so the Home Office believes. More prisons simply produce more prisoners, because the courts, urged on by the media and populist politicians, make sure all the available places are filled, splitting families, wrecking lives.

Who, in any case, are these 44,000? Are they people who have split families or wrecked live? In large measure it appears that those who are in prison are more sinned against than sinning. While it is extremely difficult to get figures on categories of people in prison— there are, for example, no statistics on the class breakdown of those in prison—it is clear that large numbers of people in prison are either petty criminals or mentally disordered or both. Many are in prison because of small debts, fine defaulting, vagrancy, drunkenness, homelessness or prostitution and the homosexual offences of importuning or having sex with people between the ages of eighteen and twenty-one. I can see no justification for any of those categories being in prison, nor is it right that so many people should be held on remand for so long especially when up to half of them will eventually be found innocent or, even under present practice, given non-custodial sentences. (48,000 were held on remand in 1982 of whom 2,000 were eventually found innocent and 16,000 given non-custodial sentences.)

A survey of a sample of the population of male prisoners in the South-East was done in 1972, however, and published in the *Home Office Research Bulletin* in 1978. It deserves wide publicity, and our democratic responsibility regarding what is being done in our name requires us to pierce the veil of Home Office secrecy and apathy to see whether its results are characteristic of the penal system generally. The following figures stand out. Eighty-two per cent of the survey were manual, semi-skilled or unskilled workers in their usual jobs, compared with sixty-two per cent in the population as a whole. Twenty-one per cent were classified as mentally disordered, and of those convicted of serious offences against the person thirty-nine per cent were mentally disordered. Only one-third of the total had been convicted of 'serious' offences. About forty per cent of the total survey were either homeless or mentally disordered or both. Many of those not actually classified as mentally disordered were regarded as unstable, and only thirty-three per cent were mentally 'apparently normal'. About one-third were regarded by the researchers as 'divertible' from prison, having committed no serious offence against the person, having made no great gains from crime, and having shown no great competence in their criminal activities. Yet over half of these were serving sentences of more than one year. Fifty-four per cent of those released from short- or medium-term sentences were reconvicted within two years while the proportion of homeless and disordered prisoners reconvicted within two years was seventy-two per cent; fifty-nine per cent of those reconvicted were sentenced to further terms of imprisonment. The picture given by this report is amplified by a National Association for the Care and Resettlement of Offenders report which shows that on 30 June 1982 there were 44,002 people in custody. Seventeen per cent were awaiting trial or sentence, twenty-five per cent were under twenty-one, forty-nine per cent were serving sentences of eighteen months or less, and over half were detained for non-payment of fines, burglary and theft (not including crimes against the person).

The conclusion from these sets of figures is that a very large proportion of those in prison are petty and incompetent delinquents, socially and mentally disadvantaged. Sending them to prison is not only, in many cases, cruel and unnecessary; it also makes it highly likely that they will return. Prison, far from solving any problems, actually creates crime and makes criminals. Why then do we tolerate it? Answering this question takes us back to the origins of the prison and forward to the social role of crime and its current definition.

The growth of the modern prison coincided not simply with the work of the reformers but also with a period of considerable social change. It coincided with the massive enclosing of common land and the suppression of the customary rights of the poor over game, wood, deadfall and the like, with the increasing use of casual, seasonal labour on the land, and hence high rural unemployment, and, increasingly, with the growth of industrial towns. All those phenomena meant that there were large numbers of small thieves and vagrants, victims of the new social conditions in that survival within the law was hard for them, who, it seemed to the propertied classes, had to be controlled in the interests of stability and of property. By the 1840s, we are told, 'summary offenders (vagrants, poachers, petty thieves, disorderlies, and public drunkards) accounted for more than half of the prison population', and a further quarter were debtors or deserters (cf. Ignatieff, 1978, p. 179). Then, as now, the criminal justice system was largely directed at small game, against the deprived and the dispossessed. One can hardly maintain that the middle and upper classes are so much more moral and honest than the rest of society as the prison population suggests or that things done by the middle and upper classes do not cause equal or greater measures of human suffering than the petty crimes of the working classes, yet our system of criminal justice—police, courts and prisons—appears to concentrate most of its efforts into fighting the working class petty offender and to proffer a high degree of tolerance towards the makers of lethal products such as asbestos, unsafe cars, thalidomide, and so on, as well as towards usury and property speculation, industrial pollution and dubious banking, insurance, legal and stock-market practices. Perhaps we should recall that Bentham saw his panopticon untying the Gordian knot of the Poor Laws.

We need to ask what function prisons and the criminal justice system as a whole performs in our society, given that it is so lopsided and so inefficacious and so many ways. Why does it carry on as it does? The answer supplied by Michel Foucault has considerable plausibility: prison in one obvious sense a failure, is in another sense a great success:

For the observation that prison fails to eliminate crime one should perhaps substitute the hypothesis that prison has succeeded

217

extremely well in producing delinquency, a specific type, a politically or economically less dangerous — and, on occasion, usable — form of illegality: in producing delinquents, in an apparently marginal, buy in fact centrally supervised milieu; in producing the delinquent as a pathologized subject (1977, p. 277).

Prisons are filled with delinquents, people who resist the disciplinary normalization of school and work, who are processed in such a way that they can hardly fail to repeat the cycle of delinquency and imprisonment over and over again. This delinquency in turn presents itself as a rising tide of crime, and justifies a greater and greater police surveillance of the milieu of the delinquents. The delinquents themselves are the subjects of massive surveillance, which, of course, naturally takes in their families, friends and neighbours. Delinquency itself is typically fragmented and marginalized, infinitely less dangerous and politically potent than the bands of vagrants and vagabonds that swarmed the country in earlier times; the delinquent himself is denied the opportunity to make common cause with his own kind, but taken up into a hierarchical network of punishment and surveillance. Moreover, despite middle-class fears, the principal victims of working classes delinquency are members of the working classes. The effect of this, of course, is to produce demands within the working classes themselves for greater policing. Prison was conceived as a panoptic structure; its logic and effect is to extend panopticism outside the prisons themselves into the heart of the potentially dangerous under-classes of society.

I would suggest further that we are extremely intolerant of those who deviate socially if they are members of the lower classes. You have to learn and you have to work in the disciplined way laid down by authority. Failure to fit in to the accepted schedules of education and work almost inevitably leads to delinquency. In this paper, I have argued that delinquents should not be sent to prison, but the deeper question is whether we are prepared to tolerate deviance—the refusal or mere inability to fit into the disciplines of society—without forcing the deviant into delinquency. The panopticism of the prison will not necessarily disappear just because we empty our prisons of delinquents, and get them to make reparation for the damage they have done, or refer the mentally disordered offender for more appropriate treatment than prison. Indeed, it might increase, with the corresponding increase of probation services, psychiatric care and the like. From the humanitarian point of view, we surely should aim to get individual petty offenders and the like out of prison, and to keep them out, as well as attempting to redress the wrongs done to the victims of petty crime. But we should also ask ourselves why petty crime concerns us so much, why people take it up as a way of life, and whether we are prepared to go on tolerating the distributions of social goods and processes of normalization which seem inevitably produce it, and the extent of the surveillance that is invoked to control it. The following words of Ignatieff, may stand as counterpoint to my opening quotation from Bentham:

> Toleration (towards the lawbreaker) does not appear to increase with the consolidation of social order. Despite the fact that the modern state has appropriated to itself a degree of power that would have thoroughly terrified our eighteenth century ancestors, public discussion about social control in Western society conveys the impression of a state barely able to hold the line against criminality and terrorism. This alarmism, which seems so exaggerated if looked at from the vantage point of a Londoner of the riotous 1770s, acts to legitimize ever more intrusive police deployment.... The historical consolidation by the 1860s of a structure of total institutions and policing did not succeed in quieting fears of disorder but only exacerbated them. Apparently, order breeds not peace of mind but greater anxiety and recurring demands for more order. It is a need that knows no satisfaction, at least not in this type of society (1978, p. 218).

I am aware that in writing about prisons I have gone far beyond abstract philosophical considerations, and also beyond the subject of prison itself. But I will end with a speculation that is more abstract and philosophical: as to whether the Benthamite philosophy, and the whole calculus approach to questions of politics and value, whose application we see in the prison system, may not be a product of a cast of mind and a society that finds human disorderliness intolerable, and is determined to push it to the margins, socially and economically. Bentham, it will be remembered, thought that the panopticon could also be used as a school, a hospital, a madhouse, a workhouse, a factory, anywhere, in fact, where 'the more constantly the persons to be inspected are under the eyes of the persons who should inspect them, the more perfectly will the purpose of the establishment have been attained' (1787, p. 40).

Bibliography

Note: I have drawn heavily on Foucault and Ignatieff on the historical background to the current prison system, while Martin Wright's *Making Good* is a comprehensive study of the present state of the prison system.

J. Bentham *Panopticon* (Collected Works), J. Bowring (ed.), Vol. IV (1787).

D. Beyleveld, 'Deterrence Research as a Basis for Deterrence Policies', *Howard Journal* **18,** (1979), 135–149.

J. P. Day, 'Retributive Punishment', *Mind* **87,** (1978), 498–516.

M. Foucault, *Discipline and Punish* (London: Allen Lane, 1977).

R. Hattersley, 'Criminal Justice in the 1980s', *Howard Journal* **22** (1983), 1–7.

M. Ignatieff, *A Just Measure of Pain* (London: Macmillan, 1978).

T. Parker, *The Frying Pan* (New York: Harper and Row, 1970).

D. Raphael, *Moral Judgement* (London: George Allen and Unwin, 1955).

R. Scruton, *The Meaning of Conservatism* (Hamondsworth: Penguin Books, 1980).

J. E. Thomas & R. Pooley, *The Exploding Prison* (London: Junction Books, 1980).

M. Wright, *Making Good* (London: Burnett Books, 1982).

The Rights Approach to Mental Illness

TOM CAMPBELL*

The concept of rights is now so dominant in the language of politics that it is becoming difficult to identify its use with any particular approach to the solution of social problems or to gain a clear picture of its significance, its advantages and its disadvantages as a way of conceptualizing and resolving contentious political issues. None the less there is a perceptible shift towards an emphasis on rights in contemporary politics which many welcome and encourage and others question and even reject, a shift which is matched in jurisprudence by the renewed stress which many theorists place on rights as a basic legal concept despite recurrent problems associated with the concept as a tool for legal analysis and moral justification.[1] Conflicting theories of legal rights are canvassed and this in turn feeds into the debate concerning the reality or significance of non-legal rights, for the process of law reform is often presented as a matter of giving legal embodiment to the rights which various interested categories of people are asserted to possess already.

One such area of political/legal debate concerns the way in which societies respond officially to the phenomenon of mental illness. The controversial topics in this area include the procedures for and justification of depriving mentally ill people of their liberty (both through involuntary civil commitment and detention as the result of criminal proceedings), the methods of ensuring that such persons receive adequate care and treatment, and the propriety of giving certain forms of treatment (such as mind-affecting drugs, behaviour modification and psycho-surgery) against their will to persons in psychiatric hospitals. These issues are standardly debated in terms of the rights of the mentally ill. Pressure groups which support reforms in the mental health sphere, such as the Australian Council for Civil Liberties, and the Citizens' Committee on Human Rights, are identifiable exponents of the rights approach to social problems, and in general the legislation which is proposed in such areas can be characterized as increasing the rights of the mentally ill. Mental illness is therefore a promising sphere in which to try out juris-

*My warm thanks are due to the Australian National University where I undertook the preparation of this article as a Visiting Fellow in 1982.
[1] See John Rawls, *A Theory of Justice* (Oxford: Oxford University Press, 1972); R. Dworkin, *Taking Rights Seriously* (London: Duckworth 1978); and John Finnis, *Natural Law and Natural Rights* (Oxford: Clarendon Press, 1980).

prudential analyses of rights and explore their relationship to the language of the political debate which motivates the processes of law reform. The proximate objective of such investigation is to see how far different analyses of rights clarify the issues at stake, thus providing some sort of testing ground for such analyses as regards their sensitivity to current uses of rights discourse. A further objective is to reach a better position to evaluate rights approaches to social problems through a more precise articulation of what they involve in practice.

I

The popularity and persuasive potency of the appeal to rights inevitably threatens its distinctive force. Much rights-talk is little more than nebulous rhetoric with no content to distinguish it from the most general type of prescriptive discourse. It is therefore necessary to place some dogmatic limits on what is to count as a rights approach. For this reason, then, I shall exclude uses of 'rights' in which statements about rights are taken as being reducible to statements about right and wrong. Firstly, for a person A to have a right to have or do X is not equivalent to A being either right or not wrong to X, although these may normally be the consequence of A having that right. True, to have a right is, amongst other things, to have available a particular sort of reason why certain of your acts or omissions are, at least *prima facie,* right (or perhaps, not wrong), but to act according to your rights is not the same as acting rightly.

Secondly, rights are not reducible in any general way to the rightness or wrongness of the acts or omissions of others in relation to the right-holder(s). A's right to X is not reducible to the wrongness of B's intervention or non-intervention in those aspects of A's affairs specified in the right (although it is the case that most types of right do correlate with the obligations of others).[2] From the bare assertion that B is wrong to act towards A in a certain way it does not follow necessarily that A has a right that B refrain from the performance of the wrongful act. Thus the utilitarian wrongness of an act which is detrimental to the happiness of another is not to be equated automatically with the violation of a right, although if, for instance, A has a (negative) right to life, it is correct to say that, other things being equal, B is wrong to kill A. That is it is standardly wrong to infringe rights, but we may do wrong in ways which do not infringe rights.

[2] For a vigorous recommendation of a theory of rights along these lines see Charles Fried, *'Right and Wrong'* (Cambridge, Mass.: Harvard University Press, 1978).

The crucial factor in distinguishing rights from right is the transition from general principles of rightness and wrongness to the presupposed or asserted existence of specific rules by reference to which it makes sense to speak, not of rightness and wrongness in general, but of obligations to act or refrain from acting in certain ways. It is rule-expressed duties not duty in general that connect with rights. In short, rights have an analytical connection with rules, either social or legal. To say that A has a right to have or do X is to say that there is a rule such that A is entitled, or warranted, or permitted to have or do X.[3] Hence the affinity between deontological morals, with its stress on fixed moral rules and principles, and the idea of rights, and the evident gap between simple act-utilitarianism and the distinctive uses of rights-talk.

Further the connection between rights and rules is one which holds only where the rules in question have a real social existence, that is, are recognized public rules, rules held to be authoritative within a particular group or community. In fact the language of rights functions paradiagmatically as an appeal to positive (in the sense of socially accepted) rules. Rights discourse is epitomized in statements of the form '*because* there is a rule in the relevant collectivity of persons to the effect that A is entitled, etc., to X, *therefore* A is right or not wrong to X and, normally, B is wrong to prevent (or not to assist) A in Xing'. That is, in rights-talk, the existence of the rule serves as the reason why certain behaviour is or is not acceptable or required in specific circumstances. Rights can therefore function only within a community in which there are such recognized rules. This excludes the use of the idea of rights in connection with a purely personal set of moral convictions, however deontological in form.

Rights-talk, if it has a distinctive content, is used in relation to the existence of rules which enable those referred to in the rules to know that they act rightly in observing those rules without standardly being required to give further justification for their behaviour. Rights serve as warrants for action or inaction which, other things being equal, require no further vindication. Rights license the specified actions or inactions and normally render inappropriate further criticism of the behaviour in question. If A has a right to X then A may X and by and large further reasons for Xing need not be given. To have a right to X is not to be accountable (to some degree) for Xing. The extent of the dispensation from further accountability given by the demonstration that a person is acting within his rights

[3] This thesis is developed in Tom Campbell, *The Left and Rights* (London: Routledge and Kegan Paul, 1982), Ch. 2 and 3.

varies with the type of rights from a total privilege of the most absolute form of 'human' rights to a highly restricted one, as in the case of relatively weak *prima facie* rights, but where the existence of a rule provides no exemption from accountability then no right exists. Rights, to be rights, must have some degree of exclusionary force in relation to the justification of action or situations.

Further, for most types of rights certain behaviour of others (B) towards the right-holder (A) (normally either not to interfere in the exercise of the right or to provide some benefit to the right-holder) is classified as non-optional in that the decision as to whether or not to act in the specified way is not left to the discretion or judgment of B. To assert the existence of A's rights is thus standardly to assert that certain behaviour of B is required, binding, non-optional, or non-discretionary. Rights have, therefore, the function of removing certain choices from persons other than the right-holders in the community in question. They are thus mandatory in their implications. To fulfil this function right-creating rules must be reasonably specific and capable of objective application so that those with the correlative obligations cannot avoid fulfilling their duties by giving their own special interpretation to highly generalized prescriptions and to ensure that following such 'rules' is not compatible with such a wide range of actions as to entail no real restriction on the freedom of the obliged persons.

A rights approach is, therefore, a particular sort of rule-based approach. It involves the demand either that rules be instituted or that existing public rules be properly applied. What sort of rules may have to be further specified, but the analytical connection between rights and rules means that it is a necssary condition for an approach to a social problem being a rights approach that it looks to the creation or implementation of generalized authoritative prescriptions of a law-like sort.

This analysis may be thought to be an unduly restrictive position from which to undertake a purportedly neutral study of rights for it seems to exclude the notion of 'moral rights' which are alleged to exist independently of the existing rules of actual groups or societies. It is however specifically designed to exclude those uses of 'A has a right to X' which are no more than an emphatic way of saying that 'A is justified in Xing' for we may translate such an assertion without loss of meaning into 'A is right to X' so that there is no need to invoke the concept of rights in such cases.

On the other hand if it is believed that there is such a thing as a natural law, that is a set of rules which has a real existence in a metaphysical realm independent of its acceptance by any actual community of persons, then rights-statements (concerning 'moral rights' or 'natural rights') can be made by invoking such a natural law. Provided there is a recognized way for ascertaining the content of such a natural law (by reference, for instance, to an authoritative way of discovering God's commandments) then it makes sense to appeal to rules, and so to invoke the notion of rights—in this case, natural rights. For some theorists natural rights of this sort are fundamental to a rights approach but belief in a literal prescriptive law of nature is clearly a minority tenet and can claim no monopoly of the language of rights.[4]

An alternative view of 'moral rights' is that they are 'ideal rights' or the rights which would exist if certain favoured rules were established. On this interpretation 'A has a moral right to X' is equivalent to 'There ought to be a rule such that A would have a right to X'. This interpretation of what have been called 'manifesto' rights does have the necessary logical connection with the idea of rules but can be misleading is so far as it implies that the rules which, it is said, ought to exist actually in some sense already do exist.[5]

If we accept the analytical tie of rights to rules then it is possible to distinguish types of rights by reference to different types of behavioural rule. Thus liberty-rights are an assertion of the absence of a rule requiring the right-holder (A) to act or refrain from acting. Claim rights, or rights in the central or strict sense, involve rules requiring persons other than A to refrain from acting in a certain manner towards A (in the case of negative rights) or to perform some action or actions in relation to A (in the case of positive or affirmative rights). Power-rights exist where there is a rule giving A the capacity to make decisions binding on or affecting the normative standing of himself or others, while immunity-rights derive from the existence of a rule limiting the power-rights of others in respect to A. Clearly a rights approach could stress any one of these rights' types and it will be important to be clear whether a particular rights approach is concerned, for instance, with pure liberty-rights, or, at the other instance, favours the enactment of a multitude of affirmative or positive claim-rights.[6]

---

[4] For more extended treatments of the concept of 'moral rights' see T. D. Campbell, 'Rights Without Justice', *Mind* **83** (1974), 445–448, and 'Humanity Before Justice', *British Journal of Political Science* **4** (1974), 1–16; also Robert Young, 'Dispensing with Moral Rights', *Political Theory* **6** (1978), 63–74, and R. G. Frey, *Interests and Rights* (Oxford: Clarendon Press, 1980), Ch. 1.

[5] See Joel Feinberg, 'The Nature and Value of Rights', *Journal of Value Enquiry* **4** (1979), 243–257.

[6] This scheme is based on Wesley N. Hohfeld, *Fundamental Legal Conceptions* (New Haven: Princeton University Press, 1919).

Further to these basic distinctions is the idea of secondary power and immunity rights which remove primary rights from vulnerability to the normal forms of constitutionally valid change, e.g. by legislation or judicial fiat. Secondary rules may require the enactment of certain primary rules or forbid the enactment or implementation of primary rules which violate certain other rules. This gives content to the idea of fundamental law and fundamental rights, that is rights which enjoy special protection in that no legislative or other act can annul the rules on which they depend or introduce rules which violate those interests.

Clearly not all rights are protected in this way but, for many, the rights approach is identified with the idea of human rights, rights which are often said to be universal, absolute and of paramount importance. Here a clear distinction must be made between the justification of such rights by reference to natural law according to which human rights are a species of moral rights grounded in a universal law which applies to all men in all situations (a background theory which is not essential to all conceptions of human rights) and the idea of fundamental law of a positive sort whereby certain rights have additional constitutional protection, either through the device of a Bill of Rights, or through adhesion to international conventions which provide for an appeal to be made beyond municipal courts against the treatment of individuals or groups which is thought to violate the internationally approved set of rights.[7]

There is some justification in thinking of the movement towards human rights as presented by fundamental law as *the* rights approach since this is an endeavour to give greater force to the exclusionary function of rights which has been identified as their dominant formal characteristic. On this view the rights approach which is most characteristic of modern politics is the attempt to give constitutional protections to certain basic rights and thereby make available legal mechanisms for overturning or limiting the normal exercise of democractic politics.

While all rights presuppose rules, not all rules establish rights. Rights-relevant rules are obligation-imposing (in the case of claim and power rights) or obligation-releasing (in the case of liberty or immunity rights), but it cannot be assumed that all obligations correlate with someone's rights. Certainly if rights are derived from obligations (or their absence) this would reduce the language of rights to that of duties or obligations. The very least that has to be

---

[7] For a clear and straightforward discussion of fundamental law see J. C. Smith, *Legal Obligation* (Athlone Press, 1978), Ch. 12.

maintained to protect the distinctiveness of rights is that rights correlate with those obligations whose fulfilment is of benefit to others (the right-holders). On this 'interest' or 'benefit' theory of rights for A to have a right to X is for others to have obligations to benefit A with respect to X. In the case of liberty-rights it is said that A benefits from the absence of obligation on his part. More broadly, for A to have a right is for A to have a rule-protected interest. This, it is alleged, does not reduce rights to obligations (even to those obligations which benefit others) since the relevant interest or benefit is the implicit reason or justification for having the rule in question. The obligation is therefore grounded in the interest, hence in this sense rights are prior to their correlative obligations.[8]

On the interest theory a rights approach is one which seeks to solve social problems by the erection and application of rules which, more or less directly, serve the interests of the classes of persons who are identified explicitly or implicitly in the rules as the rights-holders. It makes the solution of such problems depend on the selection of the interests which are to be protected or furthered and the devising of means whereby those interests may be served by regulation.

Interest theories of rights have the advantage of accommodating the broadest acceptable range of rights. Other theories are more restrictive in that they select certain types of rights as paradigmatic. They are therefore best viewed as attempts to favour a particular type of right but their proponents would also regard them as definitive of what constitutes a rights approach.

Thus the power or will theory of rights stresses that rights-holders characteristically have the power to release Bs from their obligations as well as to require them to act or refrain from acting in certain ways (not necessarily to the benefit of the right-holder). Thus for A to have a right to X is for A to be entitled to call upon some B to perform some specific action or actions and thus to impose his will on B. The rules which establish rights are, on this view, essentially power-conferring rules, it being left open whether or not these powers are to be exercised or whether their exercise is to the benefit of the power-holder. This means that A does not have a right to X merely because B has an obligation to benefit A with respect to X but only if A can, if he chooses, call upon B to act or refrain from

---

[8] A version of the 'interest' theory is expounded in Tom Campbell, op. cit., Ch. 5; see also D. N. MacCormick, 'Rights in Legislation', in P. M. S. Hacker and J. Raz (eds), *Law, Morality and Society* (Oxford: Clarendon Press, 1977), 189–209.

acting in a specific way in connection with X and hence enforce his right (or not, as he chooses).[9]

There are analytic reasons why some theorists prefer the power to the interest theory. These have to do with the open-endedness of the interest theory which seems to generate too many rights, and the apparent absence of overlap between the possession of some rights and the purported benefits which accrue to the right-holders. But there are sufficient instances of the attribution of rights to children, ill people, the old, animals and others incapable of wielding the relevant powers to suggest that the theory is descriptively too narrow. Moreover it often seems possible to distinguish between A's right to X and A's right to enforce or waive his right to X, for the power to waive B's obligation or the power to require B to fulfil a correlative obligation usually presupposes that he already has these obligations. The theory is therefore best regarded as a recommendation that all rights-conferring rules should, where possible, be accompanied by ancillary or secondary power conferring rules which enable the right-holder to take steps either to release B from his obligations or to initiate measures to ensure that B performs his obligations when requested so to do by the right-holder. To some theorists such powers are essential to a genuine rights approach. However, it does not seem necessary as a point of logic to insist that this is true of all rights (although it is more convincing to argue that some enforcement procedure is a normal rights-prerequisite).

An alternative view of competing theories of rights is to regard them not primarily as analyses of the concept of rights but as normative theories concerning the type of moral outlook underpinning the concept, the sort of reasons which have weight in the political—legislative process. Thus it has been argued that human beings have rights because they are moral agents, rights being the necessary preprequisite for living as a moral agent, that is making choices and decisions, carrying out plans of action and responding to moral values. This view has affinities with the power theory of rights through the stress on human agency and the concomitant conceptions of practical rationality and respect for persons. It suggests that rights are grounded in the furtherance of forms of human relationships which enable and encourage individual self-determination, self-respect and autonomy, hence not only the belief that rights as powers to call on others to fulfil obligations are significant, but the

[9] See H. L. A. Hart, 'Bentham on Legal Rights', in A. W. B. Simpson (ed.), *Oxford Essays in Jurisprudence*, 2nd series (Oxford: Clarendon Press, 1973), 171–201, and Stanley I. Benn, 'Human Rights—for Whom and for What?', in E. Kamenka and E. S. Tay (eds), *Human Rights* (London: Edward Arnold, 1978), 64 ff.

extension of this idea to embrace the notion that these oligations themselves have to do with protecting and enabling the exercise of moral agency. On this will-autonomy theory all rights are said to be based on the value of individuals exercising their human qualities as potentially autonomous rational and moral agents, and in a more specific variant of the theory, human rights spell out the irrevocable minimum treatment of human beings which respects their inherent dignity as persons, persons being defined in terms of thought, choice and rational action.[10] Thus in one version of the will-autonomy theory Stanley Benn lists the following requirements of 'autarchy' which he defines as 'the condition of being a chooser':

(a) it must be possible to identify a single person corresponding over time to a single physically acting subject;
(b) he must recognize canons for evidence and inferences warranting changes in his beliefs;
(c) he must have the capacity for making decisions when confronted by options, and for acting on them;
(d) changes of belief must be capable of making appropriate difference to decision and policies;
(e) he must be capable of deciding in the light of preferences;
(f) he must be capable of formulating a project or a policy so that a decision can be taken now for the sake of some preferred future state.[11]

The interest theory can then be seen as an attempt to broaden the range of right-creating factors by including aspects of human nature not directly related to autarchy or moral agency in the confine of those considerations by virtue of which human beings have significance and can make moral claims on each other. The normative interest theory incorporates anything which can be viewed as being in the interests of individual human beings or, in a more specific version, anything which people may be interested in or concerned about. This theory does not provide as distinctive a moral basis for rights-talk and it may often be for this reason that it is resisted. But the interest theory is not totally open-ended in its assumptions for it does require that any reason for the enactment or maintenance of rights-conferring rules should terminate in the identifiable interests or concerns of individual human beings. It may be that the rejection of any values which cannot be cashed out in terms of individual

[10] See Alan Gewirth, *Reason and Morality* (Chicago: University of Chicago Press, 1978), Ch. 2; Stanley I. Benn, op. cit., 66–68; and David A. T. Richards, 'Rights and Autonomy', *Ethics* **92** (1981), 3–20.

[11] Stanley I. Benn, 'Freedom, Autonomy and the Concept of a Person', *Proceedings of the Aristotelian Society* **66** (1976), 109–130, at p. 116.

interests is a defining feature of the rights approach if it is to be characterized as a particular moral outlook. Moreover, it can be refined to provide a theory of fundamental rights by the identification of those interest or concerns which are to be given special protection against and within the normal functioning of majoritarian democracy.

A rights approach may, therefore, be broadly characterized as an approach to social problems which concentrates on the creation and/or maintenance of a set of rules specifying the existence or non-existence of obligations which have a direct connection with the interests of all or certain specified types of person, these rules being such that they enable right-holders to receive such benefits or to act in specified ways to their own benefit without this having to be justified except by reference to these rules themselves. Such rules may or may not specify certain additional powers or immunities through the exercise of which the rule-beneficiaries may take steps to invoke or impose obligations, and may or may not be protected by special constitutional provisions of the type associated with the idea of fundamental law (the human rights approach), but there must be some way in which they are recognized and applied within the community to which they pertain.

II

Passing now from the general characterization of rights approaches to the application of this analysis to the controversial area of mental illness, I will focus on two topics, (1) the notion of controlling what happens to those who are considered to be mentally ill by a system of rules of the sort presupposed by the idea of rights, especially as this bears on the criteria and for involuntary civil commitment to mental or psychiatric hospitals,[12] and (2) the significance of adopting an 'interest' as distinct from a 'will' theory of rights in considering the content of such rules, particularly in relation to the so-called 'right to treatment' which has recently been claimed on behalf of mentally ill persons.[13] I shall argue that the idea of a right to involuntary

[12] In Australia at any one time about 18,000 persons are detained in hospitals under the Mental Health Acts which make provision for some form of civil commitment. This represents a rather larger percentage of the population than is the case in the UK but less than the comparable percentage in the USA. In all these jurisdictions considerably more people are compulsorily detained in mental hospitals than are in prison.

[13] For the purpose of this discussion I shall not enter directly into the controversy over whether there is such a thing as mental illness. The fact that such a concept is used in the classification of persons for the purpose of

treatment is defensible and that the 'will' theory of rights can be criticized for its inabilty to explain such a right and, more generally, for its failure to come to terms with the idea that human beings who lack many of the characteristics of what 'will' theorists call personhood should enjoy the protection and benefits which flow from the ascription of rights, including the positive claim rights which institutionalize society's duty of care towards them.

All developed societies have some system whereby those whose behaviour is considered to exhibit mental illness or defect may be confined against their will even although they have not been charged with an offence against the criminal law.[14] Official justification for this deprivation of liberty is generally along the lines that such persons are mentally ill, disordered or disabled and that they require for their own health and safety or for the protection of others custodial treatment to which they will not or cannot voluntarily submit. The officially perceived problems therefore relate both to the welfare of the confined persons and the interests of other people who might be affected by their behaviour, The controversies surrounding such systems have to do (1) with the proferred

---

different treatment in relation to the deprivation of liberty is sufficient for my purpose. Of course if there is no such thing as mental illness then systems of civil commitment may not be defensible, but since no one doubts that the behaviour which gives rise to the diagnosis of mental illness is often a social problem and a cause of distress to the allegedly ill persons, the denial that such behaviours and distresses are symptoms of illness does not in itself remove the question of what is to be done with those who are at present labelled mentally ill. The answer to such a question may well depend in part on whether there is thought to be an 'illness' and hence the relevance of medical treatment to the problem, and the nature of the problem is crucially affected by the fact that it is the mental and emotional and volitional functioning of the individual that are problematic, but a philosophical critique of the idea of 'mental illness' cannot in itself remove 'mental illness' fom the agenda of social problems. Most of what I say in this paper relates more immediately to mental illness as distinct from mental retardation although many of the general principles involved apply equally to both groups. But see Susan C. Hayes and Robert Hayes, *Mental Retardation* (Sydney: The Law Book Company, 1982), 6; 'Mental illness, wherein an individual exhibits pathologically different ways of behaving and coping, for example, withdrawal, depression, fantasy, paranoia (to name but a few widely known examples), is distinctly different from mental retardation'.

[14] For a general comparative survey see W. J. Curran and T.W. Harding, *The Law and Mental Health: Harmonizing Objectives* (Geneva: World Health Organization, 1978). For Australian data see John O'Sullivan, *Mental Health and the Law* (Sydney: The Law Book Company, 1981).

justifications for the deprivations of liberty involved, particularly where the rationale is purely paternalistic, (2) with the question of whether or not those actually confined should be so confined even if the official justifications are accepted and (3) with doubts about the care and treatment, or lack of it, which is provided in mental hospitals, especially where this involves the involuntary administration of mind-affecting drugs, electro-convulsive therapy, psycho-surgery and various forms of behaviour modification.[15]

These controversies, fuelled by a stream of revelations about the conditions in mental hospitals and recurrent doubts about the scientific nature of the practice of psychiatry, have generated recurrent demands for changes in society's responses to mental illness. Many of these demands have been couched in terms of the rights of the mentally ill and the rights of those suspected of being mentally ill. In the United States this has involved the invocation of constitutional rights of due process of law, equal protection of the laws and the prohibition on cruel and unusual punishments. In the UK it has included cases being taken to the European Court of Human Rights and judgments being obtained which condemned some restrictions placed on the rights of patients in mental hospitals and the lack of provisions for periodic review of their detention. More generally the provisions of the International Covenant on Civil and Political Rights have been applied to the condition of the mentally ill, in particular article 9 which states that 'No one shall be deprived of his liberty except on such grounds and in accordance with such procedures as are established by law'. Further the United Nations Declaration of the Rights of Disabled Persons and the Declaration of the Rights of Mentally Retarded Persons both express a detailed concern for the rights of the mentally ill, ranging over a wide range of topics from the right to qualified legal aid to the rights to receive adequate medical treatment and economic security. These declarations have been taken into account in Australia, for instance, in the articulation of demands for the reform of mental health legislation and by the Australian Human Rights Commission in its consideration of the draft Mental Health Ordinance of the Australian Capital Territory. Mental illness is, therefore, very much a topic within the sphere of human rights. But quite apart from the specific context of the human rights movement, there is an identifiable collection of opinions to the effect that the mentally ill, when they

[15] The literature on these topics is by now very extensive. Extended bibliographies are contained in Alexander D. Brooks, *Law, Psychiatry and the Mental Health System* (Boston: Little Brown, 1974), but see also David B. Wexler, *Mental Health and the Law: Major Issues* (New York: Plenum Press, 1981).

come into contact with the official organs of the state, are a deprived minority whose rights are systematically violated.

On the basis of the analysis presented in the first part of this paper the concern for the rights of the mentally ill should manifest itself in demands for the creation of clear, precise, and justiciable rules to protect the mentally ill against the unfettered discretion of those in authority,[16] and it is indeed the case that great attention is paid by those who stress the rights of the mentally ill to the reform of mental health law in such a way as to produce clear and acceptable criteria which can be applied in courts or subjected to judicial review, both as regards the criteria for compulsory commitment and the treatment of persons within mental hospitals.[17]

Such rights have essentially to do with protecting the negative liberty of all citizens in relation to the paternalistic and police powers of the state embodied in mental health legislation. The fundamental right which is at stake here is that embodied in article 9 of the International Convention on Civil and Political Rights regarding the liberty of the individual and his freedom from the arbitrary, that is non-rule governed, power of the state. The article presupposes that states may have legitimate power-rights to control the liberty of their subjects but requires that the exercise of such powers should be in accordance with legal rules. Such rules give protective rights to individuals since people whose liberty is endangered by the state can appeal to them and so challenge the legitimacy of the restriction.

For this reason dissatisfaction with existing mental health laws is not just with the content of such laws but also with their vague, undefined and open-ended nature which means that, in effect, they are scarcely rules at all since they cannot function in effective critiques of action and as the basis for objective and impartial decision making.

A typical set of rules concerning civil commitment is to be found in the Queensland Mental Health Act 1974, Section 18 of which empowers a tribunal (of two lawyers, two medical practitioners and one appointee of the Minister of Health) to admit a patient for treatment of mental illness in pursuance of an application made by a relative of the patient or by an authorized person on the grounds '(a) that he is suffering from mental illness of a nature or degree which warrants his detention in a hospital; and (b) that he ought to be so detained in the interests of his own welfare or with a view to the

[16] On the relation between rights and discretion see T. D. Campbell, 'Discretionary "Rights"', in Noel Timms and David Watson (eds), *Philosophy and Social Work* (London: Routledge and Kegan Paul, 1978), 50–77.
[17] See Wexler, op. cit. 157: 'Whatever the good will unbridged discretion won't do'.

protection of other persons'.[18] (Similar criteria apply in the Mental Health Acts of other Australian States.[19]) Not only are such terms as 'mental illness' and its synonyms which are used in mental health acts unacceptably elastic but the idea of protecting the welfare of the individuals concerned and the notion of safeguarding other people are also of such an indeterminate nature as to make them unacceptable as part, for instance, of the criminal law (although similar problems do appear where insanity is an issue within criminal proceedings). From the rights point of view the first objection to such 'rules' is that they permit excessive discretion to those applying them so that the interests of those affected by the decisions in question are at the mercy of the arbitrary judgments of officials.

Thus the objection to the term 'mental illness' and to its many synonyms such as 'mental disorder'[20] or 'mental disfunction',[21] is initially directed to the vague and open-ended nature of such a classification which could be taken to include almost any form of

[18] Section 26 of the same act permits a member of the police force 'to remove from any place to a place of safety any person who appears to him to be mentally ill and in need of treatment or control if that member thinks it necessary to do so in the interests of that person or for the protection of other persons, for a period not exceeding three days.

[19] The Victoria Mental Health Act 1959, section 42, permits detention for observation on the basis of the opinion of a medical practitioner 'that a person appears to be mentally ill and that he should be admitted for observation into a psychiatric hospital', and compulsory admission to a mental hospital for up to six months is permitted on the basis of medical opinion that 'the patient is mentally ill and requires care or treatment'. Similar criteria are laid down in the New South Wales Mental Health Act, 1958. Only slightly more precision is to be found in the South Australian Mental Health Act 1976–77, section 14 of which requires that a legally qualified medical practitioner should be satisfied

  (a) that the person is suffering from a mental illness that requires immediate treatment;
  (b) that such treatment can be obtained by admission to and detention in an approved hospital; and
  (c) that that person should be admitted as a patient in an approved hospital in the interests of his own health and safety or for the protection of other persons.

[20] 'Mental disorder' was the term introduced by the *Report of the Committee on Mentally Abnormal Offenders* (the Butler Committee) (UK, 1975).

[21] 'Mental dysfunction' is the term used in the Australian Capital Territory Draft Ordinance, section 27, where it is defined as 'a disturbance or defect to a disabling degree, of perceptual interpretation, comprehension, motivation, emotion, or some other mental function'.

statistically abnormal mental or emotional characteristics or behaviour.[22] For, while it is possible to give more or less agreed classifications of mental illness in terms of psychoses, neuroses, personality disorders and, perhaps, mental retardation there is no professional agreement about the symptoms or causes of such conditions.[23] Nor do any of the mental acts assist with the elucidation of the concept of mental illness since they confine themselves to such circularities as 'suffering or appearing to be suffering from a psychiatric or other illness which substantially impairs mental health'.[24] Perhaps the most that has been achieved so far in this area is the insertion in mental health acts of explicit statements to the effect that certain behaviours or conditions are not to be considered as exhibiting mental illness so that, for instance, no person should be committed for reasons based on 'race, ethnic origin, sex, or religious, political or philosophical beliefs'.[25]

Taking a rights approach to be in the first place a search for precise and objectively applicable rules it is difficult for a rights theorist to get beyond the glaring insufficiency in this respect of the criterion of 'is suffering from mental illness' which in one form or another is a part of every civil commitment statute. Recourse is normally had to the effort to tighten up on the other requirements which jointly with mental illness are sufficient to license commitment by specifying more clearly what sorts of harm to the self or what type of dangerousness to others are to count. However, even if such refinements are possible, if these criteria are taken as applying only to mentally ill persons, it remains the case that this category of person is being subjected to restraints on grounds not applied to the

[22] See O. V. Briscoe, 'The Meaning of "Mentally Ill Persons" in the Mental Health Act 1958–65 of New South Wales', *Australian Law Journal* **42** (1968), 207. Also, Brenda Hoggett, *Mental Health* (London: Sweet & Maxwell, 1976), 43.

[23] Indeed the 'symptoms' of such illnesses are as often to do with anti-social behaviour as with psychological malfunctioning; see N. N. Kittrie, *The Right to be Different* (Baltimore: Johns Hopkins Press), 51. 'The very symptoms of what we commonly define as mental illness, being primarily behavioural rather than physiological, mark those afflicted by them as socially deviant.'

[24] Mental Health Act 1959 (Victoria), section 3. The Mental Health Act 1958 (England and Wales) defines 'mental disorder' as 'mental illness, arrested or incomplete development of mind, psychopathic disorder or any other disorder or disability of mind' (section 4). See also Arie Freiberg 'Out of Mind, Out of Sight: the Disposition of Mentally Disordered Persons Involved in the Criminal Process', *Monash University Law Review* **3** (1976), 134–172, at pp. 135–139.

[25] Mental Health Act 1976–77 (South Australia) section 14(1).

remaining members of society for we do not similarly lock up people who decline treatment for serious physical illness or who might be a danger to others for reasons other than mental illness, except in very precisely delimited circumstances.[26]

It is often said that what is being criticized here is the excessive power of the medical profession, or the psychiatric branch of that profession, effectively on whose say-so persons are detained often indefinitely under mental health legislation. But rule of law objections to vague and open-ended rules would apply whoever administers them, be they doctors, judges, juries or policemen. It is therefore a confusion to think that merely transferring effective decision-making to a court process, even one which goes beyond rubber stamping the prior determinations of psychiatrists, is an adequate remedy for rules which have not the precision to confer effective protections.

However, a rights approach to mental illness does often involve a demand that compulsory intervention decisions be transferred from the medical to the legal profession whose forte is the impartial administration of justiciable rules. In countering this suggestion, medical professionals argue not only that they are the only ones with the relevant skills to apply tests of mental illness and make judgments about the need for treatment but also that such matters cannot readily be subjected to the governance of rules. The processes of diagnosing and prescribing treatment for illness, it is argued, cannot be reduced to rule-based decision-making. The doctor who approaches his patient so as to give him his rights in accordance with a book of rules is not practising medicine. Hence mental health decisions are impeded not assisted by the intrusion of rights-talk into the relationship of doctor and patient, particularly in the case of mental illness where it is necessary to build up a relationship of trust between doctor and patient to which the existence of rights-mindedness on the part of the patients is not conductive. This is given as a reason why mental health laws must be vague and open-ended. Psychiatry is a personalized art and its practice must allow full scope for the clinical judgment and hence the broad discretion of the medical practitioner. This means that effective decision-making with respect to the treatment of mental illness must be left in the hands of the qualified medical professional subject only

---

[26] See B. A. Brody and H. Tristram Engelhardt, *Mental Illness: Law and Public Policy* (Dordrecht: Reidel Publishing Company, 1980), 84: 'If, in the criminal law, it is better that ten guilty men go free than that one innocent man suffer, how can we say in the civil commitment area that it is better than fifty-four harmless people be incarcerated than that one dangerous man go free?'

to the normal legal safeguards which ensure that it is medicine that the medical doctors are practising and that they are not negligent in their practice according to the standards of care and efficiency determined by their peer group.

To consider possible responses of rights theorists to this line of argument we must carefully distinguish the two main rationales for civil commitment which are unfortunately frequently run together both in the rules and in people's thinking about the whole process, namely patient-protection (paternalism) and social-protection (police powers), or the health and welfare of the mentally ill on the one hand and the well-being and safety of other members of the community on the other.

It is evidently not merely a medical matter whether an individual should be placed in custody in the interest of other people. The degree and nature of the harm to be prevented which justifies incarceration are matters for legislative determination through the standard judicial and political processes. Thus the dispute of whether only serious physical prospective harm is the basis for forcible detention, and whether the likelihood of such harm be remote or highly probable, and the standard of proof required in evidencing such dangerousness, are evidently not medical matters. In the case of mental illness the medical profession's capacity to predict dangerousness may be relevant as expert evidence in connection with the application of legal rules to allegedly dangerous individuals, but whether a given type and level of dangerousness justifies commitment is clearly not in itself a medical matter.

Further, if the assessment of dangerousness, for instance, is an essential ingredient in the decision whether or not to commit a person and if this assessment is not itself an objective matter of fact, then this may be in effect to nullify the benefits of having committal rules however precise they may be in other respects. Thus it has been shown that psychiatrists are poor predictors of dangerousness at least in terms of the capacity to identify those who are highly or very likely to commit seriously dangerous acts, although it is not clear whether in fact they are simply unable to predict dangerousness with anything like the accuracy one would expect of someone with comparable scientific status in other areas, or whether the sort of decision they have to make impel them to over-predict dangerousness in order to safeguard themselves from the charge of failing to protect the public.[27]

[27] See Cocozza and Steadman, 'The Failure of Psychic Predictions of Dangerousness: Clear and Convincing Evidence', *Rutgers Law Review* **29** (1976), 1048, and Alan M. Dershowits 'Psychiatry in the Legal Process: "A Knife that Cuts Both Ways"', *Judicature* **51** (1968), 370–377, at p. 376.

If it is the case that dangerousness is unpredictable then this means that rules which presuppose that it is predictable are a threat to the interests of the mentally ill since non-dangerous mentally ill persons will be detained unnecessarily, and in effect illegally, so that mentally ill people are vulnerable to a form of preventative detention which would be unacceptable for most other groups.[28]

On a rights approach to mental illness the logic of this situation is to reject such concepts as dangerousness as constituents of acceptable rules and hence so ensure that the mentally ill are not detained on the basis of unascertainable alleged facts. This would mean that only those who can be proved to have actually committed acts of criminal harm could be detained and that for no reasons other than those for which those who are not mentally ill are similarly confined.

All this follows from the requirement that liberty should not be lost except in terms of law where law is taken to embody certain minimal standards concerning the form or nature of the rules in question.

Different considerations, however, might be thought to apply where it is the patients' health that is at stake rather than the welfare of others. Here, in the doctor–patient relationship the intrusion of rules does seem inappropriate, for it may appear to be a matter of medical judgment both whether a person is really ill and how best to go about curing that illness. In this regard doctors may well feel that their role of treating the sick would be needlessly and inappropriately hampered by the attempt to make their relationship to patients a

[28] It is interesting to note that mental patients and ex-mental patients are less dangerous as a class than non-mental patients; see B. J. Ennis, *Prisoners of Psychiatry* (New York: Harcourt Brace, 1972), 225. If the dangerousness of mentally ill persons is predictable with a satisfactory degree of probability then committal rules involving the concept of dangerousness pass the test of having the form of an acceptable rule, just as the psychiatric profession's ability to reach a consensus of the specification of mental illness, or its types, according to criteria which could be tested in court in so far as their empirical application is concerned would make 'mental illness' a formally acceptable concept within a rights approach to civil commitment. However, this still leaves open the substantive issue of whether the rules employing these concepts are acceptable in terms of their content. In the case of the prediction of dangerousness those defending the rights of the mentally ill could require that where dangerousness can be predicted of members of other groups that these be subjected to the same constraints as the mentally ill dangerous person unless reason can be given for discriminating between mentally ill and mentally healthy dangerous persons. (One such reason might be that the former are treatable whereas the latter are not but if this is accepted then detention on the grounds of dangerousness would have to be confined to those mentally ill dangerous persons who are treatable.)

rule-governed one, particularly if the rules are other than those of the medical art itself.

In contradistinction to this position the rights theorist must argue that the 'medical' thesis ignores the fundamental difference between the treatment of ordinary illness and mental illness where the latter involves involuntary hospitalization, namely that the treatment is compelled. In ordinary cases informed consent is a prerequisite of treatment failing which the treating doctor is liable to a charge of assault. Rules are therefore required to determine the point at which compulsory treatment may be given, not the separate medical matter of what the best treatment for a specific individual might be.

So, it is argued, in the case of mental illness the paternalistic power of the state to intervene in the interests of the health of a non-consenting individual should be limited to clearly defined cases in which, for instance, there is an immediate danger that the individual will inflict serious harm or death on himself. And, again, where such predictions cannot be made with a high degree of probability then paternalistic intervention should not be permitted.[29]

There is some evidence, therefore, that a rights approach to mental illness does involve the demand for the creation of clear and impartially applicable rules of the sort which can be handled in courts or whose application can be monitored by or challenged in courts. This does give the rights approach a distinctive contribution to the debate about mental illness as a social problem since it is incompatible with crucial questions bearing on the involuntary commitment of allegedly mentally ill persons being at the broad discretion of any group, judicial or medical. The logic of this approach is that if the criteria which are used to determine liability to commitment cannot be rendered precise and justiciable then the practice should cease. Whatever the content of the rules in question a rights approach to mental illness will require that the types of mental illness, the degree and nature of the harm to self or others, and the ascertainable likelihood of these harms occurring in specific cases must be specifiable with the sort of testable precision which would make it proper to speak of rights in this area. It follows also that the procedures for applying these laws should be as meticulous as those in any other area of law in which liberty is at stake, and a great deal of the effort of rights campaigners is designed to apply the procedural rules and practices which are part of the ideal of natural justice to the sphere of mental health law on the grounds that 'The procedures for achieving involuntary detention must be at least as

[29] See Ennis, op. cit. 232.

fully delineated by the general law as those applying in the criminal law'.[30]

III

Turning now to the more substantive question about the proper content of civil commitment laws, it has to be asked whether a rights approach has anything distinctive to offer in this regard. Those who say not can point to the fact that whatever position is taken with respect to the substantive rules can always be expressed in terms of rights. Moreover the issues in question can usually be set up as involving the balancing of different rights. Thus the rights of the mentally ill to freedom is pitted against the right of the rest of society to protection, or the right of the mentally ill to be treated is balanced against the right of the mentally ill to refuse treatment. To appeal to rights to settle such questions, it could be said, is only to bandy one intuition against another. So much is to be expected in the absence of a set of ascertainable moral rights on the natural law model.[31]

However, even if we eschew the appeal to intuited moral rights as the basis for determining the parameters of legitimate civil commitment, it is possible to look to theories of rights, particularly in their normative form as guides to our thinking on this issue.

Thus on the interest theory of rights, a rights approach might be thought to direct our attention to the welfare of the mentally ill as the prime, or more weakly *a* prime factor in the construction of mental health laws. Thus in pursuit of the parternalistic aims of such laws it would require that it is the interests of the mentally ill that are paramount, an emphasis which may be of great significance in counteracting pressures (such as the nuisance value of eccentric behaviour and the trouble and expense caused to the families of the mentally ill) to use the powers of civil commitment for other reasons. And in the case of the police powers of social protection the interest theory would require at least that the interests of the mentally ill

[30] Ivan Potas, *Just Deserts for the Mad* (Canberra: Australian Institute of Criminology, 1982), 74. The South Australian Mental Health Act requires intimation to patients and their friends of the rights of appeal (section 16) and requires that appellants before tribunals and Supreme Court be represented (section 39). Seven of the twenty-six recommendations of the Consultative Council of Review of Mental Health Legislation (Victoria) have to do with procedural rights. See also N. N. Kittrie, op. cit. 199–204.

[31] See R. M. Hare, 'Abortion and the Golden Rule', *Philosophy and Public Affairs* **4** (1974), 20 f, and Robert Young, 'Dispensing with Moral Rights', *Political Theory* **6** (1978), 63–74.

should be given the same consideration as those of the mentally well, an ideal which has manifestly not always been attained when extensive deprivations of liberty are justified on the basis of a minor reduction in the risk of harm to normal members of society.

The will-autonomy theorist on the other hand, whose attributions of rights depend on the existence of the capacities of personhood which the exercise of rights calls into play and which provide the telos of such rights, will contend that, if the mentally ill are to have rights they must have the qualities of personhood, the capacities to have rights. He may argue, for instance, that even those mentally ill people who are legitimately detained have rational capacities sufficient for the possession and exercise of at least some rights. And many of the demands for the rights of the mentally ill can indeed be construed in this way, objection being taken to a crude dichotomy between competent and incompetent persons. For commitment to a mental hospital, although it presupposes that the individual is not fit to take some decisions for himself, is arguably compatible with his being left free to make other decisions.[32] After all, mental illness *per se* is not equated with legal incompetence; mentally ill people may voluntarily enter mental hospitals and patients voluntarily in mental hospitals may accept treatment. So, it is argued, there is no reason why those who have to be kept in hospital custody should not make many decisions about their lives, perhaps manage their own financial affairs, and communicate normally with people outside hospital, raise legal actions, and vote, all of which are civil rights that have been denied to patients in psychiatric hospitals.

Also, it can be argued that involuntarily committed persons who are able to make choices should be entitled to refuse certain forms of treatment, such as psycho-surgery and electro-convulsive therapy.[33] This certainly makes sense when persons are committed under the police powers of mental health acts for the public can be protected

[32] See Wexler, op. cit. Ch. 2, and the *Report of the Consultative Committee on the Review of Mental Health Legislation,* para. 7.37: 'A patient may selectively retain the capacity to exercise a number of his rights, even though his freedom to refuse admission and treatment for mental illness has been temporarily withdrawn'.

[33] Quite stringent rules are now being suggested for irreversible and experimental forms of treatment and for electro-convulsive therapy. A common suggestion in relation to psycho-surgery, for instance, is that made by the Committee on Psycho-surgery in New South Wales which suggests a Psycho-surgery Review Board that would not necessarily approve applications even if they relate to illnesses of great severity if there is an absence of informed consent. This is now in part the case in the UK (see, for instance, Mental Health Act (Scotland 1984), Part x).

by the custody of the dangerous person without the patient's will being overbourne with respect to treatment. And it can be assumed that the will theorist will allow the propriety of civil commitment even of competent persons where the rationale is the police power of the state, at least in those cases where the loss of liberty to the constrained individual is balanced by even greater protection of liberty for other people.[34]

It is less clear that the right to refuse treatment makes sense when commitment is on paternalistic grounds for it seems illogical to detain for treatment and then not to be permitted to treat (although this would not apply to a right to refuse certain types of treatment when less risky and unpleasant alternatives are available). However, it is far from clear that, on the will-autonomy theory, there would be a class of persons who have the capacity to refuse treatment and yet are involuntarily committed for purely paternalistic reasons, for if rights are given overriding importance, the existence of capacity to refuse treatment would be an indicator of the possession of sufficient capacity to refuse commitment on paternalistic grounds.

Nevertheless, at the point where the person's competence is judged to be defective at that point, on the will-autonomy theory, his rights cease. Indeed this then becomes the reason why the paternalistic power of the state can have application, for where the individual is not a person he need not be treated like a person: he has no rights to stand in the way of his being detained against his will. No doubt there are moral constraints on what we may do to such non-persons—possibly we ought to treat them with benevolence of at least the type and degree we accord to other sentient animals—but they can have no rights to limit the exercise of our benevolence towards them.

The will theory can thus give us a reasonably precise line of thought in relation to the substantive rules of civil commitment. Those who lack the rationality required to possess rights may be detained, where to do so would be for their own benefit or would protect others from the risk of harm. And it is interesting to note that Standley Benn, for instance, cites types of mentally ill people (such as psychopaths, paranoics and schizophrenics) as paradigm examples of human beings who lack autarchy and therefore cannot have rights.[35] On the other hand those who possess sufficient

[34] Thus N. N. Kittrie's first article of his 'Therapeutic Bill of Rights' is that 'No person shall be compelled to undergo treatment except for the defence of society'.

[35] 'Freedom, Autonomy and the Concept of a Person', *Proceedings of the Aristotelian Society* **66** (1976), 109–130, at pp. 113–115.

rationality to be classed as autarchic may not be committed on paternalistic grounds, except perhaps as a short-term expedient to establish their autarchy, but may presumably be constrained on police grounds in order to protect the rights of the other people, at least where those rights are of a significance comparable to the loss of liberty imposed on the mentally ill but competent persons. This would mean that in considering the residual rights of those involuntarily committed we would have to make a sharp distinction between those whose non-rationality has been a necessary element in their commitment and those competent mentally ill persons who are detained for the protection of others; strictly speaking only the latter category of detained persons could have any rights at all.

This rather sweeping removal of protections from at least certain classes of the mentally ill is in line with the practice of placing the mentally ill in a distinct category from other human beings when it comes to questions of liberty and self-determination, but it should be noted that it is very stringent in its determination of what counts as being incompetent. The individuals in question have to be incapable of rational choice, that is of guiding their action in the light of beliefs which are open to alteration in the face of relevant evidence. This would not cover the large numbers of mentally ill people whose problems relate more to their distressed emotional state than to their inability to respond to objective facts, choose according to their preferences and carry out a projected line of action.

Interestingly, such a theory seems to have no place for the right to treatment in the form in which it is pitted against the right to autonomy or self-determination. The idea that a person who is mentally ill can have a right to compulsory treatment is, for the will theorist, an absurdity, for if such persons lack rationality then they can have no rights, and if they do not lack rationality then their will cannot be overbourne for paternalistic reasons. On the other hand the idea of a right to compulsory treatment does seem possible according to the interest theory in terms of which any rule which is properly construed as serving the interests of persons gives rights to that person, so that provided what is intended is to further the welfare of the individuals in question, neither the fact that the autonomy of competent individuals is being overridden, nor the fact that these individuals have no capacity to claim or to waive their right affects its status as a right. And so on the interest theory it would be possible to talk not only to the incompetent but also of the severely depressed and withdrawn but competent person who is fearful of and so refuses treatment as having a right to treatment. We have therefore in a vivid and concrete form the opposition between the two competing rights approaches to mental illness.

At this point care must be taken over the analysis of the 'right to treatment'. This concept has had its main application in the United States of America in the context of the detention both of the criminally and civilly insane, the argument being that to confine persons for the avowed purpose of treating them or on the assumption that treatment will be given, and then not to provide that treatment is statutorily or constitutionally invalid.[36]

The ideas is that if it can be shown that a person is not receiving the treatment which is an element in the justification of his confinement then he must be compensated and/or released, or, in some cases, be given such treatment. It is therefore a right which emerges in relation to those already committed and not as a reason for committing somebody.

However, the idea of a right to treatment has also been used to enforce through the courts certain standards of care and provision in state mental institutions in the United States, and this does approximate to the idea that those who are mentally ill have a positive right to receive adequate medical treatment, the right to which appeal is made to support the paternalistic power of the state to commit mentally ill persons against their will. As such it features in declarations of rights[37] and in the preambles to actual and proposed mental health acts. Explicit use of this right to support involuntary commitment is evident in a statement issued by the American Psychiatric Association to the effect that 'unfortunately a small percentage of patients who need hospitalization are unable, because of their mental illness, to make free and informed decisions to hospitalize themselves'.[38] In a similar vein a senior Australian psychiatrist is reported to have said that the suggestion that

---

[36] See *Rouse* v *Cameron* 125 U.S. App. D.C.366, 373 F.2d, 451 (1966): 'The court's duty is to test the commitment against the supposed legislative justification, the promise of treatment'; and *Wyatt* v *Stickney* 344 F. Supp. 373, 380 (M.D. Ala 1972): 'To deprive any citizen of his or her liberty upon the altruistic theory that confinement is for human therapeutic reasons and then to fail to provide adequate treatment violates the very fundamentals of due process'. Judge Johnson declared that to be adequate, 'treatment requires (i) a humane physical and psychological environment, (ii) qualified staff, in numbers sufficient to carry out the treatment plans, and (iii) individualized treatment plans'.

[37] See the United Nations Declaration of the Rights of Mentally Retarded Persons, art. 2: 'The mentally retarded person has a right to proper medical care and physical therapy and to such education, training and rehabilitation and guidance as will enable him to develop his ability and maximum potential'.

[38] *American Journal of Psychiatry* **128** (1972), 1480.

paternalistic commitments be restricted to those who have tried or will very likely try to kill or physically harm themselves 'would deny to mentally ill people a fundamental right to receive medical treatment'.[39]

Such a right to treatment is indeed an uncomfortable notion and may seem to lend weight to the will theorists' view of rights in general and the right to treatment in particular, but the nature of its oddity requires exploration.

Firstly, we should note that there is no similar discomfort in the case of many other rights which cannot be waived by the right-holder. The right to life need not involve the right to kill yourself. It is rather the right to be coerced that presents difficulties. But of course what is at issue is not a right to be coerced *per se* (like the right to be punished, which has not a distinguished history) but the right to be treated even where this involves coercion. Coercion is not the end but part of the means to a different end. Even on the interest theory there could be no right to be coerced as such unless coercion can be seen as in itself in the interests of the individual. There is no difficulty however in thinking of coerced treatment as in the interests of the patient for the end product may be such as to outweigh the evils of coercion (Indeed, even the will theorist might argue that in such cases rights are suspended in order to allow coercion which is a necessary element in treatment to restore the individual to the point where he can have rights again.)

There is therefore a relatively straightforward parallel between the rights of some mentally ill human beings who do not wish treatment and the rights of the physically sick to whom the state has an obligation with respect to medical care, in that both groups can be said to have rights because of their need for treatment, and in both cases the right is a positive right, that is, a right actually to receive treatment. The crucial difference between the two groups is that in the case of at least some mental illness the disorders requiring treatment have to do with the intellectual, emotional and volitional capacities which are brought to bear in making decisions about whether or not to seek and accept treatment. This is what is thought to make it reasonable to override their wishes where there are sufficient grounds (such as the relief of suffering) to do so.[40]

[39] *Sydney Morning Herald* 4 August 1980.
[40] Some jurisdications make the inability to recognize the need for treatment a necessary criterion for civil commitment. Thus Alabama has the criterion of not having 'sufficient insight or capacity to make responsible decisions concerning hospitalization', and New York has 'so impaired that he is unable to understand the need for such care and treatment'. See A. D. Brooks, *Law, Psychiatry and Mental Health System* (Boston, 1974), 676.

Tom Campbell

The 'right to treatment' is often appealed to by psychiatrists to justify involuntary commitment, at least of those who have a treatable and serious mental illness. It is not surprising, therefore, to find that Thomas S. Szasz, a well-known critic of psychiatry, should ridicule this notion, and it is interesting to note that at least some of his arguments are linked to his concept of what it is to have a right.

Szasz's main point against the 'right to treatment' is that it appears to validate a system which he regards as evil. Thus in criticizing the view of Benjamin Apfelberge, a psychiatrist, who wrote that 'our students come to realize that by fighting for a patient's legal rights they may be doing him a great disservice. They learn that there is such a thing as a person's medical rights, the right to get treatment, to become well', Szasz argues that 'the "medical right" to which Apfelberge refers is a euphemism for the *obligation* to remain confined in a mental institution, not the opportunity to choose between hospitalization and no hospitalization. But calling involuntary mental hospitalization a "medical right" is like calling the involuntary servitude in *ante-bellum* Georgia a "right to work".'[41] However, Szasz's position rests on the denial that it is treatment that is being offered and as such begs the question against the possibility that people can be cured by compulsory measures. It may be, as he says in another place regarding the so-called right to health, that 'the primary concern of any moral hygiene law is to empower the physicians to imprison innocent citizens under the rubric of "civil commitment" and to justify torturing them by means of a variety of violent acts called "psychiatric treatments"',[42] but this is an allegation of fact which cannot in itself undermine the concept of the right to treatment. To do this he has to appeal to the idea that the element of choice is an essential element in any right, a clear endorsement of the will theory which, if accepted would certainly render the right to compulsory treatment incoherent, but which would also destroy the right of infants to be fed and the citizens of New South Wales and South Australian (where attempted suicide is an offence) the right to life. Indeed it appears that one of Szasz's most important arguments against the right to treatment is that it would oblige doctors to treat specified persons, something which runs counter to this idea of free enterprise medicine in which the doctor must be free to treat or not to treat and the patient to seek treatment or refuse it from the physician of his choice. But this is an ideological not a conceptual point.

[41] T. Szasz, in Humber and Almeder, *Biomedical Ethics and the Law* (New York: Plenum Press, 1976), 167.

[42] T. Szasz, 'The Right to Health', in Donald S. Burris (ed.), *The Right to Treatment* (New York: Springer Publishing Company, 1969), 59–76, at pp. 72 ff.

246

There are various devices to which a will theorist can resort if he wishes to allow for a positive right to treatment on the part of those who are incompetent through mental illness. Most of these devices, which feature in many discussion of paternalism, involve the idea of a representative or agent who takes decisions on behalf of the incompetent person. However, if such an agent exercises the power of demand and waiver relating to the principal's rights simply on the basis of his view of the interests of the right-holder then this is clearly not a will theory since it is an authorized person's view of the interests of the right-holder that is decisive.

However, it is sometimes said that the representative would decide in accordance with his opinion as to what the right-holder's choice would be if he were not incompetent.[43] This, I suggest, is not something which can be determined with any acceptable degree of, probability. If the right-holder's imputed choice is arrived at by thinking of what a rational person would choose where rationality involves standard asumptions about the ordinary desires of human beings then this is not to have regard to the wishes of a particular human individual which are paramount on the will theory. Indeed this decision process comes down to allowing the invocation of rights only where the person concerned exercises them or they are exercised on his behalf according to a strong normative standard of rationality or reasonableness which the will theorist starts out denying can be applied for the purpose of restricting the exercise of rights, for the will theorist holds that if a person has a right he does not have to justify his use of that right as being justified, even in terms of his own interests.

In the case of a normal person who becomes mentally ill it might be possible to think of his prior wishes expressed while he was well

[43] This doctrine of 'substituted Judgement' is discussed in Cathy Lowy, 'The Doctrine of Substituted Judgement: Deciding for the Incompetent', *Bulletin of the Australian Society of Legal Philosophy* No. 21 (1981), 55–71. Ms Lowy quotes from the judgment concerning Earle Spring who contracted a disease of the kidneys and required regular dialysis to keep alive. He consented to treatment but became demented. His son was appointed guardian and applied to the courts to have the treatment discontinued:

> ... a competent person has a general right to refuse medical treatment in appropriate circumstances, ... The same right is also exercised through a 'substituted judgment' on his behalf. The decision should be that which would be made by the incompetent persons, if he were competent, taking into account his actual interests and preferences and also his present and future incompetency' (*In the Matter of Earle Spring*, 405 N.E. 2d. 115 Mass., 115 (1980)).

regarding what should happen to him in a condition of incompetence, but there is no way of knowing whether in his changed condition he would endorse his previous wishes, just as there is no way of knowing whether a healthy person who has said he would rather be dead than live with severe brain damage would adhere to that opinion when he is in such a condition.

Another device is to appeal to what will be the views of incompetent persons if and when they regain their former condition of health. Thus it is said that a highly depressed person who refuses treatment and is left to his misery will, if he does spontaneously recover, criticize those who did not intervene to help him.[44] An agent might take this factor into account in deciding to ask for treatment on behalf of his principal but again I suggest that this is because this a guide to what is the sensible or right thing to do in the circumstances and not a way of respecting the will of the principal.

The parallel method of justifying intervention by appealing to the views of the patient after the treatment ignores the fact that the treatment may change his personality.[45]

Even more dubious is the appeal to the 'real' will of the incompetent person who is refusing treatment. Thus it is argued that such people have a genuine desire to get better and a subconscious wish to be treated.[46] Now there is certainly much to be said for investigating the desires of a person in order to determine what is in his interests, but this does not mean that we can interpret such desires as licences to do to those persons whatever is a necessary means to obtain what they desire and still remain within the will theory, for this is to remove the relevant choice from the decision about whether to accept or reject that which is referred to in the right (namely treatment) to the decision about something that is not directly at stake (namely whether the person wishes to be free from suffering). It is perfectly possible for a person consistently to wish to be well and to refuse a particular opportunity for treatment.[47]

[44] See Health Commission of Victoria, *Report of the Consultative Committee on the Review of Mental Health Legislation* (Melbourne, 1980), para. 3.18: '...the "sick" person might later be extremely critical, and justifiably so, of family, society and medical profession which failed to take appropriate remedial action'.

[45] See Wexler, op. cit. Ch. 2.

[46] J. Katz, 'The Right to Treatment: An Enchanting Legal Fiction', *University of Chicago Law Review* **36** (1969), 770–772: 'Behind the conscious refusal of treatment, other unconscious wishes also operate—to be protected, to be cared for, to be sustained, to be helped'.

[47] See S. S. Herr, 'Protecting Human Rights of the Mentally Handicapped', *Catholic University Law Review* **26** (1977).

In short, these various ways around the will theory's incapacity to take on board the right to compulsory treatment are in effect disguised ways of abandoning that theory in favour of an indirect appeal to the interests of those involved. Moreover, if the will theory is diluted in these ways so as to be compatible with agent or proxy decision-making in regard to the power of demand and waiver, then this should lead us to say that, on the theory in question, the right is the possession of the agent. This is a good illustration of the displaced stress which the will theory places on the option feature of rights, which is present in many but not all rights, and is of fundamental importance only in some of these.

If we wish to maintain a right to treatment which can justify making decisions on behalf of the incompetent we will need to adopt some version of an interest theory according to which it is sufficient for there to be a right that there is a rule-based obligation on others to act or refrain from acting in the interests of the right-bearer. Once we do adopt this theory it is then also possible to conceptualize the idea of a right of competent but mentally ill people to have their wishes overridden in their own interests.

Our reluctance to accept this interpretation of the right to treatment stems from the normal assumption that the individual is the best judge of his own interests, an assumption which most interest theorists share. Moreover, there is a rooted suspicion of the motives of those who claim that they are acting in the interests of those whom they coerce, a suspicion which is compounded in the mental illness sphere by the fact that society, the families of 'ill' people and the psychiatrists employed in mental hospitals can be thought to have a degree of vested interest in the confinement and medication of the mentally ill.

There are also enormous problems in identifying the interests of people other than by consulting their wishes. Clearly a judgment has to be made by someone else and that person, even supposing the sort of impartiality friends, relations and professionals, both legal and psychiatric, may often lack, must bring to bear a view of life's values and priorities which may not be shared by the patient in question. Thus there is a clear need for some trained and sympathetic person to adopt the role of advocate for the mentally ill, particularly when paternalistic reasons are being used to argue for involuntary commitment and treatment.

There is no doubt that there are great dangers of unacceptable abuse in the idea of a positive right to treatment being used to override rights of self-determination, but these dangers are not best avoided by neglecting the claims to which the suffering of the mentally ill gives rise, a great deal of which is now amenable to relatively brief and safe courses of psychotropic drugs.[48] To the extent that the will-autonomy theorist forecloses this possibility he may indeed be doing a disservice to some mentally ill people for by suggesting that the self-determination of all competent mentally ill persons be respected in relation to paternalistic treatment he may be denying them the prospect of beneficial assistance which could relieve their misery and make them able to lead tolerable lives.

Indeed, the will theorists' rights approach makes it difficult to counter both the historically powerful belief that those who lack normal 'rationality' lack rights and may therefore be treated in a way which would be intolerable for any other group except criminals, and the current trend to hold back from intervening in the lives of sick but competent persons who could readily be saved much pain and dislocation to their lives, and so leaving them to 'rot with their rights on'.[49]

Also many of the pressures exerted by rights approaches to mental illness are dubiously interpreted as demands to protect the capacity for self-determination but relate more directly to the need to prevent suffering as an end of independent worth. This is perhaps the most practical significance of adopting the interest theory or rights in connection with mental illness.

It is to be expected that my line of argument will provoke a vigorous response from the will-autonomy theorist along the lines that the welfare of the mentally ill is not at risk from his theory because where there are no rights there may still be duties, duties of care, and where there are rights these may be overridden by other considerations such as the interests of those whose rights are set aside. In other words the refusal to recognize that a rule-protected interest is a right does not entail that there will not be rule-protection of interests. The disagreement between interest and will theorists is not therefore, it may be argued, over the desired institutional facts of the situation but over the labels that are put on these facts. The will theorist says that the incompetent, for instance, have no rights, but he accepts that we have duties to protect their interests, and he accepts that the competent mentally ill do have rights but thinks that this may be overriden in their own interests. Why then insist that a rule-protected interest is a right?

One answer to this line of thought is that the will theorist is insensitive to the function of rights-talk in contemporary thought, for

[48] See Leon Eisenberg, 'Psychiatric Intervention', in Humber and Almeder (eds), op. cit., 101: 'Recent discoveries hold great promise for new and better means of diminishing the misery associated with disorders of the mind'.

[49] See Editorial, *American Journal of Psychiatry* **136** (1979), 327 f.

rights have come to be regarded as priority language in that to argue that A ought to have a right to X is to argue that A's having or doing X ought to have priority over competing demands. Therefore to protect A's interest in X where there is another competing interest which is protected by a right it is necessary to urge that A's interest also be viewed as rights-creating. This means that in order to give the necessary priority to the interests of the mentally ill it is necessary to speak of the rights which they ought to enjoy.

This is particularly true in the case of human rights which is now the terminology in which the most important claims of citizens on governments are debated. If the mentally incompetent cannot have rights then they cannot have human rights; that is, their interests cannot have special protection of the sort which is afforded by a Bill of Rights or an international convention. This is a priority classification not available to mere duties.

Thus to decline to speak of rights for the mentally incompetent may well give rise to an assumption that their interests do not have the same priority and importance as the interests of rights-bearers. This is especially so where the language of rights is taken to be bound up with the notions of injustice and injury, so that it is said not to be possible to act unjustly to someone without rights or to injure or do wrong to a person except by infringing his rights.[50] This would entail that it is not possible to be unjust to the mentally incompetent or to injure or wrong them.

Further, it will still be necessary to make a clear distinction between those duties which merely concern A and those which are designed to further the interests of A. This will often be vital in the interpretation and evaluation of a rule when its meaning or implications are in doubt or when it is in conflict with other rules. Will theorists are not inclined to say we owe duties *to* a being unless that being has a right in their sense, but this at least appears to be saying that the rationale for these duties cannot be the interests of those beings, for the idea of a duty being owed to X is readily understandable as a duty which is to be performed for the sake of X, something the will theorist seems to deny.

Moreover, it may be that the linguistic impression that will theorists are playing down the importance of our duties to the mentally ill does in fact reflect a disagreement in the ordering of priorities. It is hard to believe that the analytic emphasis on the importance of individual choice in the concept of a right is not a reflection of value judgments of some sort. Thus it may not be

[50] See Stanley I. Benn, 'Human Rights—For Whom and For What?', in E. Kamenka and A. E. Tay (eds), op. cit. 65.

Tom Campbell

incompatible with a will-autonomy theorist's position to say that
mentally competent people have in general a right to refuse
treatment offered for paternalistic reasons, but that this right is
overriden or withdrawn in cases of highly depressed people, for
instance, so that involuntary civil commitment of the non-dangerous
but competent mentally ill person is permitted, but it does seem
more in line with the stress which such theorists place on the ideal of
the pursuit of autonomy to down-grade the significance of mere
happiness as against self-determination, so that what is really going
on behind the scenes of these theoretical displays is a basic conflict
between those twin goals of autonomy and happiness, the will-
autonomy theorist tending to favour the former and so reject all
forms of strong paternalism.[51]

An alternative line of defence for the will theorist is to argue that
his analysis of rights applies only to moral rights of the sort that, I
have argued, are either fictitious entities or an indirect way of
appealing to what ought to be our rights. This means that the
interest theory is allowed to apply to many legal rights, so that it
does, after all, make sense to speak of a (legal) right to compulsory
treatment even on the will theory of rights. This is, in itself, an
important modification of the will theory but it does not undermine
the implications of that theory for the content of the legal rights of
the mentally ill unless it is also asserted that moral rights do not have
overriding priority in the determination of the question of what legal
rights they (morally) ought to have. If this second move is used then
the will theory of rights loses much of its force and the dubious
concept of moral rights forfeits its traditional role in moral argument.[52]

Finally, a point which may not be welcome to all those who favour
the right to treatment should be noted. If there is such a right then it
correlates not with the right in the sense of the power of the state to
confine people for paternalistic reasons but with their duty to do so
in appropriate cases. For the central implication of a right to be
treated is the duty of society or its representative to provide that
treatment. It is not therefore that doctors and judges *may* commit
the mentally ill when this is necessary for the protection of their own
most basic interests, but that they *must* do so, and that they must

[51] This would seem to be the case with Stanley Benn's views against
strong paternalism in other spheres; see 'Benevolent Interference and
Respect for Persons', *Bulletin of the Australian Society of Legal Philosophy*
No. 21 (1981), 99–112, at pp. 111 f.
[52] See Stanley I. Benn, 'Personal Freedom and Environmental Ethics: The
Moral Inequality of Species', in Gray Dorsey (ed.), *Equality and Freedom*
(New York: Oceana Publishing, 1977), 401–424, at pp. 405–411.

commit them to institutions which do in practice provide the treatment required. This means that it would be negligent for those charged with the duty of mental health care in a society to fail to seek the civil commitment of persons whom they had reason to believe are in need of such care.

Another implication of the positive right to treatment is that advocates of those mentally ill who are committed in their own interests would be able to use the courts to ensure that adequate treatment is forthcoming at least within the level of provision which was posited at the time of commitment. Along with this would be the right of those who seek to be accepted as informal patients to be accepted and retained in care as long as their condition warrants it. This would mean that the right to treatment could not be invoked by officials to empty hospitals and so save public funds.

These are radical implications and as such may be seen either as giving further ammunition to those who are suspicious of the right to treatment or as further indications of the benefits for the mentally ill which might follow from conceptualizing society's response to their plight in terms of the interest theory of rights.

Sexual Arousal

ROGER SCRUTON

Human beings talk and co-operate, they build and produce, they work to accumulate and exchange, they form societies, laws and institutions, and, in all these things the phenomenon of reason—as a distinct principle of activity—seems dominant. There are indeed theories of the human which describe this or that activity as central—speech, say, productive labour (Marx), or political existence (Aristotle). But we feel that the persuasiveness of such theories depends upon whether the activity in question is an expression of the deeper essence, reason itself, which all human behaviour displays.

We should not conclude, however, that it is only as an active being that man displays his distinctive causality. Men are distinguished equally by the quality of their experiences, and by a receptiveness—displayed at its most complete in aesthetic experience—in which their nature may be wholly absorbed in attentive enjoyment. Those who see the distinctive marks of the human in activity, may try to discover the root phenomena of human sexuality in the stratagems of desire. I believe, however, that we can understand desire only if we first display the outline of a more passive state of mind—the state of arousal, in which the body of one person awakens to the presence or thought of another. Arousal provides the underlying circumstance of sexual enjoyment, and it contains the seeds of all that is distinctive in the sexuality of the rational being.

Sexual arousal—considered, for example, in the terms favoured by the Kinsey reports,[1] and by other such exercises in reduction—is often represented as a bodily state, common to man and animals, which so irritates those subject to it that they can find relief only in the sexual act. The sexual act, it is thought, 'discharges', or 'releases' the tensions of arousal, and so quietens it. On this view the erection of the penis, or the softening of the vagina, are the root phenomena of arousal, and are to be observed throughout the animal kingdom. Their function in stirring the animals to copulation is illustrated also by the human species. Sexual pleasure is then the pleasure, felt largely in the sexual organs, that accompanies the sexual act and which steadily accumulates to the point of discharge and release.

[1] Alfred Kinsey, W. B. Pomeroy, C. E. Martin *et al.*, *Sexual Behaviour in the Human Male* (London and Philadelphia, 1949); *Sexual Behaviour in the Human Female* (London and Philadelphia, 1953).

The attraction of that account is partly that it enables us to undersand the localized nature of so much sexual pleasure. For sexual pleasure is not simply the pleasure of 'obtaining what you desire'—on the contrary, it is precisely a *part* of what you desire. And it is undeniable that similar physiological effects, and similar sensations, can occur in the act of masturbation, and the act of love: perhaps they occur when riding a horse, or in all those chance circumstances of contact to which the Freudians draw attention in their theory of the 'erotogenic zone'. It might seem reasonable, therefore, to suggest that sexual pleasure is fundamentally a pleasure of sensation experienced in the sexual parts. On the other hand, if matters were so simple, then we should have cause to wonder at the widespread occurrence of sexual frustration. For it would be natural, in this case, to assume that sexual desire is desire for sexual pleasure: a desire that could be as well satisfied by masturbation, as by the time-consuming stratagems of courtship and seduction. (Thus Wilde's ironical commendation: 'cleaner, more efficient, and you meet a better class of person'.)

Moreover, whatever we say about the pleasure of masturbation, it has to be recognized that there is much more to the sexual act than its final stage: there is a desire to kiss and caress, and pleasures associated with those activities. A passionate kiss is both an expression of desire, and a source of sexual pleasure. Once again, someone might be tempted to say that the pleasure here is no more than pleasure *in* the lips or mouth—thus giving credence to the idea of the mouth as an 'erotogenic zone'. But such a suggestion is, to say the least, incomplete. For only in certain circumstances is the pleasure 'in' the lips to be considered either as sexual pleasure, or as part of such a pleasure. Consider two actors kissing—or in some other way going 'part hog', as Pinter might put it. ('Joey: I've been the whole hog plenty of times. Sometimes ... you can be happy ... and not go the whole hog. Now and again ... you can be happy ... without going any hog'—*The Homecoming*.) It is conceivable that these actors might feel pleasurable sensations in the affected parts— why not? To rule out the possibility would be culpable apriorism. But surely this would not be sexual pleasure. To be sexual pleasure it must be an integral part of sexual arousal. And that is precisely what is put in doubt by the supposition that the two participants are *acting*.

What, then, is arousal, and what difference does it make to the kiss? We should compare the kissing actors with a person kissing his friend in affection. It is true that in such a case there are strong proprieties at work, derived from our sense of permitted sexual relations. In the societies to which I and my readers belong, kissing has become too much a symbol of the sexual act to be regarded easily in other terms. Consider, however, a strict Islamic society, in which any such display of sexual feeling would be shocking, and indeed so shocking as not to offer itself as a possible interpretation. In such a society, as we know, friends kiss each other freely, and with evident pleasure. And the pleasure has nothing to do with any 'pleasurable sensation' located *in* the mouth, or *on* the cheek, hand or brow. Such localized pleasures have little significance beside the act of attention with which the kiss is performed. While we may think of the pleasure of the kiss as focused in the mouth, this is largely because the *thoughts of the kisser* are focused upon his gesture, upon its tender meaning, and therefore, upon the mouth only in so far as it is itself represented within the kisser's thoughts. The kiss is a recognition of the other's dearness, and its pleasure lies in the other's rejoicing in that. In such a case all idea of a 'sensation of pleasure' seems to evaporate. There may be such a thing, but it is of the least importance in explaining the act, or in accounting for its pleasurable quality.

Arousal transforms this pleasure into a sexual pleasure. But it is the pleasure of kissing—the pleasure which one person takes in another, when expressing his affection—that is transformed. It is not the 'physical pleasure' (whatever that may be) felt in the mouth or on the cheek, but what I shall call the 'intentional pleasure', involved in the recognition of the meaning of another's gesture. Arousal seems to affect, not so much the *sensation* of kissing, as its 'intentional content': although the sensation itself is by no means insulated from the thought which provides its context.

We must, indeed, always distinguish intentional from non-intentional pleasures. Some pleasures are essentially pleasures *at* or *about* an object; others (like the pleasure of a hot bath), are merely pleasures of sensation. It is not clear whether pleasures of the first kind can be attributed to the lower animals: *perhaps* they can. A dog may feel pleasure, we are apt to suppose, at the prospect of a walk, or about his master's return. There are of course highly intricate problems here, and it is not enough to be guided by our common habits of speech. Description of the mental life of animals must depend upon an overall theory of animal capacities, and it would be inappropriate at this stage to make any unwarranted assumptions. A lion dozing in the sun feels pleasure at the warmth of the sun, but the 'at' here means only 'because of'. Clearly the case is quite unlike the manifold pleasures which this situation can inspire in a human being. And it is evident that we could not begin to understand the structure of human pleasure, if we did not recognize the predominance of the intentional component: of pleasure *directed on to* an object, about which the subject, in his pleasure, is concerned. Such

257

is certainly the pleasure that expresses itself in the kiss of affection. Might the same be said of the pleasure which expresses itself, and the further pleasure which is anticipated, in the kiss of desire?

Non-intentional pleasures ('pleasures of sensation') share the defining properties of sensation: they are located in the body, at a particular place (even if that place may on occasion be the whole of the body). They have intensity and duration; they increase and decrease; and like sensations they lie outside the province of the will—a pleasure is never something that we *do*, even if we may do things in order to obtain it.[2] As I noted above, the sexual act, and much that precedes it, involves such pleasures—or at least, it does so in the normal case. And they form an important part of the experience; in particular, their capacity to 'overcome' the subject, so that he is 'mastered' by them, acquires an important role in the intentionality of desire. For the Freudian, these pleasures are the true source of sexual delight, which is entirely focused upon occurrences in the 'erotogenic zones'. And Freud's attempt to base sexuality in sensation has an important philosophical motive: it is an attempt to incorporate the body into the stratagems of desire—to show exactly why our existence as *embodied* creatures is central to the phenomenon of sexuality. However, it is undeniably paradoxical to regard the localized pleasures of the sexual act as the aim or object of desire: so to regard them is to ignore the drama of sexual feeling, and in particular to ignore the fact of the other who is desired. Many pleasurable sensations accompany sneezing, for example, or, more appositely, raising one's voice in anger and exerting oneself in the pursuit of a quarrel. In the latter case they clearly do not constitute the aim, or even the gratification, still less the fulfilment or resolution of anger.

Procopius, in his *Secret History*, has many scandalous things to say about the Empress Theodora, wife of Justinian. One particular incident is of interest to us. Theodora, according to Procopius, had the habit of lying naked upon a couch, with millet seed sprinkled over her thighs and sexual parts. Geese would be placed on her body, and the birds would nibble the seed with rough osculations from her flesh. The contact of their bills apparently sent Theodora into ecstasies (or at least pretended ecstasies—for she was on stage at the time).[3] Suppose we were to say that Theodora felt intense pleasure at the pecking of the geese. This would surely imply that her pleasure depended in some way upon the thought that it was

[2] On the classification of mental states, in terms of these formal distinctions, see my *Art and Imagination* (London, 1974), Part II.

[3] Procopius, *Secret History* ix, 20.

geese which were pecking her, rather than, say, carefully simulated automata, or any other device that could apply the gentle pressure of cartilage to her flesh. It *could* be so, but we should certainly find such a pleasure puzzling. Is she pleased *at* the pecking of the geese, or by it, or about it? (Those are not necessarily the same.) But then, why on earth? The correct description, I believe, is in terms of non-intentional pleasure. She feels a pleasurable sensation—a host of pleasurable sensations—which happen to be caused by geese. This is not necessarily abnormal, nor is it perverted, unless we suppose her to be aroused by the experience.

But it is precisely the supposition of arousal that would strike us as puzzling. For then it would seem that the geese play a constitutive role in her pleasure, that they are a kind of *object* of pleasure. Thus, in the normal case of sexual arousal, the physical stimulus cannot be detached in thought from 'what is going on': from a sense of who is doing what to whom. Tomi Ungerer has produced engravings of 'fucking machines'—machines designed to apply appropiate stimulation to the 'erotogenic zones' of those who 'consort' with them. I do not know Ungerer's purpose, but it is undeniable that the result is a vivid satire of a certain view of sexuality—the view which sees sexual pleasure and sexual arousal as purely 'physical', which is to say non-intentional, responses. Such a view corresponds to the picture of infantile sexuality given by many psychoanalysts, and indeed, the theories of child sexuality offered by Melanie Klein have been favourably described by two of her followers as involving the recognition of the child's nature, as a *'machine désirante'*.[4] Reflection upon the case of Theodora, and the idea of arousal that would be necessary to describe it, should cause us to recoil from such descriptions, which can be made to apply only by eliminating all reference to the intentional object of experience. They are, in other words, necessarily misdescriptions, and can derive their charm only from the covert recognition that this is so, from their character as 'demystification'.

Thus, in the normal case of sexual arousal, it would be quite extraordinary if the caresses of one party were regarded by the other as the accidental causes of a pleasurable sensation, which might have been caused in some other way. Sexual arousal is a response, but not a response to a stimulus that could be fully described merely as the cause of a sensation. It is a response, at least in part, to a thought, where the thought refers to 'what is going on' between myself and another. Of course, sexual pleasure is not merely pleasure *at* being touched: for that could occur when one friend touches another, or a

[4] G. Deleuze and F. Guattari, *L'Anti-Oedipe* (Paris, 1972).

child its parent. (There are countless ways in which we are pleased at human contact.) It is nevertheless (at least in part) an intentional pleasure, and if there is difficulty in specifying its object this is largely because of the complexity of the thought upon which it is founded.

The thought involves the following idea: it is *he* who is alertly touching me, intending my recognition of his act (or, who is alertly kissing me, with a similar intention). The subject's pleasurable sensation is entirely taken up in this thought and, as it were, projected by means of it towards the other person. This is brought out vividly by the possibility of deception. Someone may discover that the fingers which are touching him are not, as he thought, those of his lover, but those of an interloper. His pleaure instantly turns to disgust: it suffers, indeed, the same kind of reversal as is suffered by an emotion, when the belief upon which it is founded is shown to be false. Thus sexual pleasure, like an emotion, may be *in conflict with the facts*. The man who feels pleasure, mistaking another's touch for the touch of his lover, is to be compared with the father who feels proud, mistaking the boy who runs first past the winning post for his son. We find it no more puzzling that a lover's excitement should be extinguished by the discovery of unknown fingers about his person than that a feeling of triumph should be extinguished by the discovery that one has not, after all, won the prize. Similarly, the discovery that these fingers, while they are the fingers of my lover, are not alertly engaged in soliciting my attention—for he is asleep, say, unconscious, or dead—will extinguish my pleasure, even if it does not change the character of my sensations.

To some extent all pleasures—even non-intentional pleasures—can be undermined or compromised by a change of belief. The meat tastes differently when I discover it to be the flesh of my favourite dog. But it is important to see that the dependence of pleasure on belief is here much looser. I might have thought I was eating mutton, and learned in fact that it was moose, or kangaroo. This does not automatically alter the physical pleasure of eating it; on the contrary, the pleasure will, in a reasonable being, reconcile him to the virtues (much misrepresented, if the newspapers are anything to go by) of moose or kangaroo. Similarly, although I would be a fool not to jump out of the soothing bath after being told that what I took for water is really acid, this is not because I have ceased at once to feel pleasurable sensations in my skin. In the case of sexual pleasure, the knowledge that it is an unwanted hand that touches me at once extinguishes my pleasure. The pleasure could not be taken as confirming the hitherto unacknowledged sexual virtues of some previously rejected person. Jacob did not, for example, discover attractions in Leah that he had previously overlooked: his pleasure in her was really pleasure in Rachel, whom he wrongly thought to be the recipient of his embraces (Genesis, XXIX, 25—and see the superb realization of this scene in Thomas Mann, *Joseph and His Brothers*). If the belief changes, then it is the persistence of pleasure, and not the *change* of pleasure, that needs to be explained.

Theodora may have fantasized that the geese-bills were the pecking kisses of some imaginary lover. And when one tries to imagine a 'pure' state of onanistic arousal—combined with un-directed, or apparently undirected, sexual pleasure—it is really such a case that one is imagining. If that is so, however, then either sexual arousal, or sexual pleasure, or both, must be intentional. The function of fantasy is to *provide* an object for our states of mind, and, by making that object subservient to the will, to enable us to enjoy a magical power over the world which we frequently long for but cannot possess. (Thus sexual fantasy is no more 'undirected' than is fear felt in response to the image of danger—as in a daydream.)

Of course, as I have recognized, there are non-intentional plea-sures connected with the sexual act, and which form an important part of what we seek in the sexual act. But they gain their importance for us partly because they can be taken up, as it were, in a state of arousal, borrowing the intentionality of arousal, and becoming incorporated into the drama of the sexual encounter. It is quite conceivable that these pleasures should occur—even the pleasure of orgasm—without arousal. For arousal is a 'leaning towards' the other, a movement in the direction of the sexual act, which cannot be separated, either from the thought upon which it is founded, or from the desire to which it leads. This may sound stipulative; but as we shall see, there are sound considerations in support of such a concept of arousal. In order to understand that concept we need to analyse, first the thought and secondly the desire, to which it refers.

In speaking of 'thought' I am conscious of speaking somewhat loosely. The 'representational' nature of our mental states cannot always be comfortably described by this term: or rather, it cannot be assumed that any particular theory of 'thought' (such as that given by Frege, which argues that the identity of a thought is given by the conditions for the truth of a sentence which expresses it), will suffice to cover all the examples of intentionality. Nevertheless, for the purpose of this paper, it will be sufficient to attempt to describe at least some of the thoughts which compose the intentionality of arousal.

The first important component in the intentionality of arousal should be evident from the above discussion. Arousal is a response to

261

the thought of the other, as a self-conscious agent, who is alert to me, and who is able to have 'designs' on me. The presence of this thought is evident from our understanding of those two all-important expressions of sexual interest: the caress, and the glance.s5 A caress, when perceived under the aspect of arousal, has the character of discovery—of an 'unveiling', to use a somewhat Heideggerian idiom. A caress of affection is a gesture of reassurance—an attempt to place in the consciousness of the other an image of one's own tender concern for him. Not so, however, the caress of desire, which *outlines* the body of the recipient; its gentleness is not that of reassurance only, but that of exploration. It aims to fill the surface of the other's body with a consciousness of one's interest—interest, not only in his body, but also in him as embodied, in his body as an integral part of his identity as a self. This consciousness is the focal point of the recipient's pleasure. From the recipient's point of view, arousal, in these circumstances, is a form of permission, a silent utterance of the thought 'Go on! Make yourself familiar with what you seek to know'. Sartre—in what is perhaps the most acute philosophical analysis of desire[6]—speaks of the caress as 'incarnating' the other: as though, by my action, I bring his soul into his flesh and make it palpable. The metaphor is by no means inapposite. However, it is important to add that such 'incarnation' would mean nothing, were it not for the element of *familiarity*, which is both offered and sought by the one who caresses.

The caress is given and received with the same awareness as the glance is given and received. They each have, so to speak, an *epistemic* component, which is also an important focus of arousal and desire. It is hardly surprising, given this, that the face should have such a supreme and overriding importance in the transaction of desire. And yet, on some views of desire, including the Freudian view, it is very strange that this should be so—strange that the face should have the power to determine whether we will, or will not, be drawn towards an act which gives pleasure in quite another part. Why do eyes, mouth, nose and brow transfix us, when they have so little relation to the sexual prowess and bodily perfection of their bearer? The answer is simple: the face is the primary expression of consciousness and, to see *in the face* the object of sexual attraction, is to find the focus which all attraction requires—the focus on another's

---

[5] See the discussions of the glance in J. P. Sartre, *Being and Nothingness*, trans. H. E. Barnes (London, 1957), 379ff, and Thomas Nagel, 'Sexual Perversion', in *Mortal Questions* (Oxford, 1974).

[6] *Being and Nothingness*, cit., III, 3.

existence, as a being who can be aware of *me*. Much has been written about the glance of love, which seems so imperiously to single out its object and so peremptorily to confront him with an intolerable choice. In truth, however, it is the glance of sexual interest that precipitates the movement of the soul, whereby two people come to stand outside the multitude in which they are presently moving, bound by a knowledge that cannot be expressed in words, and offering to each other a silent communication that ignores everything but themselves. It is as true of the glance of desire as it is of the glance of love, that it concentrates into itself the whole life of the human being, constituting a direct appeal to the other to recognize my embodied existence. The experience has been well described by Robert Grant:

> (The 'love-glance') may be anything from an open, cloudless smile to a troubled, serious gaze, but it is instantly recognizable to a like-minded recipient. It differs entirely from Miss World's orthodontic grimace, the coquette's winsome leer, or the closed, resentful stare of the fashion model (which suggests nothing so much as a juvenile delinquent interrupted in the act of self-abuse). It is completely involuntary, the more obviously so the more it is fought down by modesty (the process is matchlessly and movingly depicted by Shakespeare in the courtship of Ferdinand and Miranda). What it announces is the fact of incarnation: I am here, my inmost self, in my face. The rest of my body, it says, my private parts, and therefore I myself, all are yours, if you will have it so. Being unguarded, like the naked body whose uncovering it foreshadows, it is a pledge of innocence, and an innocence not subsequently destroyed, but fulfilled, in the sexual act.[7]

It is a familiar thesis of the philosophy of language—and one which, thanks to the work of Grice, Searle and Lewis,[8] can no longer be easily disputed—that the act of *meaning* something is essentially interpersonal. It involves an intention to communicate, and also an intention that this first intention be efficacious in revealing the content of what is said. It involves, in short, an elaborate design upon the consciousness of the other, an attempt to enlist his participation in a co-operative act. Thomas Nagel has suggested that the complex intentionality-exemplified by meaning is to be found also in the glances of desire, so that if we speak of those glances as

---

[7] R. A. D. Grant, 'The Politics of Sex', *Salisbury Review* **1**, No. 2 (1983), 5.
[8] H. P. Grice, 'Meaning', *Phil. Rev.* (1957); J. R. Searle, *Speech Acts* (Cambridge, 1970); D. K. Lewis, *Convention* (Cambridge, Mass., 1969).

Roger Scruton

'meaningful' this should not be thought to be a metaphor.[9] If Nagel's suggestion were right, then, following the theory of meaning put forward by Grice, we should expect the glance of desire to involve, first, an intention to arouse sexual interest; secondly, the intention that this first intention be recognized; thirdly, the intention that, through being recognized, it play a part in precipitating what is intended. However, although there are grounds for thinking that the intentional structure of meaning may sometimes exist in the glances of desire, reciprocity is normally of a lower order. In the normal case, the intention is that the other's desire be precipitated, not by a recognition of my *intention*, but by a recognition of my *desire*. The intended reciprocity here is perhaps sufficiently like that of meaning to enable us to use meaning as a convenient metaphor for arousal, so long as we do not imagine that sexual gestures are fully 'articulate' expressions of cognitive mental states—so long as we remember, in other words, that sexual gestures cannot be 'translated'.

The experience of arousal may then be explained on the analogy with linguistic *understanding*: just as I understand your utterance by latching on to the intentions with which you thereby acquaint me, so do I respond to your glance or caress by recognizing the intention behind them, and seeing, through the intention, the possibility which might otherwise have remained concealed. A caress may be either accepted or rejected: in either case, it is because it has been 'read' as conveying the message that 'we might surely make love'. In discovering this message through the language of your caress, I receive it, not as a raw image, so to speak, a shocking presentation of an outlandish possibility, but as a thought concealed within your gesture, which you too are discovering in the very act of discovering me. Ovid's instructions to the seducer (*Ars Amatoria*, Bk 1) are finely aware of this reciprocal intentionality. They illustrate the idea that the caress and the glance must not reveal premeditation: that truly arousing conduct is that in which the awakening of the woman seduced is made to seem like a mutual self-discovery, so that *she* seems, in her own eyes, to be responsible for what he feels.

The intentional structure just described, while clearly distinct from the structure of (linguistic) meaning, has much in common with it. But we should be misrepresenting the intentionality of arousal if we saw it simply in these terms, without considering the crucial element of 'bodily awakening', which each participant both feels in himself and seeks in the other. This experience is a crucial aspect of our experience of embodiment—and of our nature as embodied beings. It may be illustrated by an example, which will

[9] Thomas Nagel, 'Sexual Perversion', cit.

264

also help to emphasize the peculiar kind of representation that is intrinsic to arousal. Consider the case of a woman, who opens to her lover's explorations—

> Ile be a parke, and thou shalt be my deare:
> Feed where thou wilt, on mountaine, or in dale;
> Graze on my lips, and if those hils be drie,
> Stray lower, where the pleasant fountaines lie ...
>
> *(Venus and Adonis)*

This opening (in the above lines, an importuning) is a fundamental gesture of arousal, and would be inconceivable without the idea of him, the lover, taking an interest in her as she is in her body. Venus's offendedness stems directly from her perception that this idea is no more than a fond illusion—having exposed herself to so much, she must then destroy the unfeeling witness of her humiliation. It is integral to the woman's thought that her lover is a conscious being, and also conscious of himself, as an agent and patient in the sexual transaction. Morover, she thinks of him as having a conception of her body, and of her in her body. Her sense of his caress is of an invitation: she experiences it as fundamentally *addressed* to her *through* her body, and *in* her body. Arousal is founded first, in the thought of his bodily presence, as a source of interest in her, and secondly in a desire to address to him the equivalent of what he addresses to her.

In the first impulse of arousal, therefore, there is the beginning of that chain of reciprocity which is fundamental to interpersonal attitudes. She conceives her lover conceiving her conceiving him.... (Sartre argued that such infinite chains of response show sexual desire to be impossible. However, the regress is indefinite, not infinite, and certainly not vicious. For just such a chain of response is involved, whenever one person understands another's meaning.)[10] There is also a specific experience of embodiment. My sense of myself as identical with my body, and of you as identical with yours, are crucial elements, both in the aim and in the reception, of the arousing caress. I am awakened *in* my body, to the embodiment of *you*. Underlying the woman's state of arousal is the thought: 'I, in my body, am something for him', and her response—the 'opening' to his approaches, and all that is entailed in that—must be understood in part as an *expression* of that thought, and of the interpersonal intentionality that is built upon it.

[10] Grice, 'Meaning', cit; P. F. Strawson, 'Intention and Convention in Speech Acts', *Phil. Rev.* (1964), reprinted in *Logico-Linguistic Papers* (London, 1971).

Although I am identical with my body, my experience of embodiment must be sharply distinguished from my experience of the body. In arousal the unity between body and person is immediately experienced, and forms the living focus of an interpersonal response. But the body is not the object of this response—as it is the object of a pathologist's examination, or an anatomist's exposure. Arousal reaches through the body, to the spirit which animates its every part. There are indeed 'bestial' inclinations, which seek to sunder the body from the spirit, and to present the first as the single focus of a sexual interest. But the interpretation of these inclinations is a matter of difficulty to us, precisely because their intentionality eludes our understanding. Consider again the female experience. In the 'normal' case of feminine bestiality the animal in question (a favourite dog, say), is treated *as if* he were a person. Not, perhaps, a very developed person, and not even a fully responsible person. But nevertheless a creature with at least one of the attributes that distinguishes persons: the attribute of the 'first person point of view', which enables him to see the world as something other than himself, and to take an interest in it, not only as the repository of warm and welcoming objects, but also as the field of action of other beings like himself. For it is the sense of this in the dog's perspective—a sense which, however erroneous, is natural to our anthropomorphic way of seeing things—which permits the gestures of arousal. The dog, too, is perceived as an embodied person.

This is not to say that there is not true bestiality in women—an interest in the animal body *as such*. John Aubrey's description[11] of the voyeuristic Countess of Pembroke, who would watch the coupling of horses in order to prime herself for the lovers who were to mount her, is perhaps a case in point—although one can see at once how vast a shadow is cast in her desire, by her own self-conscious perspective. Perhaps the countess wished to see her lovers *as* animals, in order to be excited by the thought of herself as similar, indifferent to the human attributes and interpersonal demands of the creature who is mounting her. This is a refined case of true bestiality, in which the other both is, and is thought of as, an animal. True bestiality is perverted. 'Perverted' means turned from some 'normal' aim. In this case, the arousal is turned from a person to the caricature of a person—to a creature which either is, or is thought to be, stripped of that first-person perspective which gives sense to the intentionality of arousal. The bestial act, which abrogates the responsibility of the object, abrogates also the

[11] John Aubrey, *Brief Lives*, O. L. Dick (ed.) (London, 1949), 138.

responsibility of the subject—and that is its point. It is an attempt by the subject to flee from the burden of interpersonality, to be *merely* an animal, in this encounter which could otherwise not be accomplished without intolerable disgust.

Of course, a person may take a distinctly personal pleasure in this—in the spectacle of his own degradation. But that it *is* a degradation should not be doubted. It involves a falling away from the normal condition of arousal, and a rejection of personal responsibility. No doubt there are physical sensations, and glandular transformations, that occur equally in normal human arousal and in its perverted counterpart (else there would be no call for the idea of 'perversion'). And if the *only* difference were to be found in the fact that, in the first case, the object is conceived as a person, in the second case as something essentially non-personal, and if there were no further difference that followed from this, then it would be arbitrary to distinguish them. But the differences between the attitudes, stratagems and satisfactions that arise from normal sexual arousal, and those that arise from its perversion, are so great as to justify the contrast between them. If you leave out the context, then you can always give arguments for assimilating states of mind, however different they may be. You could, for example, assimilate love to hatred on the basis of their common fascination with another's well-being, or running to swimming on the basis of their common movements. My argument implies that the glandular transformations and physical sensations that accompany arousal stand to arousal much as the movements of the legs stand to running. They are an essential part of it, but may equally occur in its absence. And, as in the case of running, what makes them what they are, is the intentionality of the state of mind which is expressed in them.

Furthermore, the sexual organs do not appear, so to speak, *neutrally* to us, at times of arousal. The sexual organ undergoes a transformation which is essentially dramatic, and not merely physiological. Both in my own eyes, and in the eyes of the other, my sexual organ becomes *me*. To be penetrated by my penis is to be penetrated by *me* (to be enclosed by my vagina is to be enclosed by *me*). Suppose there were two such organs—suppose, for example, that a man could strap on his 'tool', remove it, replace it, and exchange it. In these cases there is a kind of de-personalization of the phallus: it is, to use Hannah Arendt's useful term, 'instrumentalized'.[12] It begins to lose some of its intrinsic personal interest, and comes to seem, instead, like the lurid dildoes that are on display in sex shops, and which owe their appeal precisely to the

[12] Hannah Arendt, *The Human Condition* (Chicago, 1959).

Roger Scruton

fact that they are severed from the human body and the human will. (And which therefore have precisely *no* appeal to the person of normal sexual inclinations.) Even if, by some miracle, it would be possible to feel pleasurable sensations *in* the tool, rather than through it, it would cease to be the recipient of the kind of individualizing attention which the lover normally craves. Caresses would direct themselves, not to the tool itself, but to the body to which it is attached, perhaps at the point of attachment, which would begin to gather to itself some of the magic of the phallus, and some of its constant dialectic of modesty and pride. (There would be no point in concealing or revealing the thing itself, but much point in so 'dramatizing' its mode of attachment.)

To be aroused by another is to incorporate that other into a sexual project, the project of love-making. We feel that there is something perverted, and perhaps inexplicable, about the man who claims to be aroused by one person, in order to perform the sexual act with another. Of course there are many cases here—the extreme example being perhaps the Empress Messalina, described by Juvenal (Satire VI), of whom we might wish to say that she was the victim of an insatiable appetite for sex, which, having been roused by one man, required her to proceed to others, and so on, *ad infinitum*. But notice that an important new element has been brought into the description: that of 'appetite'. The purpose is precisely to lift the phenomenon out of the realm of normal sexual arousal, and attribute to it a character, and an explanation, which are not otherwise exemplified. There is something very important in common to the Empress Messalina's desire and that of any other normal human engaged in the sexual act. But there is also something very different. The difference lies in the intentional content, and it is this difference of intentionality that is signalled by the idea of 'appetite'.

Of course there are less serious cases than that of nymphomania: the more normal case is that of someone who, having been aroused by one person, contrives to curtail that arousal, in order to engage in the sexual act with another. Here there are in fact two states of arousal, which may be closely joined but which can never be one. The first arousal does not *point* towards the second; it has no natural history of which the second is an episode. The anticipation which is invoked in it is not for the act which is intended, but for another which is denied. The case is to be compared with that of a man who whets his 'appetite' for paintings by contemplating, say, Poussin's *Golden Calf*. It may be that, after a period of visual 'starvation', such a project has much to recommend it. But we know very well that the terms 'appetite' and 'starvation' are here being used metaphorically. We cannot conclude that the man's real interest, in studying the

268

Poussin, is one that might have been equally satisfied by a Velasquez, a Gauguin, or whatever object he may subsequently enjoy. On the contrary, he was attempting to revive in himself precisely that kind of interest in painting which compels him to treat each example 'for its own sake alone'. In other words, his interest in the Poussin cannot be satisfied by a Velasquez, say; if it could, that would only show that it was not the *Poussin* which interested him, but any painting that would 'do just as well'. In such a case we could indeed speak of 'appetite', but what kind of appetite this is, what are its meaning, value, and rationale—all these would be highly mysterious. Likewise in the case of sexual arousal. The arousal must be understood as a response to a particular person. Even if it is possible to 'whet one's appetite' for such responses, this cannot show that they are 'transferable' from object to object, like the desire for wine which leads one to sip assiduously from every glass.

To the intentionality of arousal must be added that of excitement. The 'epistemic' intentionality that I have discerned in sexual arousal has an intrinsically cumulative character, and leads the subject constantly onwards with an effect of discovery. Each phase of arousal contains an anticipation of the next. Excitement can exist in both non-intentional and intentional forms—as a general state of heightened response, and as a particular state of excitement *about* or *over* some matter of interest. In the latter case the element of anticipation and discovery—the 'epistemic' structure—is always paramount. Excitement is part of the dynamic character of arousal: and this dynamic character marks yet another difference between sexual arousal and physical hunger. At every point there is a pleasure of expectation and anticipation, which carries the subject forward, and which also forms an integral part of what is pleasurable *now*. Sexual excitement is responsible for the 'masterful' and 'urgent' quality of desire. It leads to the sense that desire 'overcomes' the agent, and deprives him of his freedom. (And therefore, according to some philosophers, notably Schopenhauer, it leads to the illusion that desire is an *exercise* of the will, and a peculiarly fruitless one, destined only to post-coital disappointment.) Excitement involves the thought of something happening, and not just a physical sensation—I am not excited in *this* way by the prospect of a cigar, a glass of ale, or a hot bath. I am excited precisely by a co-operative enterprise, in which I and the other gradually evolve within each other's perspective, changing for each other and through each other, with a constant and reciprocal anticipation of our mutual intentions.

What, however, are we excited about? Although sexual excitement is a special case (a very special case) of the excitement to be observed in all friendly conversation, it has a focus which normal conversation lacks.

Roger Scruton

This focus is our mutual embodiment, the other's 'being in' his body, and I in mine. In our excitement we sense each other's animation, and become acquainted with the pulsing of the spirit in the flesh, which fills the body with a pervasive 'I', and transforms it into something strange, precious and possessible. The penis which hardens, and the vagina which softens, to the longed-for touch, convey the whole person, just as he is conveyed in his laughter and his smile. (Hence, while you can 'possess' another in his body, you cannot possess the body alone: necrophilia, like rape, involves no fruition of desire.)

Sexual arousal has, then, an epistemic intentionality: it is a response to another individual, based in revelation and discovery, and involving a reciprocal and co-operative heightening of the common experience of embodiment. It is not directed beyond that individual, to the world at large, and it is not transferable to another, who 'might do just as well'. Of course, arousal might have its origin in highly generalized thoughts, which flit libidinously from object to object. But, when these thoughts have concentrated into the experience of arousal, their generality is put aside; it is then the other who counts, and his particular embodiment. Not only the other, also I myself, and the sense of my bodily reality for him. Thus Molly Bloom:

> and how he kissed me under the Moorish wall and I thought well as well him as another and then I asked him with my eyes to ask again yes and then he asked me would I yes to say yes my mountain flower and first I put my arms around him yes and drew him down to me so he could feel my breasts all perfume yes and his heart was going like mad and yes I said yes I will Yes.

It can readily be seen why it is that, in the normal case, arousal seeks seclusion—seclusion with the other in a private place, where only he and his point of view are relevant to my intention. Moreover, arousal attempts to *abolish* what is not private—in particular to abolish the perspective of the onlooker, of that 'third person' who is neither you nor me. Milan Kundera describes an orgy in which two of the participants catch sight of each other across the room. The passage shows what an enormous effort is involved in sustaining true sexual arousal, when the veil of privacy has been discarded. In effect, the consciousness of observation destroys the intentionality of the act:

> Both couples were in the same situation. The two women were leaning over the same way and doing the same things. They looked like enterprising gardeners working in a flowerbed, twin gardeners, one the mirror image of the other. The men's eyes met, and Jan saw the bald man's body shaking with laughter. They were united as only an object can be united with its mirror image: if one shook, the other shook as well.... The men were united by telepathic communica-

tion. Not only did each know what the other was thinking, they both knew the other knew (*The Book of Laughter and Forgetting*).

Eventually laughter gets the better of them, and their hostess, partner of one of the men, is mortally offended. The laughter, however, is the expression of a particular perception of the sexual act. When witnessed from the third-person point of view, the focus of the act is no longer the embodiment of the participants, but their *bodies*. This being witnessed by the other, tends to kill all arousal in the subject. Clearly, neither man is responding to the woman who attends to him—only to the contact of her body. The two women might have been mechanical dolls; and indeed, they have become mechanical dolls, in the laughing eyes of those who suffer their attentions. The laughter expresses the incongruity of the act, when it is divorced from the sentiment of arousal. The personal has been made public, and in the act of public recognition, it has become impersonal and routine. The frenzy of the orgy might be seen, indeed, as a reaction to the futility of sexual experience, when the urge towards impersonality is elevated into its single goal (see A. Huxley, *Ape and Essence*).

The aversion from the public which is characteristic of arousal, could also be described as a 'fear of the obscene'. The obscene is the representatiion or display of the sexual act in such a way as to threaten or ridicule its individualizing intentionality, by placing the body uppermost in the thoughts of those engaged in it. If the desire for sexual stimulation is represented as directed indifferently towards, say, the penis, or towards anything possessing a penis, or towards a human body considered independently of its agency, viewpoint and will—if, in other words, sexual arousal is represented as an urge or appetite, focused on cetain parts of the body, and satisfiable indifferently by anything with the right equipment—then the result (as in the ballad 'Nine Inch Will Please a Lady', attributed to Robert Burns) is normally obscene.

Obscenity is akin to bestiality. It standardly involves the attempt to divorce the sexual act from its interpersonal intentionality; from that epistemic 'directedness' that is contained within sexual arousal. But the divorce is effected by a peculiar shift of attention. In obscenity, attention is taken away from embodiment towards the body; the body rises up and inundates our perception, and in this nightmare the spirit goes under, as it goes under in death. Thus particular bodily perceptions—those which English children express in the sound 'ugh' and Yiddish-influenced Americans in the sound 'yuk'—play a prominent part in the experience of obscenity. The sense of the body as rotting, glutinous, adhesive—all that Sartre refers to in his celebrated analysis of *'le visqueux'*[13]—may dominate our perceptions, and

---

[13] *Being and Nothingness*, cit.

nowhere more insistently than in our experience of sex, in which bodies adhere through their viscid and agglutinative parts. In the experience of the obscene the person is as it were eclipsed by his body, which, because it fits exactly to his shape and movement, creates an absence, a darkness, where he should otherwise have been. I no longer find the person whose embodiment enticed me: only the body which, in its frightful dissolution, its character as melting flesh, fascinates and also repels me.

In the eyes of an onlooker, someone not party to our arousal, our bodies invite obscene perception. (Hence there can be obscene representation of wholly innocent sexual acts.) The observer is not engaged in the delicate negotiations whereby we coax each other into our bodies, so as to experience that intense excitement which transforms the sexual union into a union of persons. The spectator of our antics sees, first and foremost, the agglutinating bodies. The thought of his interest is precisely an obscene thought, in which our embodiment is obliterated by our bodies, and rendered alien, impersonal, prey to the fascinated curiosity of the disgusted child. We see ourselves, so to speak, under the aspect of 'yuk!' (This is one reason that might be offered for the view that, whatever else they may be, masturbation and voyeurism of the kind experienced in the video booth do not involve the release and satisfaction of the impulses which more fortunate beings may release and satisfy in the act of love.)

Sexual arousal can occur only between persons, and is an artefact of their social condition. An immense moral labour has gone into the construction of the intentionality of arousal, and while it is willing labour, constantly performed anew, by each generation of consenting adults, it might not have occurred. The state of mind that I have described is one of those achievements of civilization which it would be folly to discard and yet which can, like morality, be discarded at almost any time. There is, however, a temptation which wars against arousal: the temptation to free the sexual act from the demanding stratagems of personal communication, and to represent as appetite that which can become appetite only by losing its characteristic intentionality.

Questions about the nature of mental items are to be answered, not by scientific investigation, but by philosophical (which means equally 'phenomenological' or 'conceptual') analysis. Of course, scientific investigation of mental phenomena is also possible. There could be a science of sexual behaviour, which might show important similarities between human beings and the lower animals. It is likely that there are such similarities, since sexual behaviour is explained, in both cases, by a reproductive function. But such an investigation would not answer the questions that I have been considering. Those questions concern the perceived surface of things, from which our mental concepts take their sense. I believe that there is a significant phenomenon, to which I have given the name arousal, and that we single out this phenomenon—either by referring to it, or, more normally, by selectively responding to it—in much of our ordinary social behaviour. There may be other things that someone may wish to call by the same name—the sexual readiness of animals, or the titillations that occur in the bath. But, at the superficial level (which is the level which matters), these must be distinguished from arousal, to the extent that they lack the intentionality of arousal. I have been discussing a phenomenological problem: the problem of the intentionality of a state of mind. That such problems are (scientifically speaking) superficial should not lead us to discount them; still less should it lead us to look for a solution to them in the results of science. For persons too are superficial, as are their values, their projects, their griefs and desires. Better, however, the shallowness of persons, than the unfathomableness of things.

Child Adoption and Identity

A. PHILLIPS GRIFFITHS

I am concerned with a very problematic concept[1] of identity which one encounters in studies of practical problems concerning the adoption of children. The notion is problematic in the extreme, as I shall try to show. It seems to crop up not only in the work of researchers on this topic, but in the spontaneous and (apparently) untutored accounts of themselves given by adoptees. The question is whether there is a concept here at all: by which I mean not, instead, a family of concepts linked by family resemblances, but rather some disparate ideas linked only by verbal similarities, and run together for mistaken theoretical purposes. The notion arises crucially in attempts to deal with practical questions arising in determining policies with regard to adoption: with regard to the placement of children for adoption, and the advice to be given to adoptive parents and to adopted children, whether young or adult, who encounter, or perhaps do not even encounter, difficulties.

To avoid dealing with two problematic concepts rather than one, I had better say what I mean by the adoption of children. I mean the assumption of parental responsibilities with regard to a child by adults who are not the child's natural parents or very close relatives; and for my purposes it will be convenient to have in mind those cases where this assumption of responsibility is not merely *de facto* but legal: indeed, assumed under the relevant legal acts. (Persons can be charged with criminal neglect of a cat where they have merely by their practice made the cat dependent on them; but I am not sure whether the same is true of nurturing a waif or stray, in the way that a man can acquire legal responsibilities towards a woman by living with her without going through a formal marriage ceremony.) I am not concerned with those large number of cases where one of the parents is a natural parent who remarries and the step-parent wishes to take on the legal responsibilities and rights of a parent. Problems (including what are regarded as problems of 'identity') can arise in such cases, according to the sparse literature on the subject which deals with them mainly only for purposes of comparison; but

---

[1] I have dispensed with the usual footnotes and references. I am not dealing with the anatomization of scholarly works, but trying to pick out some features of a confused area which is nevertheless practically important. Instead, I append a short bibliography.

obviously in such cases the practical problems of placement do not arise.

Practical problems of placement and counselling with regard to adoption tend to arise not in the courts but in social work practice. The courts do of course regulate and regularize adoptions, but not at all in the same way that the courts determine custody. Adoption is regulated in that adoptions can be arranged by organized bodies which are approved, including local authorities, but once given that approval the discretion is theirs and is respected by the courts whose function is largely formal. Individuals who have parental rights can arrange adoptions through a private third party without the kind of positive concern and supervision exercised by an adoption society or local authority, except for the latter's rather negative responsibilities as guardian *ad litem*. The only way in which legal principles governing adoption can come into play is when it can be established that the child concerned is involved in a dispute—for example when a natural parent withdraws permission to adopt before the adoption is legally finalized—and is in such danger that he should be made a ward of court. In determining custody, judges are strictly bound to treat the child's welfare as paramount, though the wishes and interests of other parties such as the natural parents can be taken into account. However, organizations concerned with adoption placement have greater discretion, and their judgment can be called in question only if it can be shown that their judgment would lead to actual harm. For this reason social work practice is influenced by discussion, theory, and professional opinion in an informal way, as opposed to the courts' reliance on statute and precedent. And of course it is difficult to see how matters could be arranged otherwise. If anything, it may be thought that legalistic processes play too great a part in such matters (as in the case of divorce, where disagreement and dispute are exacerbated by being dealt with in a litigious adversary system: unlike some states in the USA where the courts will not entertain cases until they have been through a process of professional, impartial conciliation). But this necessity makes it all the more vital that social work practice should not be based on incoherent notions.

Where the courts are involved (as they much more frequently are in cases of disputed custody in separation and divorce) they too have considerable discretion. This is for the simple reason that while the law insists on the child's welfare, it provides no algorithm for deciding in what that welfare consists. This is clear from the fact that over the last fifty years or so criteria used in judicial decisions have changed considerably. In a dispute between natural parents over a child's custody in a divorce case, considerations concerning which was what was then called the 'guilty party' would not in themselves be relevant, but in earlier decisions that, in effect, tended to be the case because it was thought that a child's welfare would demand that he not be brought up by an adulterer; whereas nowadays preference would tend to be given to the mother whether or not her unreasonable behaviour were constituted by adultery. Among criteria used to decide wherein a child's welfare consists have been ones concerning identity. Thus a judge awarded custody to a natural father, where the situation would otherwise have indicated differently, on the grounds that the child should grow up 'knowing who he is'.

My first reaction to this some twenty-five years ago was one of incredulity; then as now the remark sounded to me idiotic. But idiotic or no, the judge seems to have been using a notion which, even if he could not explain it, seems to be one accepted as sensible by many; and they would find considerable support for their view in the unstudied, spontaneous language of *some* adopted children *who seek knowledge of their origins*.[2] I quote some.

I feel funny and not whole. It feels like not being you.

I don't feel I know who I am and it is a feeling I had when I was younger and if I live to be ninety it will bother me and be the same ... just the fact that you don't know who you are stays with you for life. It is a weird thing. I feel I have no identity.

When I was fifteen or sixteen I was curious to know 'who I was' and especially to know about my natural parents and their families.

If I had some description of my parents it might help me recognize myself.

A weird thing, indeed. Not, however, the weird thing that philosophers so often talk about, by which I mean the metaphysical problem of personal identity. It is not the problem of personal identity discussed by Locke, or the problem Hume was unable to solve in his famous appendix to the Treatise. It is not that they have any doubts about, or are even concerned with, Kant's conception of the noumenal self which underlies the empirical self and which must be presupposed in thinking of oneself as a moral being. It is not even the rather more commonsense philosophical problem of the necessary and sufficient criteria for the application of the ordinary expression 'same person'. Discussion of these philosophical issues will be of no help, in my view, in this area of appplication. Not, of

[2] These quotations are supplied in Triseliotis' excellent and sensible *In Search of Origins* (1973).

course, that they are not important issues, issues indeed of the first importance.

What, then, is this weird sense of 'identity' which some of these people claim to have lost, or never had? Some researchers have tried to get at it by asking people who do not feel this desperation how they would answer the question 'Who am I?'. I quote one report of such research: 'Identity is closely related to an answer to the question "Who am I?"; and when people are asked how they would answer this question they have been found to answer predominantly in terms of the social positions they occupy or in terms of the social roles they perform'. This finding is not of much help in understanding what the adopted children are asking (it can't be that they are doubtful about the jobs they do), but I think there is a clue to the weirdness of the adopted child's question if we consider what this research programme assumes. It assumes that we can find out how people conceive identity by asking them to ask themselves the question 'Who am I?' and find out what they most naturally answer, observing the best canons of unbiased research by suggesting no preconception as to what kind of answer there might be. This ignores the fact that even if no preconception is suggested, the subject will be forced to find some preconception in order to give any answer at all. (And some answer *must* be given: lay experimental subjects are notoriously respectful of men in white coats.) Imagine that you were asked face to face with your man in the white coat 'How would you naturally answer the question "Where are you?"'. It is surely a difficult question to answer even though you know perfectly well know where you are: in the psych lab; but *that* can't be the query, because the researcher knows that: he's there too. You may know you are in London, but is then the natural answer to that question 'In London'? Your wife calls from another room 'Where are you?' and the answer 'I'm on the telephone' would be a natural answer, whereas 'I'm in London' would be silly. You 'phone someone in New York who asks 'Where are you?'; 'I'm in London' would be a natural answer, but 'I'm on the telephone' would be infuriating. If there is any right answer to the question it is 'Here', which is as uninformative as the question is empty. To give any other sort of anwer to a question of this sort surely requires that one imagines some context in which somebody wants to know something of a certain sort; and indeed in asking who one is one might very well imagine one is in a social situation where what is in question is one's social role ('I'm the night porter').

The adopted child cannot put himself in this position because he is not trying to think of a context in which somebody else wants to know who he is; he is somehow asking this question of himself. Part of the weirdness arises from the fact that one simply does not normally ask this question of oneself. But there must be some explanation of what the adopted child wants to know, or thinks he doesn't or can't know. I will hazard an explanation, which suggests that a simple-minded but not entirely unusual mistake is being made, one I might christen 'the senatorial fallacy'.

Strawson has shown in his book *Individuals* that basic particulars require a structure in which individuals can be identified and re-identified. Material objects require the structure of time and space, and the other basic particulars, persons, are dependent for their identification on the identification of material objects. It will be enough for the unique identification of any basic particular, including a person, if it is individuated in terms of spatio-temporal co-ordinates which place it uniquely, and for references to it at other times and places to be satisfiable in terms of spatio-temporal continuity. However, there will be difficulties of a contingent kind in some cases of establishing spatio-temporal continuity, and these may be to some degree minimized by setting the original 'fix' in terms of one set of co-ordinates rather than another. It may be that everybody at some time and only one time passes through the turnstile at Charing Cross station, but even so having a system of referring to individuals as 'the nth person to pass the turnstile' would not be of much practical use. For different purposes, we use different criteria. So, for example, a man identifies himself in his will as 'I, John Doe, medical practitioner, of 1 High Street, Wigan'. For purposes of probate this does very well; we are more concerned with his property at and subsequent to the making of his will than whatever might have been the situation before. It would be better of course if the testator could identify himself as a person of a certain name and place at the time of his death; but few testators can be in a position to do that, unless on their deathbeds. Again, it might be most convenient to identify and re-identify persons as having a number unique to themselves tattooed on their forearms. But it would be very odd for anyone to complain of a loss of identity if one had lost one's will and forgotten where one had made it, or forgotten the number which had been erased from one's forearm. However, there is a more pervasive, one might say almost universally familiar, not arbitrary but nevertheless entirely conventional set of co-ordinates of great administrative convenience in terms of which we can uniquely individuate persons. That is, in terms of his natural parents, and the place and date of his birth, at which he is given a name proper though not unique to him, and all this is by law written down by an officer appointed for the purpose. These co-ordinates, together with the giving of the name, suffice uniquely to identify every person, even twins. The name is important, since without it one would need an impossibly long referring expression concerning dates and places of birth of the individual as well as of his ancestors for several generations (though given the name one can usually retrieve the longer description from Somerset House). Where names are not sufficiently differentiated one may need to put some other differentia into the referring expression, such as an occupation together with a reference to an immediate ancestor; for example, in Wales: Harry Parry the Hearse; which means Harry who is the son of Harry and an undertaker.

All this is trivial enough, but there is an important underlying point I wish to use later. Where we have a deeply embedded, basic method of conventional reference it may come to seem like the warp and woof of reality; even our conventional reference to time can seem like this, as it must have done to the Senator in Ohio who objected to daylight saving on the ground that if God had meant the sun to rise at 7 a.m. he would have made it rise at 7 a.m. Perhaps this is why the adopted child's question seems to him at once weird and yet about something real. It *is* interesting that adopted children who seek for their 'real identity' refer very often to their place of birth, and to names they were originally given, as well as to their natural parents. Thus, for example:

I had to find out my true identity ... to find out exactly who I was and what my original name had been.

I had to find out where I was born. Now I know I feel as if I have got rid of a barrier or a wall and an awful lot easier in myself.

Now I know my real name and where I was born. What I know is of great comfort to me.

I have not been wasting time in diagnosing the existence of a natural if somewhat simple-minded mistake here, as I shall suggest later. However, anyone acquainted with the real distress of some adopted chldren might think that what I have so far said is heartless. But I am trying to account for the question, not the distress; and it must be pointed out that the majority of those who have been found in anxiety about the question, have come to notice because of distress greater than normal. It may be that the mistake arises from the distress, not the distress from the mistake.

It may of course be that this distress and anxiety can still be accounted for by some other mistake which connects with other, more sensible, concerns. One is that the adopted child may have deleteriously mistaken notions about heredity. I quote one such: 'I think that adopted children are like their real parents. I do not care what anybody else says ... your character is formed through your heredity'.

Indeed, it may be thought that not only one's essential nature is fixed by heredity, but so also is one's social status. Thus, another: 'I read that my original mother was only a brewery worker. I became very distressed. It is two months now and I have not yet told my husband. I hate to think that all she was was a brewery worker. Once I had a desire to meet my mother but not now. If she were a teacher, or a doctor or a nurse it would be different, but a brewery worker I cannot forgive her ... Sometimes I wish I had not been born.'

One researcher suggests that it is something like this about which most adopted children seeking their origins were concerned: 'The implication of what most adoptees were saying was that without knowing about one's origins and genealogy it was difficult, if not impossible, to understand oneself, one's potentialities or one's characteristics. One's forebears are an extension of oneself and in the case of the adoptee it extends to two sets of genealogies. A sense of security and belonging was seen to be built among other things on this kind of extended genealogical identification.' The writer himself seems to underwrite this mistake, and to suggest that there is more here than simple, natural curiosity about one's ancestors.

But most practitioners in the field take the matter much more seriously. Resoundingly enough, here is the report of the Houghton Committee on the adoption of children, 1970:

> ... the child needs to know about his origins—parents—type of people, special qualities or gifts, reason for giving him up, and special medical features—for the proper development of any sense of identity.

Any sense of identity, it says. When a prestigious committee comes up with that sort of thing, we are in a pretty pass.

So with other respected writers in this field:

> The child who has no knowledge of his natural parents or only uncertain knowledge about them may become genealogically bewildered. The resulting state of confusion and uncertainty may undermine his sense of belonging or identity.

Again, '...knowledge of origins is an important part of the development of a balanced and mature sense of identity'. Again, '... most people do like to know something about their ancestors. For the adopted child this is necessary to settle for himself reality of dual background'. This is to do with 'the development of identity and an acceptable self-image'.

These writers are not quoting the weird remarks of adopted children. They are using, not mentioning, the word 'identity'. What they mean by it does not rest on the trivial mistake I have discussed, but possibly on some other.

Many of the adopted children I have quoted are concerned about their real identity; it is as if they, and the judge I quoted earlier, think there is an objective, independently real identity which each individual has and which he has to discover and could be mistaken about as he might be about his blood group. It is clear that the professionals do not have any such notion in mind when they talk about identity. 'Identity' means 'sense of identity', which someone might have without knowing who his parents were, or the number on his passport. The identity one has a sense of is not just a knowledge of such facts. What is it?

In a recently published book John Coleman writes: 'The development of the individual's identity requires not only the notion of being separate and different from others, but also a sense of self-consistency and a firm knowledge of how one appears to the rest of the world'. 'Identity', he says, 'is taken here to have essentially the same meaning as self-concept.'

Coleman's reference to 'a firm knowledge of how one appears to the rest of the world' no doubt ultimately derives from the ideas of the early American sociologist C. H. Cooley: the 'looking-glass self', in which self-image, self-appraisal and self-esteem are tied to a consciousness of the perception and judgment of others of oneself: thus making the notion of identity or 'self-concept' inherently social.

The most influential writer in this tradition, who has had a very considerable impact on theories of child development, especially on educational theorists, is Erik Erikson. What Erikson did was to take the Freudian account of the development of the ego in terms of identification with parents, or the characteristics of parents, and graft on to it an account of development through adolescence in terms of one's perception of others' perception of oneself and of others' relations with oneself.

> The sense of ego identity ... is the accrued confidence that one's ability to maintain inner sameness (one's ego in the psychological sense) is matched by the sameness and continuity of one's meaning for others. Thus self-esteem confirmed at one end of each major crisis grows to be a conviction that one is learning effective steps towards a tangible future; that one is developing a defined personality within a social reality which one understands.

It is I think only in these terms, as the underlying rationale, that one can make sense of David Kirk's view: 'Adoptive parents must be able to identify themselves with natural parents' otherwise 'the adoptee will find it difficult or impossible to fuse the images of his natural and adoptive parents into a single configuration, one which is acceptable and satisfying to him'.

Now it is clear that the adopted children I quoted, when speaking of not 'knowing who I am', of not knowing his 'identity', are not using so sophisticated a notion.

Popper once said that Freud's descriptions in psychoanalytic terms are compatible with any psychological facts, ordinarily expressed. It may be that Erikson's appeal depends on this. On the one hand he speaks of 'crises of identity', of various confusions and disturbances of adolescence, in ways which are not difficult to grasp and in terms in which one might feel happy to represent things. On the other his underlying psychoanalytic theory is supposed to give an aetiology of these states, and a diagnostic account of some of the disturbances. Even if one abandoned the psychoanalytic underpinning, the purely descriptive account of a crisis of identity, of a failure of integration, of a man as it were at odds with himself, may remain a vivid characterization of many familiar situations. (Indeed the phrase 'crisis of identity' passed into journalist cant, and was found useful in talking not only about adolescents but about nations and all sorts of associations, by people who hadn't the remotest idea of the theoretical background.) But whatever value talk of a sense of identity may have descriptively it is a very large and doubtful step to regard it as a diagnostic or aetiological tool.

Failure to realize this can lead to an illegitimate jumping to conclusions. This may be true of David Kirk's view. It is about what adoptive parents *must* do, otherwise what *will* happen. But the general notion of self-identity is an abstract one. What may or may not be the elements which are required for integration will depend on individual circumstances; and there is no reason to believe that considerations about someone's knowledge of his natural parents will play any important part among those elements. Indeed there is good evidence that more often than not they do not. The evidence is that something like 75 per cent of adoptions can be regarded by various criteria as successful, and that there is not much difference by those criteria of the successful rearing of children by their natural parents. It is also pretty well established that the more successful the adoption, the less likely that any great concern about the natural parents, over and above quite ordinary curiosity, will develop. If the description of adolescent and later problems in terms of a failure of self-identity in Erikson's sense can sometimes be applied to adopted children, it can be equally applied to disturbed adolescents who are not adopted. And since we have no even slightly reliable aetiological theory, there is no reason to think that having been adopted is particularly connected with the disturbances Erikson describes.

Of course, I do claim to be able to diagnose the state of those who *say* they don't know who they are; but that, I suggested, is that they have made the mistake I called the senator's fallacy. True, they also use the word 'identity'. They can't be using sophisticated Eriksonian language. Where do they get it from? I have my unworthy suspicions. I once heard a young man who had been adopted and who claimed that no such problem had entered his head told by a social worker, in a television discussion programme, that he was repressing his unconscious alienation from his self-identity.

There will always be a natural tendency, in attempting to explain some abnormal or out of the usual disturbance, to fix on something obviously unusual, at least particularly salient, about the subject: that he is Welsh, or a spinster, or had some unusual family history, or some disability, or the like. Or that he is an adoptee. The last is reinforced by the fact that some adoptees are prone to the senatorial fallacy, and their expression of it has a (no more than verbal) similarity to the problems discussed by Erikson. This does harm: but not only in misassessing criteria for and the desirability of adoption. It can lead to a concentration on this feature, which is no more than a symptom of some more serious difficulty which might afflict those who have not been adopted. Indeed it is all too easy a trap into which the adopted child himself can fall. Take the following, for example, said by an adopted woman:

> I feel funny and not whole. I am unable to experience things and I cannot relate emotionally to people. (*That might well be said by anybody undergoing some form of psychological distress. But she goes on*): There should be no adoption. Preferable for all girls to be aborted.

Some writers in the field are aware of similar dangers. Thus Triseliotis writes of some results produced in Sweden:

> The study found an over-representation of behavioural, but not of social, disturbances among adopted boys and that this was possibly connected with the adoptive situation itself and the disturbances that this involves in the relationship between parents and child. The study relied heavily on teachers' ratings and may have recorded a bias. What the studies were possibly recording was the teachers' perception of adopted children as a minority group and of adoption as a state of deprivation bound to have some effect.

I am inclined to conclude two things, the second stronger and therefore more tentative than the first.

First, a crisis of identity or problem of identity in Erikson's sense may and in most cases must have an aetiology unconnected with any facts of adoption. That is not to say that it may never be connected with such facts; but its aetiology, even if connected with facts resulting from adoption, and the Eriksonian problem of identity itself, must not be confused with the adopted person's own anxieties about 'identity' expressed by adoptees.

It may be that those undergoing Eriksonian or other crises may be more likely to commit the senatorial fallacy than others: grasping at a broken straw. But some may make the mistake just because they are not sharp enough to see through it: like the senator.

Nothing I have said is intended to be an objection to the inclusion in the Children's Act of 1975 (as a result of the Houghton Committee) of the right of all adopted persons to have access to any publicly recorded information about their natural parents; but not altogether for the reasons given by the Houghton Committee. It is not a specific right peculiar to adopted children: it is simply a consequence of the general right of any adult person to have access to any publicly recorded information concerning him (now further enshrined in the Data Protection Act), including his credit rating.

Bibliography

J. Coleman, *The Nature of Adolescence* (London: Methuen, 1980).

C. H. Cooley, *Human Nature and the Social Order* (New York: Scribners, 1922).

E. Erikson, *Childhood and Society* (New York: Norton, 1963).

I. Goodacre, *Adoption Policy and Practice* (London: Allen & Unwin, 1959).

D. Kirk, *Shared Fate* (Glencoe, Glencoe, 1963).

G. S. Klein, *Psychological Issues* (New York: International Universities Press, 1959).

L. Raynor, *The Adopted Child Comes of Age* (London: Allen & Unwin, 1980).

J. Rowe, *Parents, Children and Adoption* (London: Routledge & Kegan Paul, 1966).

P. F. Strawson, *Individuals* (London: Methuen, 1959).

J. P. Triseliotis, *In Search of Origins* (London: Routledge & Kegan Paul, 1973).

Notes on Contributors

G. E. M. Anscombe is Professor of Philosophy in the University of Cambridge. She is a contributor to *Philosophy* and her *Collected Philosophical Papers* were published in 1981.

Tom Campbell is Professor of Jurisprudence in the University of Glasgow. His latest book is *Left and Rights: A Conceptual Analysis of the Idea of Socialist Rights* (1983).

David E. Cooper's latest book is *Authenticity and Learning: Nietzsche's Educational Philosophy* (1983). He is a contributor to *Philosophy* and to previous volumes of Royal Institute lectures. He is Reader in Philosophy at the University of Surrey.

A. Phillips Griffiths, Professor of Philosophy at the University of Warwick, is Director of the Royal Institute of Philosophy.

R. M. Hare, until recently White's Professor of Moral Philosophy at the University of Oxford, is now Professor of Philosophy at the University of Florida, Gainesville. He has contributed to *Philosophy* and to a previous volume of Royal Institute Lectures ('Contrasting Methods of Environmental Planning' in *Nature and Conduct,* ed. R. S. Peters, 1975). His latest book is *Plato* (1982). He is the author of *The Language of Morals* (1952), *Freedom and Reason* (1963), and *Moral Thinking* (1981).

Martin Hollis is Professor of Philosophy at the University of East Anglia. His latest book is *Invitation to Philosophy* (1985). He has published a number of articles in *Philosophy* and contributed to the Royal Institute lecture series (1983).

Ted Honderich is Professor of Philosophy at University College, London. A contributor to *Philosophy,* his *Punishment: The Supposed Justifications* was published in 1969 and his *Violence for Equality: inquiries into political philosophy* in 1980.

Don Locke is Professor of Philosophy at the University of Warwick. He has contributed articles to *Philosophy* and to the Royal Institute lecture series (1968–69). His *A Fantasy of Reason: The Life and Thought of William Godwin* was published in 1979.

William Newton-Smith is Fellow and Senior Tutor in Philosophy at Balliol College, Oxford. His *The Structure of Time* was published in 1980 and his *Rationality of Science* in 1981.

Notes on Contributors

Anthony O'Hear is the co-founder (with Brenda Cohen) of the Society for Applied Philosophy. His latest books are *Experience, Explanation and Faith* (1984) and *What Philosophy Is* (1985), and he is a contributor to *Philosophy*. He is Professor of Philosophy at the University of Bradford.

Anthony Quinton (Lord Quinton) is President of Trinity College, Oxford. He has contributed to *Philosophy* and to the Royal Institute lecture series. His latest book, *Thoughts and Thinkers,* was published in 1982.

Roger Scruton's latest book, *Sexual Desire, its Meaning and its Goal* is to be published in the autumn of 1985. He has contributed to *Philosophy* and to previous Royal Institute lecture series. He is Reader in Philosophy at Birkbeck College, London.

Richard Tur is the Benn Law Fellow at Oriel College, Oxford. He is author of many articles in legal and philosophical journals. He has contributed to the *Journal of Applied Philosophy*. His 'American Legal Philosophy' will appear in the forthcoming Royal Institute volume of lectures on American Philosophy.

Martin Warner is Programme Director of the Centre for Philosophy and Literature at the University of Warwick. He is a member of the Council of the Royal Institute and of the Executive Committee of the Society for Applied Philosophy. He contributed to *Philosophy* and to previous Royal Institute lecture series, and his *Ethics and Religion* accompanied the videorecordings of the Royal Institute Christmas Discussions (1984).

Index of Names

Index of Names

Lawton, L. J., 78
Leibniz, Gottfried, 166
Lejeune, Jerome, 111–112
Leo, Pope, 155–156
Levi-Strauss, Claude, 49
Lewis, D. K., 263
Locke, Don, *v*
Locke, John, 18, 150, 277
Lukes, S., 69

Mackie, John, 139
Mann, Thomas, 261
Manning, H. E., 183ff.
Marx, Karl, 255
Melbourne, Lord, 27
Mountbatten, Earl, 215

Nagel, Thomas, 263
Newton-Smith, William, *vii*
Nietzsche, Friedrich, 32, 43, 44, 48
Nino, C. S., 127n, 140n

Owen, G. E. L., 166

Parker, Tony, 207
Plato, 18, 48
Popper, Sir Karl, 283
Potas, Ivan 240n
Prickett, Stephen, 151, 158
Putnam, Hilary, 64ff.

Quine, Willard, 660

Ramsey, Ian, 160
Raphael, David, 213
Ricoeur, Paul, 165
Robinson, Ian, 151
Ross, J. F., 167
Rousseau, J. J., 213
Ryle, Gilbert, *vi*

Sartre, Jean Paul, 262, 265, 271
Saussure, Ferdinand de, 46
Schopenhauer, Arthur, 19
Scruton, Roger, *vi*, 210
Searle, John, 163, 262
Simpson, Alfred, 80
Smart, J. J. C., 119
Smith, J. C., 75, 77, 83ff.
Stephen, James F., 89, 142
Strawson, Sir Peter, 96, 160, 279
Szasz, Thomas, 18, 31, 246

Triselotis, J. P., 277, 284

Voltaire, Francois, 18

Warner, Martin, *vi*
Warnock, Baroness, 160, 203
Wiles, Maurice, 159
Williams, Bernard, 119n
Williams, Glanville, 77, 79, 85–86
Wittgenstein, Ludwig, *vi*, 162, 166
Wright, Martin, 219

Zander, Michael, 78

290

DUE DATE _____